RETHINKING Early Childhood EDUCATION

Edited by
Ann Pelo

A Rethinking Schools Publication

Rethinking Early Childhood Education
Edited by Ann Pelo

A Rethinking Schools Publication

Rethinking Schools, Ltd., is a nonprofit educational publisher of books, booklets, and a quarterly magazine on school reform, with a focus on issues of equity and social justice. To request additional copies of this book or a catalog of other publications, or to subscribe to *Rethinking Schools* magazine, contact:
Rethinking Schools
6737 W. Washington St. Suite 3249
Milwaukee, Wisconsin 53214
800-669-4192
www.rethinkingschools.org

First edition

Cover Design: Patrick Flynn
Cover Illustration: David McLimans
Production Management: Jacqueline Lalley Communications
Book Design: Kate Hawley
Proofreading: Jennifer Morales
Business Manager: Mike Trokan

Special thanks to the Peppercorn Foundation for its support of Rethinking Schools' early childhood education work.

Library of Congress Cataloging-in-Publication Data
Rethinking early childhood education / edited by Ann Pelo. -- 1st ed.
p. cm.
Includes bibliographical references and index.
ISBN 978-0-942961-41-6
1. Social justice--Study and teaching (Elementary) 2. Environmental education. 3. Education, Elementary--Social aspects. I. Pelo, Ann, 1965-
LC192.2.R48 2008
372.21--dc22
2008036726

Acknowledgments

As a childcare teacher and a long-time reader of *Rethinking Schools* magazine, I was thrilled when I learned of the editorial board's plans for an early childhood book. But I gulped when they invited me to serve as editor of the book: rethinking early childhood education is no small effort. But this book has certainly not been a solo effort; this book has been shaped by many people.

Rita Tenorio, a kindergarten and 1st-grade teacher for many years before becoming principal at La Escuela Fratney, was one of the founding members of Rethinking Schools. This book builds on her long leadership on early childhood issues as a member of the editorial board of Rethinking Schools. Her commitment to social justice teaching in early childhood contributed to the birth of this book.

In 2004, the Peppercorn Foundation generously funded an early childhood writing retreat led by *Rethinking Schools* editors Linda Christensen and Bill Bigelow. Teachers and caregivers from childcare centers, Head Start programs, elementary schools, and community college early childhood programs came together at Menucha Retreat Center in Oregon. Out of that gathering came the first-ever early childhood special issue of *Rethinking Schools.* A year later, Peppercorn supported another gathering of early childhood educators to advise the editorial board of Rethinking Schools on its early childhood work. The participants at both these gatherings offered insight and challenge that deepened my understandings of social justice work in early childhood and that shaped this book.

Fred McKissack, managing editor of *Rethinking Schools*, worked closely with several contributors to the book, and offered me big-picture guidance and warm encouragement. Kelley Dawson Salas helped craft the contents and the emphasis of the book, sharing her experiences as a 4th-grade teacher and a parent of young kids. Jacqueline Lalley shepherded the book from start to finish with patience and good humor. Members of the Rethinking Schools editorial board offered suggestions and support; thanks to each of them: Wayne Au, Bill Bigelow, Terry Burant, Linda Christensen, Stan Karp, David Levine, Larry Miller, Bob Peterson, Kelley Dawson Salas, Rita Tenorio, and Stephanie Walters. Mike Trokan, business manager of *Rethinking Schools*, did his usual behind-the-scenes magic. Amalia Oulahan put in plenty of hours on the small details that need to be done with precision.

Bill Bigelow was a partner and coach for me at each step of the journey. He continues to teach me about writing, teaching, and living with integrity.

Amanda Abarbanel-Rice and Bonnie Robbins sent encouragement along with their suggestions of children's books for a social justice classroom. Deb Curtis jumped in at the eleventh hour with photos to fill a gap.

Margie Carter gave me my first subscription to *Rethinking Schools* many years ago. She has been my first and best example of social justice teaching in early childhood education.

Contents

Introduction: Embracing Social Justice in Early Childhood Education *ix*
by Ann Pelo

Language Matters *xv*
by Ann Pelo

Part One: Prioritize anti-bias, culturally sensitive teaching and learning. 1

What Color Is Beautiful? 3
by Alejandro Segura-Mora

Why an Anti-Bias Curriculum? 7
by Louise Derman-Sparks

Developmental Themes, Tasks, and Goals in Anti-Bias Work 13
by Margie Carter and Deb Curtis

Raising Issues of Race with Young Children 17
by Rita Tenorio

Using Persona Dolls to Help Children Develop Anti-Bias Attitudes 23
by Trisha Whitney

Miles of Aisles of Sexism: Helping Students Investigate Toy Stores 29
by Sudie Hofmann

Where Are the Game Girls? 35
by Ann Pelo

Rethinking 'The Three Little Pigs' 41
by Ellen Wolpert

What If All the Kids Are White?:
Anti-Bias Themes for Teaching Young Children 43
by Louise Derman-Sparks

Unwrapping the Holidays: Reflections on a Difficult First Year 49
by Dale Weiss

Part Two: Make ample time for play and exploration. **55**

The Scripted Prescription: A Cure for Childhood 57
by Peter Campbell

What About Play? 61
by Sharna Olfman

Confession: My Students Play in the Classroom—and It's Good for Them 65
by Seth Shteir

Playing with Gender 67
by Ann Pelo

Cybertots: Technology and the Preschool Child 75
by Jane Healy

Part Three: Use curriculum approaches that are responsive to children's developmental and intellectual pursuits. 85

Why We Banned Legos: Exploring Power, Ownership, and Equity in the Classroom 87
by Ann Pelo and Kendra PeloJoaquin

'Lego Fascists' (That's Us) Vs. Fox News 95
by the Editors of Rethinking Schools *Magazine*

'I Just Want to Read *Frog and Toad*' 99
by Melanie Quinn

Tuning In to Violence: Students Use Math to Analyze What TV Is Teaching Them 103
by Margot Pepper

Talking with Children About War and Peace 108
by Ann Pelo

Testing Tots: Why We Need a Better Means of Evaluating Our Nation's Children 109
by Richard Rothstein

Testing Lang 113
by Amy Gutowski

Think Less Benchmarks: A Flawed Test Does More Harm than Good 115
by Amy Gutowski

From Critique to Possibility: New Zealand's Radical Approach to Assessment 119
by Margie Carter

Part Four: Cultivate a sense of place—of belonging to a particular patch of earth and sky—and a connection to the earth and its creatures. **121**

A Pedagogy for Ecology 123
by Ann Pelo

Bringing the Earth Home: Professional Development on Ecology 131
by Ann Pelo

Don't Know Much About Natural History: Education as a Barrier to Nature 133
by Richard Louv

Food Is Not for Play 137
by Jean Hannon

Lessons from a Garden Spider: How Charlotte Transformed My Classroom 139
by Kate Lyman

Part Five: Emphasize children's social-emotional learning. **145**

Holding Nyla: Lessons from an Inclusion Classroom 147
by Katie Kissinger

Fairness First: Learning from Martin Luther King Jr. and Ruby Bridges 151
by Stephanie Walters

Staying Past Wednesday: Helping Kids Deal with Death and Loss 155
by Kate Lyman

Part Six: Learn from and stand with families. **159**

Welcoming Kalenna: Making Our Students Feel at Home 161
by Laura Linda Negri-Pool

Holiday Lessons Learned in an Early Childhood Classroom 165
by Julie Bisson

Strawberry Fields Forever?: An Early Childhood Teacher Draws on Her Past to Teach Children of Migrant Farmworkers 171
by Cirila Ramírez

Talking the Talk: Integrating Indigenous Languages into a Head Start Classroom 175
by Cathie DeWeese-Parkinson

Heather's Moms Got Married 177
by Mary Cowhey

Bringing the Lives of Lesbian and Gay People into Our Programs 180
by Ann Pelo

Activism Brings Us Power, An Interview with Hilda Magana 183
by Jacqueline Lalley

Part Seven: Advocate for children, families, and early childhood workers. 187

Who Cares for Our Children?: The Child Care Crisis in the Other America 189
by Valerie Polakow

It's All of Our Business: What Fighting for Family-Friendly Policies Could Mean for Early Childhood Educators 197
by Ellen Bravo

Improving Conditions and Status for Early Childhood Educators 201
by Charles Bruner

Caught in a Quagmire: The Effort to Improve Wages and Working Conditions for Childcare Teachers 203
by Patty Hnatiuk

Part Eight: Resources 209

10 Quick Ways to Analyze Books for Racism and Sexism 211
by the Council on Interracial Books for Children

Music for Social Justice 215
by Rita Tenorio

Books and Multimedia 219
Recommendations from Contributors

Organizations and Websites 223
Recommendations from Contributors

Introduction

Embracing Social Justice in Early Childhood Education

BY ANN PELO

There's a small town in Italy with an international reputation for its early childhood programs. The teaching and learning that happens in their schools is certainly compelling—but more compelling is the story of how the community came together to create an early childhood education system. The town of Reggio Emilia, like much of Italy, was devastated by World War II; as the war ended, the townspeople were fiercely determined to create a new culture, a culture in which the fascism that had taken hold of Italy in the decades leading up to the war would find no foothold. The citizens of Reggio Emilia were clear about how to begin this work of culture-building: they would create schools for young children.

Parents occupied an abandoned building near the town square, demanding that the city government make that building available to them for their first school, while the teachers and children set up school each day on the courthouse steps where the city officials would be sure to encounter them. Parents and teachers didn't set out to create private schools available to a few; they wanted publicly funded schools, open to all families in the community, organized around the values of critical thinking and joyful collaboration. One of the founders of the schools, Loris Malaguzzi, explained the vision of the community this way: "We are part of an ongoing story of men and women, ideals intact, who realize that history can be changed, and that it is changed starting with the future of children."[1]

This story has resonance for us today. It reminds us that early childhood education is a political act, and that it necessarily involves values and vision. Early childhood is the time in our lives when we develop our core dispositions—the habits of thinking that shape how we live; our work as early childhood educators is to nurture dispositions in young children towards empathy, ecological consciousness, engaged inquiry, and collaboration. These dispositions undergird just and equitable communities; they are at the heart of activism and in the hearts of activists. Early childhood educators must believe, with the founders of the schools in Reggio Emilia, Italy, that history can be changed, and that our work is to contribute to that change. That is the premise of this book: quality early childhood education is inseparable from social justice teaching and ecological education. It is essential to rethink early childhood education, and it is essential to ensure that quality early education—programs for children from their first months through the primary grades—is offered to all children.

Fostering Social and Ecological Dispositions in Young Children

Early childhood programs that put social justice and ecological teaching front and center share particular characteristics.

They prioritize anti-bias, culturally sensitive teaching and learning. Teachers call attention to the ways in which people are different and the ways in which people are the same, honoring individual and group identity. They intentionally introduce issues of fairness and unfairness, and coach children to think critically and to take action. Teachers learn about children's family and cultural identities and integrate those identities into the daily life of the classroom, at the same time as they acknowledge the ways in which their own cultural identities shape their teaching.

They are organized around play and ample time for exploration. Teachers create time and provide open-ended materials for children's imaginative, self-directed play. They talk with families, with other teachers, and with community members about the value of play for children's healthy development and for their learning.

They use curriculum approaches that are responsive to children's developmental and intellectual pursuits. Teachers pay attention to children's play and conversations, watching for the developmental themes, compelling questions, understandings, and misunderstandings expressed in their play. They use what they observe to develop curricula that challenge children to think deeply and to explore collaboratively.

They cultivate a sense of place—of belonging to a particular patch of earth and sky—and a connection to the earth and its creatures. Teachers take the children outdoors and bring the natural world into the classroom, inviting the children to engage their senses and their minds as they come to know and care about—and to care for—the place where they are spending their days.

They emphasize children's social-emotional and dispositional learning. Teachers seek to cultivate in children the disposition to pay attention to their own and others' emotions and needs. They emphasize the importance of collaboration and offer children coaching and practice about understanding multiple perspectives. Teachers create opportunities for children to think critically and engage intellectually with ideas and with each other—and to take action based on their critical thinking.

They learn from and stand with children's families. Teachers recognize that they have much to learn about children from their families, about children's particular ways of being in the world, about their family rituals and rhythms, and about their cultural identities. As they learn from families about their strengths and challenges, they can then offer themselves as allies to families, in ways specific to individual families and in the arena of broader community activism and justice efforts.

They advocate for children, families, and early childhood workers. Teachers acknowledge the broader social conditions that impact the lives of children, families, and teachers. They take action—speaking out in their community, writing letters to news media and to legislators, participating in demonstrations. They know that their activism is an extension of their teaching, contributing to social justice efforts and modeling for children what it is to live in the world as a change-maker.

This is early childhood education at its best: teachers, children, and families opening themselves to each other and to the earth in ways that invite joyful play, collaborative inquiry, thoughtful observation, and deep caring that gives rise to action. These ways of being are a foundation for children's lives in community. They foster the social and emotional well-being that is at the heart of just communities, and they strengthen the intellectual development that is at the heart of academic learning.

Challenges to Early Childhood Education

This vision for top-notch early childhood programs is a stark contrast to the cultural belief system that now threatens early childhood education. Early childhood, we're told, is a time to get children ready for school and for work. Play is nice, but school is about learning and skill development, and that means memorization and drill and testing.

Pressure from federal policy has pushed assessment-driven, academic instruction into programs for the youngest children: most federal- and state-funded programs use standardized, scripted curriculum packages that emphasize literacy and numeracy at the cost of open time for play, and administer a barrage of tests to the 4- and 5-year-old children enrolled in their programs. This emphasis on a "teacher-proof" drill-and-skill curriculum communicates to families that early childhood ought to be about "school and test readiness," defined in the narrowest and most hollow academic terms. Families, in turn, are confused: should they accede to this vision for their children's earliest years, hoping to insure their children's school success, or press for a more generous and spacious experience for their young children, anchored in their intuition that childhood ought to be about more than literacy drills and tests?

Families carry their confusion to teachers, looking for reassurance that their children will be ready for school—and for the tests they're sure to encounter there. Teachers are squeezed between this push towards early academics and their commitment to children's right to play and to meaningful curricula anchored in their lives and questions. And teachers are weighed down by the emphasis on narrowly technical teaching centered on discrete skills, which stands in stark contrast to the intellectually engaging work of reflective study and inquiry that is teaching at its best and most sustaining. Teachers face wrenching pressure to abandon their desire to be reflective, responsive educators who think critically about their teaching and the children's learning, and, instead, to organize their teaching around assessments and scripted curricula.

In addition to this daily intellectual and emotional challenge, childcare teachers and caregivers work with the constant strain of low wages and no health care or retirement. Their work is dismissed as unskilled, jobs that anyone can fill—an attitude born of the view that early childhood work is women's work. Caring for and educating very young children comes naturally to women, the thinking goes: women do that work by instinct, and have been doing it forever—it certainly doesn't require any particular education or professional development. That attitude has been institutionalized in the field of early childhood education: there are only minimal requirements for childcare workers in most states—typically, passing a criminal background check and having a high school diploma. No specialized training, no internships, no particular experience needed.

The attitude that "anyone can do this work" is one reason for the current emphasis on "teacher-proof" curricula. Early childhood agencies provide scripted curricula in place of professional development for early childhood educators. This communicates a startling disrespect for teachers' ability to generate engaging, thoughtful, instructive experiences for children without a script to follow, and drives people from the field who are eager to engage intellectually with children, families, and colleagues.

Given these stresses, it's no wonder that the annual national turnover rate in child care stands at around 40 percent.[2] And that turnover compounds the challenges that early childhood education faces. Children and families are shaken each time a cherished caregiver leaves; the effort of developing trust in new caregivers becomes a too-familiar detour away from learning. And teachers, too, are shaken as their colleagues come and go; they face a daunting uphill struggle to create a community of thinkers anchored by a shared understanding of the work. The disruption created by teacher turnover is felt especially in impoverished communities, where teachers typically earn rock-bottom wages and struggle with an appalling lack of resources and a corresponding high degree of stress.

Early childhood education is in a precarious situation.

We believe that social justice and ecological teaching offers a much-needed vision for early childhood education in the face of the challenges weighing on the field and confronting the planet.

Social Justice and Ecological Teaching Is Responsive Teaching

Social justice teaching grows from children's urgent concerns. If we listen to the themes embedded in children's play and conversations, we hear questions about identity and belonging, about community and relationships and fairness: *Can boys be part of the game about the kitty family, or just girls? The bad guy is the one with brown skin and a funny way of talking, right? Can we have two moms in this family?* And, in their everyday negotiations, children are working to make sense of the ways in which people are the same and different: *Your lunch has food in it that I've never seen before. Why don't you have a dad in your family? You have Easter at your house, but I don't. Why is your skin a different color than your mom's skin?* Children are fundamentally concerned with making sense of their social and cultural world; teachers and caregivers can join them in this pursuit, guiding them towards understandings rooted in accurate and empathetic understandings—or we can leave them to figure out their questions on their own, coming to conclusions based on misinformation and cultural bias. When we engage with children in questions about identity and equity, we participate in the work of reshaping our society.

Ecological teaching grows from an understanding that current ways of living on this planet are unsustainable and destructive and must be replaced. Young children are forming the fundamental understandings that will shape how they engage with the earth. Will they learn that the earth is a resource to be used and abused by humans with little attention to the price of that use, or will they grow a more intimate relationship with the earth that ranks the environment high on the list of "things to consider" in every decision? Our planet cannot afford another generation of children to grow up disregarding the earth, the sky, the water, and all who live in them. And children cannot afford to grow up ignorant of the earth and its ways, displaced from their ecological home terrain by lack of intimate knowledge.

Changing the Discussion about the Purpose of Early Education

Social justice and ecological teaching relocates the meaning of early childhood education from school readiness to social and emotional learning and intellectual development. It offers another way to understand childhood, reminding us that this is a time when children ought to be developing core social and ecological dispositions rather than cramming for the tests ahead. Social justice and ecological teaching reframes our work as educators from a too-heavy focus on academic skills that actually diminishes the capacity for deep learning, and offers, instead, an emphasis on thoughtful observation, reflection, and planning on behalf of children's dispositional and developmental learning. This is teaching at its best: responsive to children's developmental questions and pursuits and attentive to building a sturdy intellectual foundation for the academic work that children will encounter in later schooling.

In these ways, social justice and ecological teaching becomes a form of resistance to the view that early childhood education is unskilled work, important only inasmuch as it prepares children to recite the alphabet, identify colors, and count to 10. Social justice and ecological teaching is intellectually and emotionally engaging work; it sustains, rather than drains, teachers and caregivers. It asks that teachers listen closely to the social and cultural questions embedded in children's play, and that they think carefully about how best to engage the children around those questions. It demands that teachers stay present to the children's developing understandings about the world and themselves in order to best support their learning. This is a far remove from scripted curricula and preplanned lessons; it is authentic teaching—and it is the kind of teaching our society urgently needs. We need teachers who are engaged and curious, who create in their classrooms cultures of deep listening, compassionate perspective-taking, and critical thinking. We need teachers who, in the words of Terry Tempest Williams, cultivate "democracy as a way of life: the right to be educated, to think, discuss, dissent, create, and act, acting in imaginative and revolutionary ways."[3]

Our Work Extends Beyond the Classroom

When we embrace social justice and ecological teaching, we participate in changing history, "starting with the future of children." But the challenges we face and the vision we hold of just communities carry us beyond our teaching practices into the arena of broader activism.

We can resist and subvert assessment-driven, standards-based curricula in our daily teaching, but our individual efforts won't safeguard children's right to education that is anchored by their questions, passions, and pursuits. There is a growing movement to remake the government mandates that locate drills and tests at the heart of education; until recently, that movement hasn't much involved early childhood educators. Now, though, Head Start directors, community childcare leaders, administrators in state-funded preschools, and other early childhood educators are coming together with colleagues in elementary and secondary education to strengthen the movement against packaged curricula and assessments.

The push to create universal prekindergarten (UPK) programs offers another entry point for activism on behalf of children, families, and teachers. Universal prekindergarten is a movement to provide preschool programs to all 4-year-old children as preparation for the academic work that they'll encounter in kindergarten; it's a state-funded drive—each state legislates its own mandates for prekindergarten programs. Universal prekindergarten offers increased access to early education for low-income families, something to celebrate given the large numbers of children who currently aren't served by affordable, quality early childhood programs in their communities. Yet UPK classrooms typically adopt (often by the mandate of funding agencies) standardized curricula characterized by rote learning and skill-and-drill teaching. This compromises the assertion that these are top-quality programs. And it is especially problematic for low-income communities most deserving of education that fosters critical thinking and social awareness: as children's opportunities seem to be expanding because of the increased access that UPK offers, the type of education that they're offered is narrow and intellectually numbing. In addition to these contradictions, UPK threatens to disrupt community-based childcare programs, as families and teachers exit these programs to move into UPK classrooms. UPK is in its infancy; this is the time for concerned educators, parents, and community members to get involved in shaping how it unfolds.

Another challenge that carries us into action beyond our daily teaching arises from the ongoing discrimination that early childhood educators face. In the late 1970s, teachers and caregivers of young children began to organize in protest of the unlivable wages and lack of benefits that characterize early childhood education. They created the Child Care Employees Project, a national effort to draw attention to poor working conditions in early care and education and to jumpstart initiatives that would make early childhood education a sustainable career. The Child Care Employees Project gave rise to the Worthy Wage Campaign, as early childhood educators across the country took part in creative, bold acts of protest and challenge, and began to form and join unions in an effort to improve working conditions. That effort has been folded into the current Center for the Child Care Workforce, a project of the American Federation of Teachers. In the three decades since this movement began, important ground has been won—and new struggles have emerged. There is work for us to do beyond our classrooms, stepping into the terrain of broad social action aimed at transforming the working conditions for early childhood educators.

There is an even broader arena of social concerns to acknowledge. Inadequate health care, immobilizing poverty, unstable housing, lack of access to decent nutrition—the best early childhood programs that we can imagine won't fix these broader social conditions. There is much work to be done, and all of it is interconnected. Caring about young children means caring about—and taking action to improve—the social conditions that shape their lives and determine their opportunities.

When we embrace a vision of social justice and ecological teaching in early childhood education, we join a lineage of educators who are intent on changing history, participating in the "ongoing story of men and women, ideals intact," who understand that how we engage with the youngest children in our communities speaks volumes about the kind of society in which we hope to live. ■

Ann Pelo is an early childhood teacher and teacher mentor in Seattle, Wash.

References

1. Loris Malaguzzi. "When We Got the News," in *Brick by Brick: The History of the XXV Aprile People's Nursery School of Villa Cella.* Renzo Barazzoni, ed. Reggio Emilia, Italy. Reggio Children. pp. 14-15. 2000.
2. Dorrie Seavey. *The Cost of Frontline Turnover in Long-Term Care.* Washington, D.C. Institute for Future of Aging Services. 2004.
3. Terry Tempest Williams. *The Open Space of Democracy.* Great Barrington, Mass. The Orion Society. 2004.

Language Matters

BY ANN PELO

The words we use to describe early childhood programs come layered with meanings. "Child care," "preschool," "prekindergarten"—each of these conveys social and political ideas and images, and each is problematic.

"Child care" is an umbrella that overarches licensed and unlicensed family childcare homes, childcare centers, and a plethora of informal arrangements among family members. Some folks say "day care," though that's becoming less common, as caregivers remind us, tersely, "We take care of children; it's child care, not day care." Both phrases—child care and day care—are commonly used dismissively, shorthand for bare-bones, minimal quality caregiving: "It's just child care; they don't do much for kids' learning."

To counter the sting of that disrespect for their work, childcare providers increasingly refer to themselves as "teachers"; it's painful to have one's work patronizingly dismissed as unskilled babysitting. And "early childhood education" is becoming increasingly common—we use it throughout this book—as people who work with the youngest children seek to raise up the social and political image of their field by calling attention to the significant teaching and learning that happens in programs for young children. ("Early childhood education" is in itself problematic, though, as it highlights "education" but leaves out "caregiving"; this distancing from the caregiving aspect of work with young children implies that education happens separately from caregiving, and is more important than caregiving, and, so, contributes to the second-class status accorded to that traditional women's work.)

There are other layers of meaning to "child care." In its origins and, still, at its core, child care represents a political commitment to provide structural support for women to pursue work for pay, in addition to their parenting. Child care was fought for and hard won by feminist activists. Now, that meaning has been distorted by welfare laws that require women to leave their children in inexpensive (and, too often, poor quality) childcare programs in order to work for pay, as part of their "welfare-to-work" benefits.

"Preschool" typically refers to part-time programs that emphasize children's social learning through group interactions. Increasingly, these programs also explicitly focus on school preparation—becoming, literally, pre-school programs. Because they have limited hours (often three or four hours a day), preschools often offer "extended care," child care for children whose parents aren't able to pick them up at the end of the preschool session. Usually, the extended care staff is paid less than the preschool staff, because they're seen as "just doing child care" rather than "teaching."

The word "preschool" carries an explicit, and troubling, meaning: it frames childhood as a time before, a time of preparation for some later context. But childhood is worthy in its own right, and the lives of young children hold a richness of play, emotion, relationships, questions, and exploration that deserves to be honored and celebrated.

"Prekindergarten" is a near-cousin to "preschool." It makes explicit an orientation to future schooling and to the values of academic learning. There are prekindergarten programs for affluent families, aimed at preparing children for academic success in private schools. And there are publicly funded prekindergarten programs for low-income families, aimed at preparing children to navigate the terrain of public schools and, minimally, not to fail (often confounded with the idea of "success" for these children). These publicly funded prekindergarten programs have been the testing ground for standards-based curricula and assessments in early childhood education.

"Head Start" was the prototype for publicly funded prekindergarten programs. It grew out of the War on Poverty and was created with an overt political acknowledgment that families living in poverty had fewer resources to offer their children to prepare them for school success than families who were economically privileged—and that the hierarchy that grew from that was wrong. But it's an easy slide from a strong political critique of the social and economic class system in our country to a patronizing, racist, classist attitude that "those children" need extra help, need a head start, if they are to keep up with "the rest of us." In everyday parlance, "Head Start" connotes a deficit understanding of poor children and of children of color.

Each of these ways of describing early childhood programs is problematic, but each can be reclaimed and used to honor children and their caregivers and teachers. Jonathan Kozol, in his book *Ordinary Resurrections*, reminds us to keep childhood at the heart of our programs, however we describe those programs:

> Childhood ought to have at least a few entitlements that aren't entangled with utilitarian considerations. One of them should be the right to a degree of unencumbered satisfaction in the sheer delight and goodness of existence itself. Another ought to be the confidence of knowing that one's presence on this earth is taken as an unconditioned blessing that is not contaminated by the economic uses that a nation does or does not have for you. ■

Ann Pelo is an early childhood teacher and teacher mentor in Seattle, Wash.

Part I

Prioritize anti-bias, culturally sensitive teaching and learning.

"[Paulo Freire writes about] 'the practice of freedom: the means by which men and women deal critically and creatively with reality and discover how to participate in the transformation of their world.' The 'practice of freedom' is fundamental to anti-bias education … [An] anti-bias curriculum is value-based: Differences are good; oppressive ideas and behaviors are not. It sets up a creative tension between respecting differences and not accepting unfair beliefs and acts. It asks teachers and children to confront troublesome issues rather than covering them up. An anti-bias perspective is integral to all aspects of daily classroom life."

Louise Derman-Sparks and the A.B.C. Task Force
Anti-Bias Curriculum: Tools for Empowering Young Chilldren

ROSANA FARA/NIÑA BONITA

What Color Is Beautiful?

BY ALEJANDRO SEGURA-MORA

Most of my kindergarten students have already been picked up by their parents. Two children still sit on the mat in the cafeteria lobby, waiting. Occasionally, one of them stands to look through the door's opaque windows to see if they can make out a parent coming. Ernesto*, the darkest child in my class, unexpectedly shares in Spanish, "Maestro, my mom is giving me pills to turn me white."

"Is that right?" I respond, also in Spanish. "And why do you want to be white?"

"Because I don't like my color," he says.

"I think your color is very beautiful and you are beautiful as well," I say. I try to conceal how his comment saddens and alarms me, because I want to encourage his sharing.

"I don't like to be dark," he explains.

His mother, who is slightly darker than he, walks in the door. Ernesto rushes to take her hand and leaves for home.

Childhood Memories

Ernesto's comment takes me back to an incident in my childhood. My mom is holding me by the hand, my baby brother in her other arm, my other three brothers and my sister following along. We are going to church and I am happy. I skip all the way, certain that I have found a solution to end my brothers' insults.

"You're a monkey," they tell me whenever they are mad at me. I am the only one in my family with curly hair. In addition to "monkey," my brothers baptize me with other derogatory names—such as Simio (Ape), Chineca (a twisted and distorted personification of being curly, and even more negative by the feminization with an "a" at the end), and Urco, the captain of all apes in the television program *The Planet of the Apes*.

As we enter the church, my mom walks us to the front of the altar to pray before the white saints, the crucified white Jesus, and his mother. Before that day, I hadn't bought into the God story. After all, why would God give a child curly hair? But that day there is hope. I close my eyes and pray with a conviction that would have brought rain to a desert.

"God, if you really exist, please make my hair straight," I pray. "I hate it curly and you know it's hard. So at the count of three, please take these curls and make them straight. One, two, three."

With great suspense I open my eyes. I reach for my hair. Anticipating the feel of straight hair, I stroke my head, only to feel my curls. Tears sting my eyes. As I head for one of the benches, I whisper, "I knew God didn't exist."

For Ernesto, the pill was his God; for me, God was my pill. I wonder how Ernesto will deal with the failure of his pill.

A Teachable Moment

I can't help but wonder how other teachers might have dealt with Ernesto's comments. Would they have ignored him? Would they have dismissed him with a, "Stop talking like that!" Would they have felt sorry for him because they agree with him?

As teachers, we are cultural workers, whether we are aware of it or not. If teachers don't question the culture and values being promoted in the classroom, they socialize their students to accept the uneven power relations of our society along lines of race, class, gender, and ability. Yet teachers can—and should—challenge the values of white privilege and instead promote values of self-love.

Young students, because of their honesty and willingness to talk about issues, provide many opportunities for teachers to take seemingly minor incidents and turn them into powerful teaching moments. I am grateful for Ernesto's sincerity and trust in sharing with me. Without knowing it, Ernesto opened the door to a lively dialogue in our classroom about white privilege.

To resurface the dialogue on beauty and skin color, I chose a children's book which deals with resistance to white privilege (a genre defined, in part, by its scarcity). The book is *Niña Bonita*, written by Ana María Machado and illustrated by Rosana Fara (1996, available in English from Kane/Miller Book Publishers). The book tells the story of an albino bunny who loves the beauty of a girl's dark skin and wants to find out how he can get black fur. I knew the title of the book would give away the author's bias, so I covered the title. I wanted to find out, before reading the book, how children perceived the cover illustration of the dark-skinned girl.

"If you think this little girl is pretty, raise your hand," I said. Fourteen hands went up.

"If you think she is ugly, raise your hand," I then asked. Fifteen voted for ugly, among them Ernesto.

I was not surprised that half my students thought the little girl was ugly. Actually, I was expecting a higher number, given the tidal wave of white dolls which make their way into our classroom on Fridays, our Sharing Day, and previous comments by children in which they indicated that dark is ugly.

After asking my students why they thought the girl on the book cover was ugly, one student responded, "Because she has black color and her hair is really curly." Ernesto added, "Because she is black-skinned."

"But you are dark like her," Stephanie quickly rebutted to Ernesto, while several students nodded in agreement. "How come you don't like her?"

"Because I don't like black girls," Ernesto quickly responded. Several students affirmed Ernesto's statement with "yes" and "that's right."

"All children are pretty," Stephanie replied in defense.

Carlos then added, "If you behave good, then your skin color can change."

"Are you saying that if you are good, you can turn darker?" I asked, trying to make sure the other students had understood what he meant.

"White!" responded Carlos.

"No, you can't change your color," several students responded. "That can't be done!"

"How do you know that your color can change?" I asked, hoping Carlos would expand on his answer.

"My mom told me," he said.

"And would you like to change your skin color?" I asked.

"No," he said. He smiled shyly as he replied and I wondered if he may have wished he was not dark-skinned but didn't want to say so.

Carlos's mother's statements about changing skin color reminded me of instances in my family and community when a new baby is born. "Oh, look at him, how pretty and blond-looking he is," they say if the baby has European features and coloring. And if the babies came out dark, like Ernesto? Then the comments are, "¡Ay! Pobrecito, salió tan prietito"—which translated means, "Poor baby, he came out so dark."

I hear similar comments from co-workers in our school's staff lounge. A typical statement: "Did you see Raul in my class? He has the most beautiful green eyes."

It is no surprise that so many students must fight an uphill battle against the values of white privilege; still other students choose not to battle at all.

Challenging the Students

In an attempt to have students explain why they think the black girl in *Niña Bonita* is ugly, I ask them, "If you think she is ugly for having dark skin, why do you think her dark skin makes her ugly?"

"I don't like the color black," volunteers Yvette, "because it looks dark and you can't see in the dark."

"Because when I turn off the light," explains Marco, "everything is dark and I am afraid."

Although most of my kindergarten students could not articulate the social worthlessness of being dark-skinned in this society, I was amazed by their willingness to struggle with an issue that so many adults, teachers included, ignore, avoid, and pretend does not exist. At the same time, it was clear that many of my students had already internalized the values of white privilege.

At the end of our discussion, I took another vote to see how students were reacting to *Niña Bonita*; I also wanted to ask individual students why they had voted the way they had. This second time, 18 students said the black girl was pretty and only 11 said she was ugly. Ernesto still voted for "ugly."

"Why do you think she is ugly?" I asked, but this time the students didn't volunteer responses. Perhaps they were sensing that I did not value negative answers as much as I did comments by students who fell in love with *Niña Bonita*. In their defense of dark skin, some students offered explanations such as, "Her color is dark and pretty," "All girls are pretty," and "I like the color black."

SKJOLD

Our discussion of *Niña Bonita* may have led four students to modify their values of beauty and ugliness in relation to skin color. Maybe these four students just wanted to please their teacher. What is certain, however, is that the book and our discussion caused some students to look at the issue in a new way.

Equally important, *Niña Bonita* became a powerful tool to initiate discussion on an issue which will affect my students, and myself, for a lifetime. Throughout the school year, the class continued our dialogue on the notions of beauty and ugliness. (One other book that I have found useful to spark discussion is *The Ugly Duckling.* This fairy tale, which is one of the most popular among early elementary teachers and children, is often used uncritically. It tells the story of a little duckling who is "ugly" because his plumage is dark. Happiness comes only when the duckling turns into a beautiful, spotless white swan. I chose to use this book in particular because the plot is a representation of the author's value of beauty as being essentially white. I want my students to understand that they can disagree with and challenge authors of books, and not receive their messages as god-given.)

When I have such discussions with my students, I often feel like instantly including my opinion. But I try to allow my students to debate the issue first. After they have spoken, I ask them about their views and push them to clarify their statements. One reason I like working with children is that teaching is always a type of experiment, because the students constantly surprise me with their candid responses. These responses then modify how I will continue the discussion.

I struggle, however, with knowing that as a teacher I am in a position of power in relation to my young students. It is easy to make students stop using the dominant ideology and adopt the ideology of another teacher, in this case my ideology. In this society, in which we have been accustomed to deal with issues in either-or terms, children (like many adults) tend to adopt one ideology in place of another, but not necessarily in a way in which they actually think through the issues involved. I struggle with how to get my students to begin to look critically at the many unequal power relations in our society, relations which, even at the age of 5, have already shaped even whether they love or hate their skin color and consequently themselves.

At the end of our reading and discussion of the book, I shared my feelings with my students.

"I agree with the author calling this girl 'Niña Bonita' because she is absolutely beautiful," I say. "Her skin color is beautiful."

While I caressed my face and kissed my cinnamon-colored hands several times happily and passionately, so that they could see my love for my skin color, I told them, "My skin color is beautiful, too."

I pointed to one of my light-complexioned students and said, "Gerardo also has beautiful skin color and so does Ernesto. But Gerardo cannot be out in the sun for a long time because his skin will begin to burn. I can stay out in the sun longer because my darker skin color gives me more protection against sunburn. But Ernesto can stay out in the sun longer than both of us because his beautiful dark skin gives him even more protection."

Despite our several class discussions on beauty, ugliness, and skin color Ernesto did not appear to change his mind. But, hopefully, his mind will not forget our discussions.

Ernesto probably still takes his magic pills, which, his mother later explained, are Flintstones Vitamin C. But I hope that every time he pops one into his mouth, he remembers how his classmates challenged the view that to be beautiful one has to be white. I want Ernesto to always remember, as will I, Lorena's comment: "Dark-skinned children are beautiful and I have dark skin, too." ■

* Names have been changed.

Alejandro Segura-Mora is a facilitator and speaker and is founder of Mind Growers, a consulting organization dedicated to helping schools close the achievement gap.

Why an Anti-Bias Curriculum?

By Louise Derman-Sparks

"Why can't we just let children be? Children don't know anything about prejudice or stereotypes. They don't notice what color a person is. If we just leave them alone and let them play with each other, then everything will be fine," argue many parents and early childhood teachers. Many adults assume that children are unaffected by the biases in U.S. society. Nevertheless, what we know about children's identity and attitude development challenges this comfortable assumption. Research data reveal that:

- Children begin to notice differences and construct classificatory and evaluative categories very early
- There are overlapping but distinguishable developmental tasks and steps in the construction of identity and attitudes
- Societal stereotyping and bias influence children's self-concept and attitudes toward others

Data about how young children first develop awareness about different physical abilities are still sparse, but do suggest that the same three points apply. Awareness of other types of disabilities seems to appear later than the preschool years.[1]

Children construct their identity and attitudes through the interaction of three factors:

- Experience with their bodies
- Experience with their social environments
- Their cognitive developmental stage

Thus, their growing ideas and feelings are not simply direct reflections either of cultural patterns or of innate, biological structures.

Phyllis Katz, writing about racial awareness, suggests that from 2 through 5 or 6, children (1) make early observations of racial clues; (2) form rudimentary concepts; (3) engage in conceptual differentiation; (4) recognize the irrevocability of cues (cues remain constant—skin color will not change); (5) consolidate group concepts; and (6) elaborate group concepts. Evaluative judgments begin to influence this process at step 2.[2] Kohlberg's stages of gender identity development suggest a similar developmental sequence to Katz.[3] Marguerite Alejandro-Wright also finds that racial awareness begins in the preschool years, but cautions that full understanding occurs much later (age 10 or 11). She states that "knowledge of racial classification evolves from a vague, undifferentiated awareness of skin color differences to knowledge of the cluster of physical-biological attributes associated with racial membership and eventually to a social understanding of racial categorization."[4]

Even Toddlers Are Aware

Let's look briefly at what these developmental patterns mean. During their second year of life, children begin to notice gender and racial differences. They may also begin noticing physical disabilities, although so far indications are that this may begin a year or two later. By 2½ years of age, children are learning the appropriate use of gender labels (girl, boy) and learning color names, which they begin to apply to skin color.

By 3 years of age (and sometimes even earlier), children show signs of being influenced by societal norms and biases and may exhibit "pre-prejudice" toward others on the basis of gender or race or being differently abled.

Between 3 and 5 years of age, children try to figure out what are the essential attributes of their selfhood, what aspects of self remain constant. They wonder:

Will I always be a girl or a boy?

If I like to climb trees do I become a boy?

If I like to play with dolls, do I become a girl?

What gives me my skin color?

Can I change it?

If I interact with a child who has a physical disability, will I get it?

Will I always need a prosthesis in place of my arm?

During this time, children need a lot of help sorting through the many experiences and variables of identity as they journey the path to self-awareness.

By 4 or 5 years of age, children not only engage in gender-appropriate behavior defined by socially prevailing norms; they also reinforce it among themselves without adult intervention.[5] They use racial reasons for refusing to interact with children different from themselves and exhibit discomfort, and rejection of differently abled people. The degree to which 4-year-olds have already internalized stereotypic gender roles, racial bias, and fear of the differently abled forcefully points out the need for anti-bias education with young children.

What Is Our Responsibility?

Early childhood educators have a serious responsibility to find ways to prevent and counter the damage before it becomes too deep. Selma Greenberg forcefully argues for active intervention to remedy the cognitive, social-emotional, and physical deficits brought about by constraining gender stereotypes that limit growing children's access to specific areas of experience:

> When they enter an early childhood environment, children are more open to friendships with members of the other sex, and more open to non-stereotypic play experiences than they are when they leave. Clearly, while the early childhood environment cannot be held solely responsible for this biased development, it cannot be held totally guiltless either.[6]

Greenberg suggests that early childhood teachers re-evaluate existing early childhood curricula and develop ways to prevent and remediate the developmental deficiencies created by gender stereotyping.

Other researchers also conclude that active intervention by teachers is necessary if children are to develop positive attitudes about people of different races and physical abilities. Contact with children of various backgrounds is *not* enough. For example, Shirley Cohen states that "in the absence of a variety of supports, direct contact can exacerbate mildly negative reactions."[7] Moreover, Mara Sapon-Shevin finds that "interventions not handling the direct confrontation of difference seem doomed, or do little more than bring temporary changes in the patterns of social interaction and acceptance within integrated groups." Consequently, "mainstreaming should not be viewed as an effort to teach children to minimize or ignore difference, but as an effort to teach them *positive, appropriate* response to these differences (p. 24)."[8]

Mary Goodman's research about young children's racial attitudes adds further substantiation to the position that direct contact is not enough. She documented numerous examples of biased behavior and feelings as she watched children play "freely" with each other in interracial, "nonbiased" preschool programs.[9] Catherine Emihovich, looking at children's social relationships in two integrated kindergartens, found that structure and teaching methodology significantly affected the amount and quality of children's interracial peer interaction.[10] Even though both teachers espoused pro-integration attitudes, interracial interaction was high and positive in one classroom but low and negative in the other.

In sum, if children are to grow up with the attitudes, knowledge, and skills necessary for effective living in a complex, diverse world, early childhood programs must actively challenge the impact of bias on children's development.

Common Questions and Answers About an Anti-Bias Curriculum

Won't an anti-bias curriculum make things worse? "If you point out differences, won't children start seeing differences they haven't been noticing?" "If you talk about stereotypes, won't you be teaching them things they would otherwise not learn?" "Isn't it better to emphasize the positive than the negative (how we are different)?"

Concern about addressing differences arises from a mistaken notion of the sources of bias. *It is not differences in themselves that cause the problems, but how people respond to differences.* It is the response to difference that an anti-bias curriculum addresses. If teachers and parents don't talk about differences, as well as similarities, then they can't talk about cultural heritages, or about the struggles of groups and individuals to gain equality and justice. For example, if teachers don't talk about differences in physical ability, children can't figure out ways to modify the environment so that the differently abled child can be as independent as possible. Similarly, celebrating Martin Luther King Jr.'s birthday means little unless teachers talk about his role in organizing millions of people to challenge racism.

The question "Won't an anti-bias curriculum make things worse?" comes out of a "colorblind" or "color-denial" philosophy of how to deal with racial differences. This attitude assumes that differences are insignificant and is exemplified in statements such as "We are all the same" and "A child is a child. I don't notice if they are brown, purple, or green." Child development research is frequently based on a colorblind position and therefore makes the serious error of assuming that the issues of development are the same for all children and that they all share similar contexts for growth.

Colorblindness arose as a progressive argument against racial bigotry, which ranks racial differences, putting "white" on top. However well-intentioned, this is not an adequate response to children's developmental realities. It has been a soothing view for whites, while blatantly ignoring the daily experience of people of color. It establishes the white experience as the norm, and the differences in others' experience become unimportant. It promotes tokenism and a denial of the identity of persons outside the mainstream. Within it, curricula need not address the fact of diversity nor the specifics of a child's identity. Paradoxically, however, people espousing a colorblind position do often recognize the need to bring children of diverse backgrounds together so that, by playing with each other, they can discover that "we are all the same."

> "I don't like Indians. They shoot bows and arrows at people and burn their houses," a 4-year-old informs his class after a visit to Disneyland. "Oh, those aren't real Indians," explains his white teacher. "Real Indians are nice people. They live in houses and wear clothes just like us."

The teacher obviously means well. But, does the "colorblind" teacher's explanation mean that Native Americans who don't live "just like us" (i.e., "just like whites") are not nice people?

Ultimately, the colorblind position results in denial of young children's awareness of differences and to nonconfrontation of children's misconceptions, stereotypes, and discriminatory behavior, be they about race, culture, gender, or different physical abilities. Many caring parents and early childhood teachers make mistakes of this kind. In contrast, an anti-bias approach teaches children to understand and comfortably interact with differences, to appreciate all people's similarities through the different ways they are human, and to recognize and confront ideas and behaviors that are biased.

In an environment in which children feel free to ask questions and make comments about disabilities, gender, and race, there will be an increase in adults' and children's interactions over issues of bias. Sometimes children will test limits set by teachers or parents on unacceptable biased behavior. This does not mean that directly addressing bias is a mistake; it means that children understand that bias is an important issue and are testing to find out how clear and how firm the rules/limits are, as they do when adults set other types of behavioral boundaries.

How does an anti-bias curriculum differ from a multicultural curriculum? The approach of choice among early childhood professionals today is multiculturalism. Its intent is positive: Let's teach children about each other's cultures, so they will learn to respect each other and not develop prejudice. However, deterioration into a *tourist curriculum* often keeps this approach from accomplishing its intent.

A tourist curriculum is likely to teach about cultures through celebrations and through such "artifacts" of the culture as food, traditional clothing, and household implements. Multicultural activities are special events in the children's week, separate from the ongoing daily curriculum. Thus, Chinese New Year is the activity that teaches about Chinese Americans; a dragon is constructed, and parents are asked to come to school wearing "Chinese" clothing to cook a "Chinese" dish with the children, who have the opportunity on this one day to try eating with chopsticks. Mexican American life is introduced through Cinco de Mayo, another celebration. Indeed, some multicultural curricula are written in the form of calendars, suggesting foods, crafts, and perhaps a dance to do on specific days. Paradoxically, the dominant, Anglo–European culture is not studied as such. Christmas is not perceived as an "ethnic" holiday coming from specific cultural perspectives, but is treated as a universal holiday.

The tourist curriculum is both patronizing, emphasizing the "exotic" differences between cultures, and trivializing, dealing not with the real-life daily problems and experiences of different peoples, but with surface aspects of their celebrations and modes of entertainment. Children "visit" non-white cultures and then "go home" to the daily classroom, which reflects only the dominant culture. The focus on holidays, although it provides drama and delight for both children and adults, gives the impression that that is all "other" people—usually people of color—do. What it fails to communicate is real understanding.

Patricia Ramsey highlights other problems that may characterize the multicultural curriculum:

- It frequently focuses on information about other countries—learning about Japan or Mexico—rather than learning about Japanese Americans or exploring the diversity of culture among Mexican Americans.
- It may be standardized, with the assumption that there should or can be one set of goals and activities for all settings, ignoring the importance of taking into account the backgrounds of the children, their experience or lack of experience with people from other groups, and their attitudes toward their own and other groups.
- Teachers may assume that children only need a multicultural curriculum if there is diversity in the classroom. This seems to be an issue particularly for teachers in all-white classrooms, when, in fact, white children may be the most in need of learning about the differences that exist in American society.[11]

An anti-bias curriculum incorporates the positive intent of the multicultural curriculum and uses some similar activities, while seeking to avoid the dangers of a tourist approach. At the same time, an anti-bias curriculum provides a more inclusive education: (a) it addresses more than cultural diversity by including gender and differences in physical abilities; (b) it is based on children's developmental tasks as they construct identity and attitudes; and (c) it directly addresses the impact of stereotyping bias and discriminatory behavior in young children's development and interactions.

Is it developmentally appropriate to openly raise these anti-bias issues of injustice with young children? Certainly, they have lots of experience with the day-to-day problems and conflicts generated by their own differences. They have lots of experience with problem solving "fair" or "not fair." They have the capacity for expressing hurt and enjoying empathy and fairness. Adults often want to defer children's exposure to the unpleasant realities of bias, to create a protected world of childhood. By so doing, however, they leave children to solve troublesome problems by themselves.

The anti-bias curriculum should be grounded in a developmental approach. In order to develop activities that respond effectively to children's specific interests and concerns, it is first necessary to understand what a child is asking, wants to know, or means by a question or comment. Moreover, unless the curriculum consistently takes into account children's perspectives, it may become oppressive to them. They must be free to ask questions about any subject, to use their own ideas in problem solving, to engage in real dialogue with adults, to make choices, and to have some say in their daily school life. If we are to facilitate children's sense of self-esteem, critical thinking, and ability to stand up for themselves and others, then our methodology must allow them to experience their intelligence and power as having a constructive effect on their world.

I already have so much to do, how am I going to find time to learn the necessary skills and add anti-bias activities to my curriculum? A teacher has no choice if she or he wants to enable children to develop fully. The point to remember is that an anti-bias approach is *integrated into* rather than *added onto* an existing curriculum. Looking at a curriculum through an anti-bias lens affects everything a teacher does. Much classroom work will continue, some activities will be modified, some eliminated, some new ones created. Beginning is hard, not because of new activities, but because teachers have to re-evaluate what they have been doing. This means being self-conscious and learning by trial and error. After a while—six months, a year—it becomes impossible to teach without an anti-bias perspective. ■

Excerpted from *Anti-Bias Curriculum: Tools for Empowering Young Children.* Washington, D.C. National Association for the Education of Young Children. 1989.

Now retired, **Louise Derman-Sparks** was on the faculty of Pacific Oaks College in Pasadena, Calif., for more than 30 years. She has taught and directed early childhood programs and authored/co-authored several books on anti-bias and anti-racism development and learning. She speaks publicly, consults, and is an activist for peace and justice.

References

1. Eugene Levitt and Shirley Cohen. "Attitudes of Children Toward their Handicapped Peers." *Childhood Education.* 52. pp. 171–173. 1976.
2. Phyllis A. Katz. "Development of Children's Racial Awareness and Intergroup Attitudes." *Current Topics in Early Childhood Education.* 4. pp. 17-54. 1982.
3. Lawrence Kohlberg. "A Cognitive-Developmental Analysis of Children's Sex-Role Concepts and Attitudes." E. E. Maccoby, ed. *The Development of Sex Differences.* Stanford, Calif. Stanford University Press. pp. 82–172. 1966.
4. Marguerite N. Alejandro-Wright. "The Child's Conception of Racial Classification." In M. B. Spencer, G. K. Brookins, and W. R. Allen, eds. *Beginnings: The Social and Affective Development of Black Children.* Hillsdale, N.J. Erlbaum. pp. 185–200. 1985.
5. Alice Sterling Honig. "Sex Role Socialization in Early Childhood." In *Young Children.* 38 (6). pp. 57–70. 1983.
   Jaipaul L Roopnarine. "Sex-Typed Socialization in Mixed Age Preschool Children." In *Child Development.* 55. pp. 1078-1084. 1984.
6. Selma Greenberg. "Eliminating Sex Bias in Early Childhood." In *Equal Play.* 1 (4). p. 5. 1980.
7. Shirley Cohen. "Fostering Positive Attitudes toward the Handicapped: New Curriculum." In *Children Today.* 6 (6). pp. 7–12. 1977.
8. Mara Sapin-Shevin. "Teaching Young Children about Differences: Resources for Teaching." In *Young Children.* 38 (2). pp. 24-32. 1983.
9. Mary E. Goodman. *Race Awareness in Young Children.* New York. Collier. 1964.
10. Catherine A. Emihovich. "Social Interaction in Two Integrated Kindergartens." In *Integrated Education.* 19 (3–6). pp. 72–78. 1980.
11. Patricia Ramsey. "Multicultural Education in Early Childhood." In *Young Children.* 37 (2). pp. 13–24. 1982.

Developmental Themes, Tasks, and Goals in Anti-Bias Work

By Margie Carter and Deb Curtis

This chart is republished from *Training Teachers: A Harvest of Theory and Practice* (Redleaf Press, 1994). It is adapted from *Anti-Bias Curriculum: Tools for Empowering Young Children*, by Louise Derman-Sparks and the A.B.C. Task Force (National Association for the Education of Young Children, 1989). The chart offers an overview of children's understanding of gender identity, physical disability, racial differences and silimarities, and cultural identity as well as anti-bias goals for children's learning in these areas.

—Editor

GENDER IDENTITY

Twos	Threes and Fours	Fives
Curious about anatomy; notices differences in gender. Nonverbally explores differences (looking, pointing, touching). Learning names of body parts. Confused about anatomical differences; may think they have both types of genitals or that they can change their body parts. Learning attitudes of dominant culture toward gender; learning from different behaviors and messages towards boys and girls. *Developmental Goal:* To gain simple matter-of-fact information about anatomy. Acceptance regarding curiosity. Construct a healthy non-sexist identity based on anatomy as what determines gender, rather than looks, e.g., hair length or clothing.	Know whether they are a boy or girl. Strongly influenced by dominant culture attitudes toward gender behavior; have definite ideas about how boys and girls are supposed to do things differently. Confused about gender constancy. Have questions about whether they will remain the same gender as they grow. *Developmental Goal:* To develop a clear, healthy gender identity through understanding that being a boy or a girl depends on anatomy, not on what they like to do; to expand understanding.	Have established gender identity constancy; know that they are and will remain a boy or girl. Have learned to be embarrassed about gender anatomy and show this through teasing, giggling, and secret genital play. Curious about how babies are born. Defining own gender identity; acting out prevailing gender stereotypes. *Developmental Goal:* To expand ideas regarding gender roles to counter prevailing biases; to acquire accurate information and terms about gender anatomy and differences; to be aware of a variety of role models who cross gender lines.

LEARNING ABOUT PHYSICAL DIFFERENCES AND DISABILITIES		
Twos Notices the more obvious differences in physical abilities, such as a person using a wheelchair, a brace, or crutches to move around. Uses nonverbal behavior to explore differences such as staring, imitating, pointing. Shows signs of "pre-prejudice," discomfort, or fear with physical differences. *Developmental Goal:* To gain words for observations; to receive acceptance for curiosity; to develop comfort and familiarity with physical differences.	**Threes, Fours and Fives** Able to see shared abilities and similarities. Notices and asks questions about disabilities. Curious about equipment and devices people use to help with disability. Confusion about what a person with a disability can or can't do. Has anxiety and fear about being hurt or "catching" the disability through contact with the person or equipment. May reject or show fear or impatience with someone differently abled; lack skills for interacting with differently abled.	*Developmental Goals:* Children with disability—to see themselves reflected in the world around them; to receive acceptance for who they are; to develop autonomy and independence. Children without disability—to ask questions and express feelings about disabilities; to gain information about and comfort with those who are disabled.

RACIAL DIFFERENCES AND SIMILARITIES

Twos	Threes and Fours	Fives
Notices differences in skin color; learning color names. Curious about differences in hair texture. Uses nonverbal cues to signal noticing differences; may react with curiosity or fear. Overgeneralizes common characteristic such as skin color, e.g., "those are some of the Cosby people." *Developmental Goal:* To develop a positive awareness of own racial identity; to learn words for observations of differences; to develop a comfortable awareness of others.	Continued curiosity about racial differences; wonder where they fit in. Aware of and sensitive to attitudes toward skin color and other racial characteristics; becoming aware of societal bias against darker skin and other physical differences. Wants to know how they got their color, hair, and eye characteristics. Aware that getting older brings changes; wonders if skin color, hair, and eyes remain constant. Confusion about racial group names and actual color of their skin. *Developmental Goal:* To understand that racial identity does not change; to learn accurate information about racial identity to counter bias; to understand that one is part of a large group with similar characteristics (not "different") and to feel comfortable with exactly who one is.	Can begin to understand scientific explanations for differences in skin color, hair texture, and eye shape. Can understand more fully the range of racial differences and similarities. *Developmental Goal:* To understand and value the range of differences among racial groups.

CULTURAL DIFFERENCES AND SIMILARITIES		
Twos	**Threes and Fours**	**Fives**
Aware of cultural aspects of gender and ethnic identity. Can understand different words from different languages. *Developmental Goal:* To see self as a part of a family group.	Understands cultural identity as it relates to their family; knows one has individuality and a group connection. Confused about criteria for ethnic/cultural group membership. Acquiring information and bias from the dominant culture's prevailing attitudes and images. Cultural understanding is based on concrete, daily living with family members through language, family stories, values, celebrations, spiritual life. Beginning to understand that everyone has a culture or group identity and that there are similarities and differences among children and adults. *Developmental Goal:* For white children—to counter the developing belief that the dominant white culture is superior to other ways of life. For children of color—to build a positive sense of person and group identity; to see themselves as of equal value to others.	Begin to make connections between their individual and family cultural identity and the larger cultural/ethnic group. Begin to understand people's struggles for justice and a better quality of life. *Developmental Goal:* To understand the broader context of how individuals and families relate to the larger community; to begin to identify bias and find ways to take action to challenge and change injustice.

Margie Carter began her work in early childhood education as a teacher of 1st grade, kindergarten, and preschool children and has gone on to direct childcare programs, create staff development videos, and co-author seven books. She is on the web at ecetrainers.com.

Deb Curtis has worked as a preschool teacher and a teacher educator. She is the co-author of seven books about joyful, reflective teaching and learning and about designing engaging environments for young children. She is on the web at ecetrainers.com.

SUSAN LINA RUGGLES

Raising Issues of Race with Young Children

BY RITA TENORIO

Before I became principal of La Escuela Fratney, an ethnically diverse school in a racially mixed working-class Milwaukee neighborhood, I taught kindergarten and 1st grade for many years. I still remember sitting down one day with children in my 1st-grade class, early in the year when we were getting to know each other. We talked about how we were alike, how we were different. "Our skin is different," one of the children said. I asked everyone to put their hands together on the table, so we could see all the different colors.

One of my African American students, LaRhonda,* simply would not. Scowling, she slid her hands beneath the table top, unwilling to have her color compared to the others.

It was a reaction I had seen before. Even for students with only six or seven years of life experience, the centuries-old legacies of bias and racism in our country have made an impact on their lives. I have seen fair-skinned children deliberately change places in a circle if African American children sit down next to them. An English speaker won't play with a Latino child because, he says, "He talks funny." On the playground, a group of white girls won't let their darker-skinned peers join in their games, explaining matter-of-factly: "Brown kids can't be in our club."

Early in my teaching career, I might have told LaRhonda we were all equal and we were all the same, and left it at that. But much has changed, and

I've learned that it is part of my job to help students to learn how to discuss issues of race.

I now know that while early childhood students are too young to intellectually understand the complexities of issues such as racism or prejudice, their behaviors show the influence of societal stereotypes and biases. Throughout my career I have had children who vehemently believed that Indians all live in "teepees" or, even worse, that there were no more Indians "'cause the cowboys killed them all."

I had wanted to believe that children arrived in kindergarten with an open mind on all subjects. But the reality is different. Children mirror the attitudes of society and of their families. Researchers have found that between the ages of 2 and 5, children not only become aware of racial differences but begin to make judgments based on that awareness. Having watched on average over 5,000 hours of TV by age 5, it is no wonder that some children believe all Indians are dead. Television's influence is further compounded by the segregated lives many children lead prior to coming to school.

A New Anti-Racist Curriculum

In the 1970s and 1980s, multicultural education meant moving from holiday to holiday, learning about cultures all over the world. As a teacher in those years, I changed bulletin boards and literacy activities to correspond to the holidays, and proudly integrated the activities into my daily lessons. We learned about our "differences" and celebrated our "similarities." I insisted that "we can all live together" and forbade words or actions that would "hurt" anyone.

My message was that everyone would be treated fairly and equally in our classroom, and I thought it worked. My classroom was filled with active, playful, well-disciplined children. I held high expectations for all the children and by all obvious measures they were growing and learning in ways that pleased both me and their parents. Yet over the years I became uncomfortable with my approach.

Even in my fair and "equal" classroom environment, there were frustrating conflicts. Sometimes they centered around a verbal put-down, other times they involved body language—such as when white or lighter-skinned children would get up and move if a brown Latino or African American child sat next to them. Life on the playground could be even rougher and certain students would be isolated or ridiculed if they were different. Even the children's "make-believe" stories were at times defined by race. Comments like, "You can't be the queen; there are no black queens," caught me off-guard. Equally disturbing, more often than not the children accepted these hierarchies without complaint.

As part of the group of educators who founded La Escuela Fratney, a two-way, English/ Spanish bilingual school, I had my chance to forge an entirely new kindergarten curriculum that was multicultural and anti-racist. Fratney envisioned students not only learning about the history and culture of the major ethnic groups, but also understanding racism's influence on all of us.

At Fratney, which serves 400 students from kindergarten through 5th grade, we discuss issues of social justice with all of our students. Teachers strive to build classroom community by helping children learn about each other's lives and families. They ask students to collect and share information about their families and ancestry. For example, they might talk about how they got their names, how their families came to live in Milwaukee, which holidays they celebrate and how. And at every step teachers help the children to explore the nature of racial and cultural differences and to overcome simplistic notions of "who's better" or who is "like us" and who isn't. Some years ago, as part of a 1st-grade team, I helped to develop a series of activities and projects that help children to discuss issues of race and social justice in a meaningful, age-appropriate way.

These activities include:

Me Pockets

This was always a class favorite. Each child took home a letter-sized clear plastic sleeve, the kind used to display baseball cards. We asked students to fill the pockets with photos, pictures, drawings, or anything else that will help us know more about them and the things that are important in their lives. They returned the pockets within a week and put them into a three-ring binder that became the favorite classroom book to read and re-read.

The individual pockets reflected the cultural and socioeconomic diversity of the families. Some students put lots of photos or computer images in their pockets. Others cut pictures out of magazines or made drawings. Every family was anxious to share in some way, and family members took time to help their children develop the project.

If someone didn't bring their Me Pocket sheet back, the teachers stepped in to help them find pictures or make the drawings they needed to add their page to the binder.

I was always amazed at how quickly the children learned the details about each other's lives from this project: who had a pet, who took dance classes, who liked to eat macaroni and cheese. The children knew there were differences among them, but they also love to share the things that are alike.

"Look, Rachel has two brothers, just like me."

"I didn't know that Jamal's family likes to camp. We do, too!"

Each of the teachers also completed a Me Pocket. The students loved looking at the picture of me as a 1st-grader, seeing my husband and children, and learning that chocolate cake is my favorite food.

Partner Questions

Each day we took time to teach the social skills of communicating ideas with others and listening to another person's perspective. We used this time to "practice" those skills with role-playing activities and problem-solving situations they or we brought to the group. For example, we asked such questions as: What is the meanest thing anyone has ever said to you? Why do you think some people like to use put-downs? The children took a few minutes to talk about this with a partner. Afterwards some were willing to share with the whole group. We sometimes then role-played the situation as a group and looked for ways to respond, such as speaking back to insults.

"Someone Special"

By the end of October, during the time of Halloween, Día de los Muertos, and All Souls' Day, we learned about how people remember their ancestors and others who have died or who are far away. We set up a table and students were encouraged to bring in pictures or artifacts to display. They brought a remarkable variety of things: jewelry, a trophy won by a departed relative, a postcard that person sent them, or perhaps the program from a funeral. And they brought many, many stories. Again, the teachers also participated and shared stories of those who have gone before us. We got great responses from our students, and from their families.

MARILYN NOLT

Let's Talk About Skin

Another important conversation I had with my students focused on the varieties of skin color we had in our group. Usually when we began this discussion, some children were uncomfortable about saying "what they are" or describing the color of their skin. In particular, children with very dark skin—like LaRhonda, who would not even put her hands on the table—were often reluctant to join in. Meanwhile, the white kids often boasted about being "pink." Though we'd never talked about this in class before, there was definitely a strong implication that it was better to be lighter.

Many children were amazed that this topic was put out on the table for discussion. The looks in their eyes, their frequent reluctance to begin the discussion, told me that this was a very personal topic.

As part of the lesson, we asked the students if they had ever heard anyone say something bad or mean about another person's skin color. The hands shot up.

"My mom says that you can't trust black people."

"My sister won't talk to the Puerto Rican kids on the bus."

"Mara said that I couldn't play, that I was too black to be her friend."

They continued to raise their hands and this conversation went on for a while. We talked about ways we'd heard others use people's skin color to make fun of them or put them down. We talked about what to do in those situations.

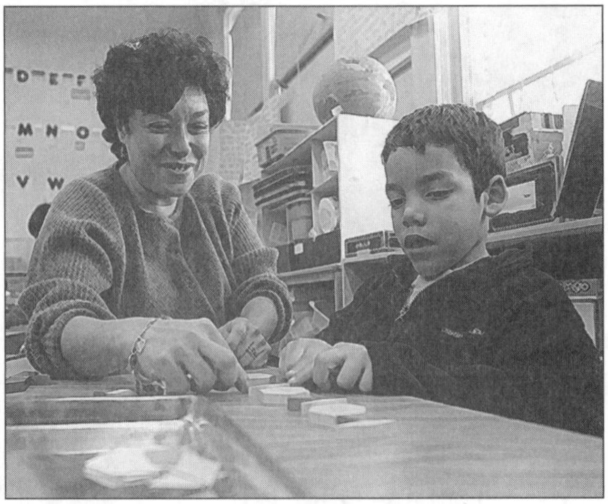
PETER ZUZGA

Rita Tenorio with one of her students.

As we continued to discuss issues of race, we teachers often introduced our personal experiences. I told them about the first time I realized that black and white people were treated differently. I shared my experience being one of the few Latinas in my school. And we tried to ask questions that really intrigued the students, that invited them to try to look at things with a different perspective, to learn something new about the human experience and be open-minded to that idea: Do people choose their colors? Where do you get your skin color? Is it better to be one color than another? Lots of our conversations revolved around a story or a piece of literature.

With a little work, we were able to expand this discussion of skin color in ways that incorporated math lessons, map lessons, and other curricular areas. We did surveys to see how many of our ancestors came from warm places or cold places. We asked children to interview their relatives to find out where the family came from. We created a bulletin board display and a graph that we used to compare and learn about the huge variety of places our students' relatives were from.

Skin Color and Science

Our class discussions of skin color set the stage for lots of "scientific" observations.

For example, I brought in a large variety of paint chips from a local hardware store. The students loved examining and sorting the many shades of beige and brown. It took a while for them to find the one that was most like their own skin color.

In the story *The Colors of Us*, by Karen Katz, Lena learns from her mother that "brown" is a whole range of colors. Like the characters in the story, we took red, yellow, black, and white paint and mixed them in various combinations until we'd each found the color of our own skin. Then we displayed our research as part of our science fair project.

In another exercise, inspired by Sheila Hamanaka's *All the Colors of the Earth*, students were asked to find words to describe the color of their skin, and to find something at home that matched their skin color. Then we displayed the pieces of wood and fabric, the little bags of cinnamon and coffee, the dolls and ceramic pieces that "matched" us.

As we continued these explorations, dealing concretely with a topic that so many have never heard discussed in such a manner, students began to see past society's labels. It was always amazing to children that friends who call themselves "black," for example, could actually have very light skin. Or that children who perceived themselves as "Puerto Rican" could be darker than some of the African American children.

Writing About Our Colors

As children began to understand the idea of internalizing another's point of view, they could apply that understanding by examining different ideas and alternatives to their own experiences. As they learned to express themselves through reading and writing, they learned to challenge stereotypes and speak back to unfair behavior and comments.

Once students had a chance to reflect on skin color, they wrote about it. Annie wrote: "I like my skin color. It is like peachy cream." James wrote: "My color is the same as my dad's. I think the new baby will have this color too." And Keila wrote: "When I was born, my color was brown skin and white skin mixed together."

When LaRhonda wrote about mixing the colors to match her skin, she said: "We put black, white, red, and yellow [together]. I like the color of my skin." How far she had come since the day she would not show us her hands.

Tackling Issues

These activities had an impact. Parents spoke to us about the positive impression that these activities made on the children. Many children had taken their first steps toward awareness of race. They were not afraid to discuss it. They had developed more ways in which to think about and describe themselves.

Yet these activities are no guarantee that children will internalize anti-racist ideas. So much depends on the other forces in their lives. Teachers are still working on making these activities better: doing them sooner in the year, integrating them into other subjects, deepening the conversations, finding other stories or activities to support them. Each year's student group is different, and we need to incorporate their experiences and understandings. We learn something new every time. The students challenge my consciousness too.

Are They Too Young for This?

Many people would say that children at this age are too young to deal with these serious issues. I too had real questions at first about what was actually possible with young children. Can you have "real" conversations with 6-year-olds about power, privilege, and racism in our society? Can you make them aware of the effects that racism and injustice have in our lives? Can they really understand their role in the classroom community?

The answer to all of these questions is "yes." Even very young children can explore and understand the attitudes they and their classmates bring to school each day. They have real issues and opinions to share, and many, many questions of their own to ask. In this way they can begin to challenge some of the assumptions that influence their behavior toward classmates who don't look or talk the same way they do.

Children at this age can explore rules and learn about collecting data, making inferences, and forming conclusions. They can compare the experiences of people and think about what these experiences mean. They can, that is, if they are given the opportunity.

We rely on our schools to be the place for a multicultural, multiracial experience for our children. We want to believe that learning together will help our students to become more understanding and respectful of differences. Yet so often we do not address these issues head-on. Teachers have a responsibility to recognize the influence of racism on themselves and their students. And we can help children learn the skills and strategies they will need to counteract it in their lives. It is unlikely that sensitivity and tolerance will develop, that children will bridge the gaps they bring to school from their earliest days, without specific instruction.

I want to see more than tolerance developed. I want children to see themselves as the future citizens of this country. I want them to gain the knowledge to be successful in this society. Beyond that, though, I want them to understand that they have the power to transform society, and to live in a world where children won't hesitate to share the color of their skin. ■

Rita Tenorio is the principal of La Escuela Fratney in Milwaukee, Wis.

DEB CURTIS

Using Persona Dolls

to Help Children Develop Anti-Bias Attitudes

BY TRISHA WHITNEY

The foundation of the *Kids Like Us* storytelling method is a set of dolls. These dolls can be homemade or bought from a catalog. They can be as small as 10 inches or as large as life-sized. They can be made of cloth or plastic and dressed in handmade clothing or thrift store baby clothes that look like older kid clothes. In other words, many types of dolls are useable for storytelling. *Kids Like Us* dolls are special. They are not the same as the dolls found in the housekeeping area of many classrooms. Classroom dolls are usually babies, meant to be diapered and fed, held as one's own baby in each child's imaginings. *Kids Like Us* dolls are not babies. They are the same age as your students. Each doll represents a real person and maintains its own identity: personal traits, family, and culture. Some of these details are invented before presenting the dolls to the children, and some are added as they relate to stories the dolls take part in. But these details stay the same over time, just as the details of a real student's life would.

For example, when I made a doll with dark brown skin and black cornrows, I decided it was a girl, named her Ianthe, and set her age at 6 years old and her race as African American. I decided that she lives with her mother and father and her younger brother Henry, one of my other dolls. As I told stories about Ianthe, I added to her biography that she is a very close friend of another doll named Julio and that she likes to jump rope and climb trees.

These are the basic facts of Ianthe's life. Children meet Ianthe early in the year and can always say, "I know her!" when she comes to talk to them. All kinds of things happen to Ianthe throughout the year. The children see her at storytelling sessions. They listen to her problems and hear about her joys. They help her think of ways to solve her problems. They are happy for her and sad for her. They relate to her much as they would a classroom friend.

A classroom collection of *Kids Like Us* dolls can be as few as four and as many as twenty. The dolls are introduced one at a time, helping the class get to know each one individually. The collection should represent the population of students in the class and many other kids who are not represented in the class. Take into account a number of details when creating the dolls' lives—gender, age, race and ethnicity, religion, family structure, culture, class, likes and dislikes, languages, special abilities and disabilities. In this way each student will see herself in parts of the dolls and will also become comfortable with diversity.

DEB CURTIS

To make the storytelling situations as real as possible, the dolls are treated much as if they were students in the class. They are kept in a special place in the classroom where they can "observe" what is happening in the room. They are available to come to talk with the group at a moment's notice but are not within a child's reach. When they are brought down from their observation point, they are treated with respect. They like hugs but do not want their hair pulled or their clothes taken off. The teacher sets the tone for this scenario of "real kids, just like us," and the children love to be part of it. "Ianthe has a problem she is hoping you can help her with," is answered with cries of "*What's wrong, Ianthe?*" and "*We'll help you, Ianthe! Don't worry!*"

Telling stories with your dolls will allow you to easily involve your students in practicing pro-social skills, problem solving, cooperation, and dealing with emotions. Being involved in discussions about the stories enables each student to develop empathy and anti-bias attitudes. Doll stories are the perfect way to gently correct incorrect beliefs or stereotypes your students may have picked up.

The bias that children experience may take several forms. You will tell stories in which children experience name-calling, exclusion, hurtful teasing, and other biased behaviors.

> "When everyone went around the circle to tell what they want to be when they grow up, Brad said he would like to be a nurse. Then Rajit laughed and said 'You can't be a nurse, dummy. That's for girls!'"
>
> "When Henry went to play in the boat, two kids yelled at him, 'Go away! No black kids in here!'"
>
> "When Ianthe was at play practice, one of the other kids told her to give up her chair. Ianthe told him no, because she was sitting in the chair. He said she should go sit on the floor because her family comes from Africa. He said everybody in Africa sits in the dirt, so Ianthe should too."

Don't be afraid to tell stories like these. Children need to experience the feelings these dolls have in order to understand how much bias hurts. They will learn by empathizing with the dolls, discussing strategies for dealing with the situations, and seeing themselves as a person who will not act in this way.

Remember that although many such situations feel heartwrenching to us, children listening to the same story may not be aware of the implications of hundreds of years of history that we feel behind such comments. And many of these situations are likely to be occurring in their everyday lives. Many times children will have even more intense experiences to relate when you bring these issues up in a story. In fact, the last two stories are real ones. The first was observed in a childcare setting with 4-year-olds, and the second was related by a 10-year-old.

The stories you tell will have a different meaning for each student. Some children will relate to the story as something that might or already has happened to them or the people they know. Others will recognize their own biased behavior. Both groups of children will benefit by hearing the story.

This is not to say that students will be unaffected by the feelings inherent in the stories that you are telling. As part of the planning process, you will need to prepare to support students who might relate personally to the story you are planning.

The main goal for all of the children when listening to these stories is the same: to learn that acting in a biased way is unfair, hurtful, and, most important, not something any of us ever want to do. They will learn to recognize common biased behaviors such as name-calling, exclusion, and hurtful teasing. As they critique these situations, all the children will practice the critical thinking skills that are essential to recognizing and rejecting bias as they experience it in their lives. This ability will make it possible for them to avoid incorporating biased ideas into their belief systems and allow them to stand up against bias when they encounter it.

To plan a story line about a bias situation, decide what bias the story will present and in what way the bias will be expressed. Determine whether the doll you use as the main character will be acting in a biased way or experiencing the bias. Then choose the doll that best fits these details.

It is important to deal extensively with the issue of exclusion. You can do this as part of the process of learning about the common biased behaviors. Because behavior that involves excluding others is very likely to occur among your students, you will probably find yourself needing a story about exclusion at the beginning of the year, before you have even had a chance to tell many other stories. As with any bias incident, be sure to intervene in these situations *at the time they happen.* Then you can use your *Kids Like Us* dolls in an exclusion story, even if you have not yet practiced all the preparatory skills. You can always go back and work on those later. It is more important to deal with the issue immediately.

Children often use exclusion, based on any bias that comes in handy, to wield social power. Yelling a derogatory name and insisting on making someone an outsider gives a child a sense of power and superiority if the group goes along with her. Your goal, then, in telling *Kids Like Us* doll stories about exclusion is to unmask the reasons for this behavior and turn the "kid culture" against it. This will make it impossible for anyone in your group to use this method since the others will see through the bias to this child's motivation and refuse to cooperate with the exclusion:

> "The other day at recess Julio was watching a basketball game some kids were playing. He really wanted to play, but when he tried to get in the game one of the kids said, 'Man, you can't play ball with those lame shoes!' Julio ran and hid in the bathroom."

> "Lucia wanted to sit with Brad at lunch time. But Brad told Lucia she couldn't sit next to him because she was a stupid girl. He said only boys can sit with him."

> "Umoja and Ianthe started a doggie club with the kids on their street. Everybody got a great doggie name. But when River came by and asked to join the club, they told him, 'This club is only for us African American kids. You're white, so you can't be in it.'"

To help students understand what bias is and how hurtful it can be, you will want to tell stories about subjects common to most of your students' lives. Telling stories about things that might happen at school are easiest to create accurately and uses an environment that is familiar to the children.

Language bias; Hurtful teasing: "Julio is doing very well learning English. One thing he has a hard time with is saying the V sound. In Spanish that letter sounds almost like 'buh.' And then yesterday Julio told the class he was working very hard on his science project. Rajit laughed and said it sounded like Julio was working 'berry hard.' He said, 'Is your project about berries, Julio?' And the whole class laughed."

Family structure bias; Insistence on conformity to another's beliefs: "One of the kids looked at Lucia's drawing of her family and said, 'Where's your mom and dad? You can't have a family with just a grandma in it!'"

Racial bias; Exclusion: "The kids were having fun up on top of the jungle gym. When Mei Lin came and tried to climb up, Rachel yelled 'NO! ONLY AMERICANS UP HERE!'"

Single incident bias; Name-calling: "One day Rachel got the flu while she was at school. Her stomach hurt really bad and then she threw up on her desk. Melly yelled, 'Stinky! Stinky! Don't come near me, Stinky!' when Rachel walked past her. The next day Melly called her Stinky again, and so did some of the other kids."

Disability bias; Constant focus on one characteristic of another person: "Henry talks with his hands. When he first came to Saed's class, he wanted to teach Henry words with his mouth. He went to speech class to learn how to do this. But Saed would take him around the classroom and say words to him and make him try to copy him. At recess he would take his hand and make him go with him to learn more words all round the playground. But Henry wanted to play in the sandbox."

Gender bias; Name-calling: "Brad was very excited because he got to go to dance class with Elizabeth one day. But when he told Mickey about it, Mickey said, 'A boy at dance class? What are you, a fag?'"

Culture bias; Put-downs: "Julio could hardly wait for lunch because he had some special yummy tamales left over from the party the day before. But when he got out his lunch, Elizabeth looked at his tamales and asked, 'What's that blucky thing?'"

Remember to tailor these situations to your own class. In a class that is mostly Latino, this story might happen from the following perspective: "Elizabeth could hardly wait for lunch because she has some special yummy potato salad left over from the party the day before. But when she got out her lunch, Julio looked at her lunch and said, 'What's that junk?'"

Each group of students has had different experiences. Your knowledge of them and the issues important to them will be the best guide as to which stories they are ready to discuss. Later you can examine biases they may not have any experience with yet.

It will be important to tell the stories based on many different biases. In this way students learn that biased behavior is not really about the subject of the bias itself but about a lack of knowledge, the wielding of power, or the need to feel better than someone else. Knowing that the problem lies with the person expressing the bias helps children avoid believing in the bias themselves.

All of your students will experience bias aimed at them. This is not just an issue for the "diverse" students in your class. While some children will experience more bias throughout their lives because the bias against them is backed by the institutional power in our society, every single one of the children will feel the threat of having bias leveled at them at one time or another. If a child doesn't get teased about her race or religion, there are always other targets—a nose that is too freckled, hips that are too wide, the "dorky" shoes, or the time she threw up in class. You will want your doll stories to represent this fact and not focus on a few dolls for whom bias might be "a problem." Bias is a problem for all of us.

The story line is only the beginning of the story process. With your students, you will examine the feelings of the character being treated unfairly. They will discuss the problem with the way the doll is being treated. They will brainstorm strategies to deal with the situation, and you will relate how the doll successfully handled it. Your students will take a journey through the story to the successful conclusion, right along with the doll.

Some stories should be told from the perspective of the doll that acts in a biased manner. This way you have an opportunity to discuss how a person is feeling when they do this and to help them understand the motivations behind it. An easy story line to create is one that tells about a doll who experiences something new and then rejects it.

> "River had never met anyone with cerebral palsy before. When Mickey first came into River's classroom, River asked his teacher, 'How come that kid's all jerky? He gives me the creeps!'"

> "Rachel's class learned a lot about what it is like to live in India. Then one day they had a special India party. Some of the kids tried on beautiful saris and jewelry from India. Everybody enjoyed a shadow puppet show. Rachel said that the saris were pretty costumes but she liked real clothes better."

Another story line that comes from the perspective of a doll acting in a biased way shows the doll actively avoiding other people due to its incorrect beliefs. This is a common reaction to diversity. These stories are especially good for bringing out the feelings that cause children to act in a biased way.

> "Elizabeth saw a man with a missing hand at the library. He had a metal claw that could grip things. Elizabeth cried and tried to pull her mom out of the library because she thought the man was a bad man and that he would grab her with the claw."

> "When Marcy first came to her child care she didn't want to hold hands with Henry. She thought his brown skin was like dirt and would rub off on her."

Dolls can also tell about a stereotype or other bias that they have come to believe. In these stories, the dolls tell about a mistake they made because of a stereotype or incorrect belief they had and how they learned from it. The feelings of both characters will be examined. The doll believing the stereotype will come to the circle to help the children understand that everyone acts in a biased way sometimes. The doll who has been treated unfairly will be named, to help the children begin to look at both perspectives in one situation.

> "Lucia was all excited about Christmas coming. She asked Saed if he was excited too. Saed told Lucia that his family is Muslim and they don't celebrate Christmas. Lucia thought everyone celebrated Christmas."

I tell another story, usually around Thanksgiving, to counteract the stereotypes to which I know the children will be exposed.

> "When River learned that Melly was Native American, he was excited. He asked her, 'Will you show me how to hunt for buffalo?' Melly said she belongs to the Siletz tribe, because her mom and dad do. She told him Siletz are water people and never hunted buffalo, even a long time ago."

DEB CURTIS

Most bias stories should be told from the perspective of the doll being treated unfairly since children need much practice in putting themselves in this doll's place. To focus on how it feels to experience bias, bring a doll to circle to relate how another doll or dolls acted in a biased way toward her.

"Marcy got permission from her mom to invite Brad over to play. But when Marcy asked Brad if he could come, he said, 'Naw, I don't wanna. You don't hardly have any toys to play with at your house. Don't your parents ever buy you anything?'"

"When Lucia got mad at Mei Lin, she pulled her eyes into little slits and said, 'I don't have to do what you say. You have ugly eyes!'"

"Last week all the kids made flower vases for their mothers for Mother's Day. Rajit made two vases so he would have one to give to each of his moms. Then Umoja said, 'You can't have two moms! Everybody has only one!' When Rajit told Umoja he *did* have two moms, she said Rajit was weird."

Some stories should show how a doll used to believe in a bias against herself. This is the reality for many children (and adults too). The children really like the dolls, and so taking part in a *Kids Like Us* doll story where the entire class encourages the doll not to believe those biased ideas can help them feel better about themselves.

"Umoja hates her name. She wishes she could change it to Susan. Or maybe Hilary. When she first came to her school and the teacher told the class her name, some of the kids laughed. Now Umoja is afraid someone will laugh again."

"Mei Lin hates her straight black hair. She thinks it is ugly. She wishes she had long blond hair like River."

"Elizabeth loves dancing. Whenever she hears music, she just has to move. She even got her mom to sign her up for dance class so she could learn more. But then one of the kids at the dance class said to her, 'What are you doing here? Don't you know elephants can't dance?' Now Elizabeth never dances any more. In fact, at recess time she sits on a bench and reads a book instead of running and playing tag like she did before."

"Ianthe used to think she wasn't pretty because she has dark brown skin. She used to put herself down about it. Then her class got a brown bunny for a pet. Everyone said what a beautiful brown coat the bunny had—and then Ianthe realized her skin is almost the same beautiful brown color as that bunny." ■

Excerpted from *Kids Like Us: Using Persona Dolls in the Classroom.* St. Paul, Minn. Redleaf Press. 2002.

Trisha Whitney is teacher and director at The Drinking Gourd Elementary School in Eugene, Ore. *Kids Like Us* is her first book.

STEPHEN KRONINGER

Miles of Aisles of Sexism

Helping Students Investigate Toy Stores

BY SUDIE HOFMANN

You sure wouldn't know our society has experienced almost 40 years of significant changes in the area of gender equity in education after a trip to the mall.

Toy stores are stubbornly resistant to change and remain entrenched in sex-role stereotypes and the unabashed glorification of war. Boys are still blasting, crushing, striking, and pulverizing their way through playtime. And girls are cleaning, diapering, and primping through theirs.

Unfortunately, toy stores continue to support levels of male and female gender bias not unlike what we saw before Title IX was passed in 1972. The aisles of girl toys are designated with pale pink letters and the names of the girl toys are in oval signs framed in purple or pink. The boys' aisles are marked with green letters or blue frames—even today in Toys 'R' Us, one of the nation's leading toy stores. And in many stores, child-sized Dirt Devils and Easy Bake Ovens crowd the girls' department and plastic power tools fill the boys'.

Some say corporations are just giving consumers what they want by providing friends and family with the products that will put smiles on kids' faces at weekend birthday parties. Yes, trendy toys and gadgets reflect societal values, habits, and the quest for stimulation. But let's look at the long-term messages that are sent to kids. Are toys providing innocent fun, or are children being socialized in ways that could ultimately influence career and life choices? Are boys encouraged to demonstrate power and control during playtime by simulating violence and war?

In 2005, I attempted to answer these questions. I started by taking a look around Wal-Mart, Target, Kaybee Toys, and Toys 'R' Us to consider the possible effects of gender-based toys. I came up with several areas of concentration such as gender segregation, career-related toys, militarism, and themes in packaging such as color usage and marketing language. After completing my investigation, I designed an exercise that required my students in a university gender issues course to explore a local toy store and report back to the class.

JOSEPH BLOUGH

Investigating Stores

A visit to several chain toy stores at the Mall of America and suburban shopping centers in the Minneapolis/St. Paul metro area taught me a powerful lesson about how toy manufacturers operate. I began by recording the categories of toys in the girls' and boys' sections. The boys' section was dominated by weaponry. Using Myriam Miedzian's powerful critique included in her 1991 book *Boys Will Be Boys: Breaking the Link Between Masculinity and Violence*, I observed that boys' toys have become even more "lethal" since 1991. But much of the language used on the packaging now justifies the use of force or violence in the name of being a "peace keeper," completing a "mission," or being a "superior defender." The text used on the war toys Miedzian observed was honest about being the aggressors. The Rambo 81 mm Mortar Thunder-Tube Assault, on the other hand, declares the "army will stop at nothing to control the world" and the motto for the Rampage Transformer is "those who conquer act; those who are conquered think." Madison Avenue now encourages violence during playtime in the name of peace and justice.

The colors commonly used on the packaging are black, red, and deep yellow to provide images of flames. Jagged letters suggest lightning, the icon for speed and power.

Words such as "bashing," "kicking," "deadly," and "assault" are standard fare used to promote these children's toys. Toys such as Power Brutes, Battle Arena, and Big Brother (whose box states, "Get Ready for the Real Confrontation") can be purchased at just about any discount or toy store.

Kaybee Toys committed more than one third of one aisle to Power Team Elite, manufactured by Hong Kong-based M&C Toy Centre; featured were about two dozen action figures with guns, scopes, grenades, Humvees, and an A-F Combat Helicopter. These toys offer children a particular perspective: Patriotism and superiority are the ultimate goals, and aggression and training for war are justified through a simplistic lens of "us" versus "them."

In addition to the war toys, the male area offers word games, chess, and other challenging board games. Boys—and presumably their dads —are prominently featured on the boxes of Pavilion's Backgammon and Chess Teacher. Planetariums, globes, interactive world maps, atlases, 3-D Dino Adventure, Legos, science kits, and GeoGenius fill the shelves.

I tried to find one female—child or adult—on any of the many science kits at Toys 'R' Us. I thought my research results would look a bit questionable if, in 2005, I claimed that not one female appeared on any of the science kits. I was determined to find at least one. I found a small plastic chair and attempted to reach the top shelf to see if that very last science kit would have a female on it. A friendly —albeit skeptical—store clerk asked if I needed assistance. I told him about my research and he brought the box down. For one joyous moment I thought I had found a female. Alas, it was not to be. The boy on the back panel just had long hair.

The girls' area, or should we say fantasyland, is well-stocked with vanity mirrors, combs, brushes, nail kits, makeup, and polyester hair extensions. The focus is on being popular with boys. The shelves are overflowing with Mattel Barbies and endless paraphernalia, including Barbie's scale, set at one weight: 110 pounds.

Shopping is a focus of many of the girl toys such as Lil Bratz Fashion Mall, which warns girls, "Don't forget to stop at the makeup shop." Packages provide fashion advice and tips about how to be trendy and get noticed. Crowns, pompoms, and phones in lavender and pink hang on the separate carousels near the small, upholstered furniture. Jump ropes, umbrellas, tea sets, and sticker books are in abundance. Unlike the colors used on the panels of the boys' toys, pastels reign here. The edges of the letters are smooth and an i or a t is dotted or crossed with a heart, butterfly, or star. Glitter is on everything—from the packaging to the product itself. The copy usually includes words such as "kitten," "princess," "fairy," "precious," "wish," "dream," and "wonder."

The girls' section does not have many board games that stimulate creative thinking or require higher-order reasoning. It has bingo and simple activities such as coloring books and car or travel games. Although the female area appears to be a pink fantasyland, the dream soon ends. After getting the guy, by playing Milton Bradley's Mystery Date or through sheer vanity and competition, the girls get the brooms, mops, vacuums, diapers, and plastic food. And they are smiling in every packaging photo.

Boys are noticeably absent from any of the advertisements, promotions, store posters, or packaging for toy household cleaning products, kitchen items, or childcare toys such as baby dolls and strollers. The product lines do not model social acceptance for boys to play homemaking or parenting.

When young boys engage in dress up, pile on the necklaces, enjoy painting their nails, or select other girl toys, cultural norms or homophobia often correct the behavior immediately. In fact, in Fisher Price Playlab studies where staff members observed children behind one-way glass, they found that boys will play with "girl" toys if they think they are in a safe environment.

My students frequently offer supporting evidence about boys crossing these gender lines, from their part-time jobs at after-school programs. They believe that young boys relish the chance to get their nails painted and have their hair styled when girls are doing it as a special activity. As one student told my class recently, "I think boys just like the closeness of being with a staff member, being touched while we paint their nails, and talking with us." Perhaps it is the tactile, calming aspect of this activity that draws boys and girls to it. However, sex roles are reinforced very early in boys' lives, and toys play a part in that socialization.

Jackson Katz in *Tough Guise: Violence, Media and the Crisis in Masculinity*, a Media Education Foundation video, explores the ways boys are taught to be tough and how they're encouraged to define manhood in ways that hurt themselves and others. Katz provides an insightful analysis about how boys are socialized to be solitary, independent, and often violent through toys, video games, and Hollywood movies. According to Katz, the cultural message is that emotional connections are for sissies. Beyond the obvious problems of violence and aggression that many of the toys engender, even the science-based toys are solitary and don't present opportunities for verbal or social development. Packaging hints at being the best or creating and building superior models or designs. There is little evidence that toys help boys in social and emotional development or in Katz's words, help boys to be "better men" some day.

Toys for girls implicitly urge them to find husbands in order to get their dream lives. Girls are taught to compete with each other for male validation. One makeup kit states, "Wait 'til they see you." Female rivalries, jealousies, and other negative behaviors such as bullying and harassment pose a host of problems for girls. Yet girls' toys promote unattainable physical perfection and materialistic values. Mary Pipher, author of *Reviving Ophelia*, a groundbreaking book about the emotional lives of adolescent girls, including depression, eating disorders, and declining self-confidence, refers to contemporary society as a "girl poisoning culture" and offers many empowering approaches for addressing issues of self-esteem. The toys available to girls typically strengthen the cultural messages of inferiority and second-class status that have influenced and continue to affect self-image and academic performance for many girls.

Most women work because they have to, and girls should be aware of this fact early on in their lives. According to the Ms. Foundation for Women, women make on average 77 cents to a man's dollar, and the disparity is worse for African American women, who earn 62 cents, and Latinas, who earn 53 cents. Nearly 10.5 million women are single parents (as compared with 2.5 million single fathers). Economic self-sufficiency and a sound understanding of money are essential for girls and boys. But it's hard to get even a glimpse of that reality in the fantasyland of toy stores.

Action Research for Students

After completing my own toy store research, I designed an exercise for my students where they navigated a store of their choice, aisle by aisle. The students were enrolled in a gender issues course in the College of Education at St. Cloud State University. I had originally intended the course to be an elective for teacher education students but the course has filled with non-licensure students every time I have offered it. In the first few weeks of the course, we examine a wide range of common gender socialization practices for young children, from parental biases in decorating the nursery, to the clothes and toys selected for children, to the verbal messages given to them regarding their gender roles.

In most of my classes I favor projects that send students out into the real world and these assignments frequently send the students into retail stores. For example, I send my students to seasonal stores in the fall to determine which Halloween costumes perpetuate racism, and in the spring I ask students to analyze the colors and fabrics used in children's spring jackets. We begin the action research project in my gender issues course by reviewing class material on gender socialization. Students generate a list of things to look for in a toy store such as messages about gender expectations and general issues such as cost, quality, and amount of toys in the boys' section versus the girls' section. The students can use the list of questions the class formulated together to complete their research or they can use their own.

Part of the action research assignment is a written and oral report to the class summarizing their findings. Some students have asked if they can give their report as a group and I have found these presentations to be lively and interactive. One group somehow came up with the funds—or credit card—to buy many of the toys they researched. They provided the class with an array of war toys, Barbies, and GI Joes. The men in the group were the most vociferous in their critique of the messages sent to children, particularly boys, who play with war toys. One of the students had been in the military and said he felt angry about the socialization he had absorbed from toys, like assumptions that men make war, war is exciting, and new weapons are fun to use. The students took their show on the road and shared their research with classes in the College of Education, and they also provided a session at a student-sponsored conference on nonviolence on campus.

Each class has found different things to review in their research. For example, one student found that there were, "twice as many toys for boys than girls." She went on to write that the smaller girls' section was located in the front of the store and shared space with seasonal toys.

Another student noticed the facial expressions on the packaging of toys. She observed this in one item in particular, a bean-bag chair. She wrote the following:

> The girls' bean-bag package displayed two pictures of girls sitting back in their chairs, smiling and looking very relaxed. One girl was talking on the phone and the other girl was talking to another girl. The boys' bean-bag package showed two pictures of boys leaning forward in their chairs. Both boys were gritting their teeth as the one played an electronic game while the other raised his fist and cheered for a sports team.

Other packages portray girls taking instruction or baffled by some accomplishment. A student noticed that the cover of Marvin's Magic Mind Blowing Card shows four boys in the front row and two girls in the back row watching a card trick being performed. The facial expressions of the two girls make them look flummoxed by the trick, while the boys seem to be studying it. In addition to these observations, almost all students reported that women were highly sexualized in many marketing promotions. One student reported that Toys 'R' Us had 126 covers of video games displayed on a wall and the only women shown were in "compromising positions" with "major cleavage." The only non-sexualized female was a furry yellow "Sonic Hero."

Toy Segregation

The effect of toys and playtime may not be as benign as some parents and educators think. Although great strides have been made in many social areas, boys are still pushed toward higher levels of unhealthy competition and stoicism during playtime while many girls are reinforced in their unrealistic beliefs that they will always be taken care of or that employment outside the home is optional. The segregation under those neon lights is a fairly good predictor for what is to come, both in terms of earning power and career choice. The power and labor inequities in homes and work places—and the damaging messages sent to boys about their roles in society—are often shaped and defined in the types of toys that are mindlessly thrown in the shopping cart. ■

Sudie Hofmann is a professor of human relations and multicultural education at St. Cloud State University in Minnesota. Hofmann teaches courses on gender bias and other related issues of oppression in educational settings.

Where Are the Game Girls?

BY ANN PELO

"Why are there Game Boys, but not Game Girls?" 4-year-old Katrina asked over lunch at her childcare program one day.* This simple, incisive question launched a small group of 4- and 5-year-old children and their teacher, Emily Viehauser, on a three-month research project about the gendered nature of toys.

Emily invited five children—all outspoken in their daily informal observations and assessments about "girl stuff" and "boy stuff"—to take up Katrina's question. At the group's first meeting, Emily launched their investigation by asking, "What *is* a Game Boy? And why are there only Game Boys, not Game Girls? Katrina was wondering about that, and I think that's an important question for us to think about."

Michael: "You can play games and if you mess up, there's a button if you want to try again."

Bridget: "That's why it's called a Game Boy, because boys like to play it."

Katrina: "It's called a Game Boy because it has boys' games in it."

Michael: "If it has girl games in it, it's called a Game Girl."

Bridget: "If it's for anyone, it's called a Game Kid."

Katrina: "If you were a girl and you wanted a Game Girl, it felt not fair."

Bridget: "Only boys get to play it."

Michael: "Girls do play it—my sister does."

Katrina: "It wouldn't be fair to the girls if they

have boy games like hockey."

Eliot: "And they have Batman."

Katrina: "And that makes it *very* not fair."

Bridget: "It's not fair for the kids that are girls."

Michael: "Girls want to play it a little and boys want to play it a lot."

Eliot: "Girls don't like Batman."

This initial round of conversation was an opportunity for Emily to gather information about the children's understandings of "girl games" and "boy games," information that she and I, the mentor teacher working alongside teachers to plan curricula, used to craft the next steps that Emily and the children would take in their research. Our attention was caught by the notion of Game Kids. What sort of game would the children consider to be "for anyone," boys and girls? We decided to invite the children to invent Game Kids, thinking that an exploration of gender-inclusive games would help them clarify what makes a game gender-specific.

The children's designs for Game Kids were remarkable in their variety.

In Michael's game (drawing above), "you throw the ball and catch it with the bat three times to win." Bridget commented that "girls don't like this one." Katrina protested Bridget's assessment. "I would like it," she said. "But it seems kind of tricky. It's really hard to catch the ball three times and it's really hard to win and you might want to win."

Katrina's game design (drawing on page 35) was evocative of Duck-Duck-Goose: "The girl is trying to run around her before she catches the girl. If they get caught, they take a time-out and do something else. They try to kick the soccer ball. The winning prize is a pair of dresses. They wear crowns for helmets. They have elbow pads and knee pads. Some kids get frustrated; some kids can kick it and some kids can't." Eliot exclaimed, "No way would I play that game!" Bridget understood why: "You have to wear dresses and boys don't like dresses." Michael confirmed her explanation: "No way with dresses!"

Eliot's game (drawing above) was "a Batman game. You have to get Green Goblin with a net before Joker catches Batman."

Katrina was encouraging; "That sounds fun!" Michael offered some advice to make the game more gender-inclusive: "There could be a woman Joker."

Lilly's game (next page, first column) included active play and dessert: "The girl is trying to kick the ball to her. The cookies are for eating when they're done."

Enid's game (next page, second column)was dramatic: "The princesses are in the castle and they're trying to find their way out, before the bad guy comes." Michael recoiled, exclaiming, "I wouldn't want to play that game, because I don't like princesses."

When we met to study the children's designs and their exchanges about them, Emily and I were intrigued by the element of physical play that crept into several games: baseball, soccer, tag.

The princess and Batman scripts stood in striking contrast to these games, throwbacks to the sort of gendered video games that the children referenced in their initial conversation about girls' games and boys' games. The Game Kids designs reflected the contradictions that the children experienced about gender and play. They enjoyed many of the same games, especially physical, outdoor games like soccer and chase. Yet, as preschool-aged kids, they'd begun to play in groups delineated by gender, and their Game Kids designs reflect that: all-girl games of soccer and Duck-Duck-Goose. And, increasingly, the girls and boys engaged with different play scripts: princesses and Batman rarely encountered each other in the children's dramas. As the children crafted designs for Game Kids, they wrestled to untangle these contradictions—and seemed not to find their way to clear resolution about games that would appeal to "anyone."

Emily and I decided to call the children's attention to the contradictions around gender and play by teasing apart the threads in their Game Kids designs. First, Emily would follow the thread that evoked active outdoor play, inviting the children to notice how gender was a factor—or not—in that play. Then, she'd tug on the thread that led to toys and drama scripts.

Emily packed up clipboards, paper, and pens, and took the children to the nearby park to observe kids at play. She asked the children to draw what they noticed about how boys and girls were playing. After a stint of observation, the children shared their notes with each other.

> Michael: "Boys liked being goofy and getting chased."
>
> Katrina: "I drew some girls getting chased, because I saw them playing chase, too."
>
> Bridget: "Boys and girls played ball."
>
> Enid: "Girls and boys like to go down the slide."
>
> Eliot: "Everyone likes everything at the park."

Outdoor play, the children decided, was play "for anyone"; these games were good candidates for Game Kids.

From this open-air observation and its agreeable findings, the children moved their research indoors, to a room used by one of the other groups of children in our childcare program. Emily and I were curious to learn how the children would assess the toys that anchor our program—blocks, art materials, dramatic play props. This was the arena that was beginning to be marked by gender-specific play, as these children moved squarely into preschool life: girls playing together without boys, boys playing together without girls—still playing with the same materials, but separate from each other. How would this experience show up in the children's assessment of the toys in the room?

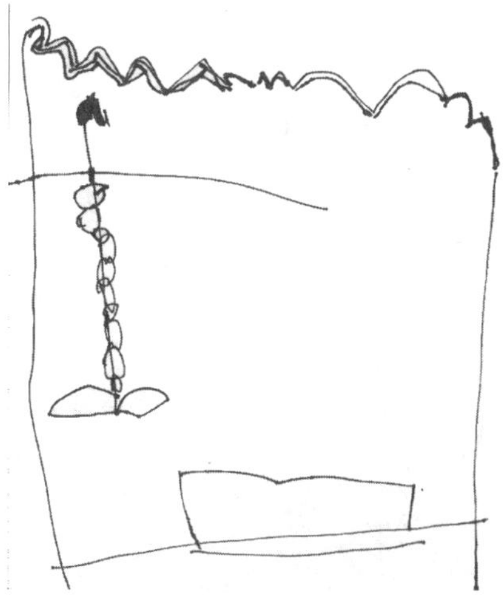

Emily asked the children to put "G" sticky notes on toys they thought that girls used and "B" sticky notes on toys they thought that boys used. She directed the children to decide as a group about whether a toy should get a G or a B or both. The children debated a bit—but not fiercely—as they moved around the room.

> Eliot: "Should there be girls' books and boys' books?"
>
> Bridget: "All of them are for both."
>
> Michael: "Because they could be interested in any books."
>
> The books got both a G and a B note.
>
> ...
>
> Katrina: "Girls definitely like dancing."
>
> Michael: "Boys like dancing when they're rock stars."
>
> The CD player got both a G and a B note.
>
> ...
>
> Michael: "Girls and boys like to dress up, because in our room, Eliot and me dress up in these cool clothes with numbers on them."
>
> Katrina: "But not dresses."
>
> Michael: "Actually, I saw Henry wear a dress the other day."

The dress-up clothes got both a G and a B note—books, art supplies, the CD player, foosball, drama props, and Legos. Then the children wrote a note to the group of children whose room they'd assessed, asking them, "Did we make the right guesses about the toys?"

The children from the other room replied with a simple and affirming note: "You were right about every toy."

The children and Emily did one more round of research together. With Emily's support, each of the children crafted a survey to administer to other children in our program. They asked questions like, "Do you like soccer?" and "Do you like to read magazines?" They carried their surveys to girls and boys, jotting down the responses to track their data. Michael's and Katrina's surveys capture the spirit of the research (see sidebar below):

> Do you like soccer?
>
> Do you like to paint?
>
> Do you like to dance?

Michael's Survey

Katrina's Survey

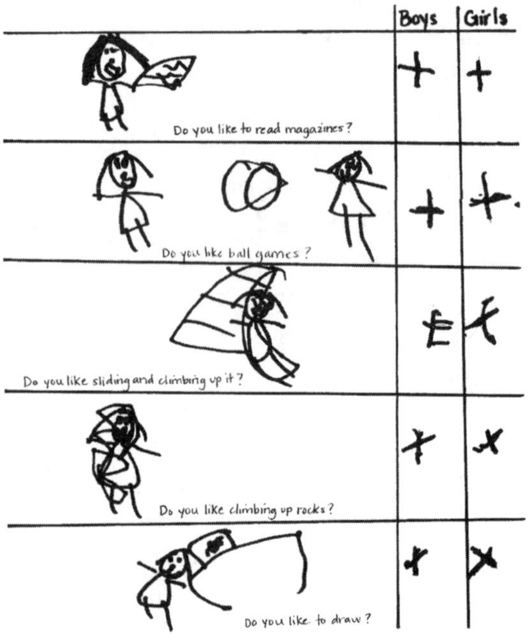

Do you like to pick flowers?

Do you like to play music?

Do you like to read magazines?

Do you like ball games?

Do you like sliding and climbing up it?

Do you like climbing up rocks?

Do you like to draw?

The surveys were conclusive: Girls and boys said yes to every question.

After this research, the kids returned to the subject of Game Boys, more irate than ever about the injustice they represented. Emily and I were curious to see that the children hadn't revised their understandings of who could play Game Boys, or who the games might appeal to: the notion that there are games that boys like and games that girls like wasn't at issue, from the children's perspective. The problem with Game Boys was that there was no corresponding game for girls, nor was there one that would appeal both to girls and to boys. Their research had pointed out that there are games that everyone likes, and games that girls like—and those games were not represented by Game Boys.

Emily suggested that the children write to the people who make Game Boys, voicing their objections. Their letter speaks volumes about the children's sense of themselves as researchers whose study generated clear conclusions:

> Dear Sir or Ma'am,
> There's no Game Girls and there's no Game Kids. We're a little bit mad about that, because the girls don't think it's fair. We did a lot of research. Since we've done a lot of work, we learned what boys and girls like. We learned what they like to play. They like to play chase, tag, going down the slide, drawing, singing, playing music, picking flowers, playing soccer, and playing tennis. If you want to watch us do it, we can show you. Boys and girls like the same games. This is from the research we did and the ideas of how it should look. We have some ideas for Game Kids; you could choose one of our pictures.
>
> From Michael, Lilly, Eliot, Bridget, Katrina, and Enid ■

Ann Pelo is an early childhood teacher and teacher mentor in Seattle, Wash.

Rethinking 'The Three Little Pigs'

BY ELLEN WOLPERT

There's scarcely a parent or young child who isn't familiar with "The Three Little Pigs." It has a simple plot line, is easily remembered, and it's so much fun imitating the big bad wolf as he huffs and puffs and "blo-o-ws" the house down.

I find the story is also useful to talk about the stereotypes in many of our favorite tales.

I first became aware of the story's hidden messages when we were doing a unit on housing at my daycare center. As part of the unit, we talked about different homes and the many approaches to solving a basic human need: a place to live.

During the discussion I suddenly thought to myself, "Why are brick homes better than straw homes?"

To this day, I'm not completely sure why that question popped into my mind. I do know, however, that I had been sensitized by the movement for a multicultural curriculum, which had taught me to take a questioning approach to even the most seemingly innocuous materials and to look beneath the surface for hidden assumptions.

After thinking about it, I realized that one of the most fundamental messages of "The Three Little Pigs" is that it belittles straw and stick homes and the "lazy types" who build them. On the other hand, the story extols the virtues of brick homes, suggesting that they are built by serious, hardworking people and are strong enough to withstand adversity.

Is there any coincidence that brick homes tend to be built by people in Western countries, often by those with more money? That straw homes are more common in non-European cultures, particularly Africa and Asia?

Once I realized some of these hidden messages, the question became what to do about it. In my experience, the best approach is not to put down such beloved tales and refuse to read them, but to use them to pose questions for children. One might explain, for example, that in many tropical areas straw homes are built to take best advantage of cooling breezes. In some areas, straw homes are on stilts as protection from insects and animals or to withstand flooding.

Such a perspective then becomes part of a broader process of helping children to understand why homes are different in different parts of the world—and that just because something is different doesn't mean it's inferior. ■

Ellen Wolpert has been an early childhood educator since 1970 and is the coordinator of the Cambridge Community Partnerships for Children in Massachusetts.

JEAN-CLAUDE LEJEUNE

What If All the Kids Are White?

Anti-Bias Themes for Teaching Young Children

BY LOUISE DERMAN-SPARKS AND PATRICIA RAMSEY

"What if all the kids are white?" has been one of the most frequently asked questions in my many years of working with early childhood teachers on anti-bias teaching and learning. Three misconceptions about the role of anti-bias education for white children underlie the confusion reflected in that question. One is that racial, ethnic and cultural diversity refers only to people who are "different from" whites. This misconception sometimes leads to white people feeling excluded from dialogues about diversity. A second misconception is that we can only teach white children about diversity if they are in a group with children of color. This erroneous idea denies the range of diversity among white children and leaves white children unsupported in their learning about diversity—which they are doing whether or not their teachers address the topic. A third misunderstanding is that an anti-bias curriculum only needs to focus on white children's attitudes towards children of color, not on their own identity development. This idea ignores the reality that racism impacts white children's socialization, the other side of the coin from its impact on children of color. White children begin to learn the power codes and benefits of racism early on. They absorb messages about white superiority or "rightness" at the same time that they absorb negative messages about people of color.

In our book *What If All the Kids Are White? Anti-Bias Multicultural Education with Young Children and Families* (Teachers College Press,

2006), we identify core anti-bias learning themes for white children. These are:

1. Develop authentic identities based on personal abilities and interests, family history and culture, rather than on white superiority.
2. Know, respect, and value the range of the diversity of physical and social attributes among white people.
3. Build the capacity for caring, cooperative, and equitable interactions with others.
4. Understand, appreciate, and respect differences and similarities beyond the immediate family, neighborhood, center/classroom, and racial group.
5. Learn to identify and challenge stereotypes, prejudice, and discriminatory practices among themselves and in the immediate environment.
6. Commit to the ideal that all people have the right to a secure, healthy, comfortable, and sustainable life and that everyone must equitably share the resources of the earth and collaboratively care for them.
7. Build identities that include anti-bias ideals and possibilities and acquire skills and confidence to work together for social justice in their own classrooms and communities, and eventually in the larger society.

The following excerpt highlights the book's discussion of learning theme 5. Keep in mind that this learning theme builds on the four that precede it.

***

Learn to identify and challenge stereotypes, prejudice, and discriminatory practices in the immediate environment.

Many young white children already hold ideas about white superiority and "normalcy" and negative, stereotyped attitudes toward people of color that they have absorbed from images and messages all around them, including from books, television, video games, holiday decorations, greeting cards, and toys. Moreover, children will continue to be exposed to racist ideas for the rest of their lives. However, the experience of early childhood anti-bias educators tells us that by 4 years of age, children can profit from learning opportunities that encourage them to contrast accurate images and information with incorrect and stereotypical ones. They can also learn to recognize and challenge the concrete ways that whiteness is presented as the norm and, in many cases, superior. Because of their cognitive developmental stage and continual exposure to misinformation, it is impossible to eradicate all of their stereotypical ideas. However, we can help them develop their capacities to think critically and flexibly.

As you work to counter children's stereotypes and discomforts, be conscious of the reality that every day they are being exposed to misinformation. At times it may feel like a losing battle. Do not get discouraged; expect that it will take a long time and many discussions for children to learn to resist this pull.

Use children's biased remarks as teachable moments. Although children may not understand the full meaning of their biased comments, these can become the basis for more developed prejudice if adults do not respond to them. When you hear such a comment, immediately follow up with exploratory questions to gain a deeper understanding of the child's thoughts and feelings ("What do you mean by that?" "How do you know that?" "Do you think that all the people there do ___? What about moms and dads and kids?") Use an exploratory, rather than accusatory, tone. Ask questions in ways that let you into the children's thinking, rather than close them down. Then plan both immediate and longer-term experiences, as illustrated by the following example from Eric Hoffman:

> "Did you hear what those children said?" The parent's question drew my attention to four 4-year-olds sitting at a table, talking and giggling. To me, they looked like they had found a good way to get away from the crowd and relax, but when I focused on their words, I understood the parent's distress. They were repeating a jingle that made fun of Chinese people. The children were clearly unaware

that their language was racist. Their interest was in the silly sounds and their feelings of friendship.

"I hear you saying a rhyme that makes you laugh." They started to repeat the words, but I stopped them. "Do you know what the word Chinese means?" They all shook their heads. I explained that it referred to people from a part of the world called China, and that Chinese people would be insulted by the jingle. They were taken aback—that was not their intention.

"I know one that's not about Chinese," a child said, and he started saying another rhyme that made fun of Asian eyes. I explained that even though the new rhyme didn't mention Chinese people, it was still making fun of people. I started to explain about Asia and China, but I could see that my geography lesson was beyond their comprehension.

"It looks like you're not trying to hurt anybody's feelings. You want to be friends and laugh about silly words. So let's think of some that won't upset anyone." We came up with a great list of ridiculous rhymes that left them rolling on the floor with laughter. I felt good about how I handled the situation, until I heard one of the children say to another, "You shouldn't say Chinese. That's a bad word."

In discussing with my staff how we should respond, I was struck by a dilemma that is common in anti-bias work: How do you help people unlearn racism without hurting those who are the targets of that racism? We wanted to create a curriculum that would help the children develop positive feelings about ethnic and national differences. However, we knew that we ran the risk of uncovering more racist ideas. We didn't want the children to censor themselves out of fear they would be punished; it felt important to get those misconceptions out in the open so they could be challenged. On the other hand, allowing children to voice racism, even when it is unintended, can damage children who are members of the targeted group. People of color shouldn't be forced to listen in while white people work out their racism. I find this especially important to keep in mind in groups where there is little ethnic or racial diversity, because it's so easy to dismiss the feelings of the minority when there is no one around to express them.

One way to make sure those feelings are heard is through persona dolls. By introducing a variety of dolls at the beginning of the year, I can bring people to my class who can voice the unfairness of name-calling and discrimination. If I have used the dolls correctly and brought them to life, young children will respond to those voices with compassion and work hard to correct the injustice.

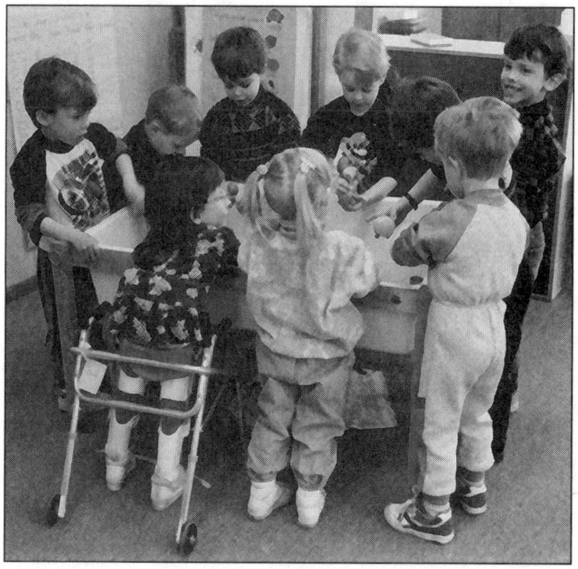
JEAN-CLAUDE LEJEUNE

So when my staff and I planned our new curriculum we didn't start with lectures and geography lessons, we started with feelings. One of the dolls talked about her wonderful Vietnamese family and how much she hated being made fun of for her differences. She spoke with great pride and great pain. That opened the door for many discussions about ethnic labels, places in the world, ancestors, and how much it hurts to have someone make fun of the way you look, speak, or act.

Help children recognize stereotypes and incorrect information, and appreciate the harm they can do. When you read stories or show pictures that have stereotypes, encourage the children to identify them and talk about why they are not fair. Ellen Wolpert suggests playing a "Stereotype or Fact" game with older preschoolers and kindergartners to help them explore the differences between a stereotype and a fact.[1] The teacher makes exaggerated statements that the children know from experience are obviously not true, such as, "All children hate ice cream." Then she asks if the statement is true or false and how the children know. Some of the teacher's statements can also be tested out by the children, as in, "Only boys know how to run." After trying out several similar kinds of statements, the teacher explains that the untrue statements are called stereotypes, because they say "all children" or "all boys," and so on, even when it isn't true for everyone. Then, when children make a stereotypical comment about a person/group not in their experience, the teacher can refer to the "Stereotype or Fact" game as one way to introduce critical thinking about misinformation.

JEAN-CLAUDE LEJEUNE

Start exploring stereotypes with statements about gender. Preschool children are very concerned about gender identification, often express gender stereotypes, and exclude peers along these lines. Thus, addressing gender-related assumptions is a good way to begin. Moreover, children can "test" these beliefs against their own experiences. For instance, make a list with the children of the activities boys like and the activities girls like. Then take photographs of play in the classroom and compare the photographs with the list. What do children notice? Should any changes to the list be made? Encourage children to talk about times that they have been teased, rejected, or told that they couldn't play with a particular toy, because of being a girl or a boy. How did they feel when that happened?

Next, work in a similar way with children's ideas about people of color. Provide images and books that challenge the common stereotypes to which children are exposed in society and help children see and think about the contrast between what they may think and what is real. For example, contrast young children's common belief that all American Indians live in teepees or shoot people with bows and arrows with photographs and books about real contemporary American Indians.

Engage children in critiquing children's books that only include images of whites or that depict inaccurate images of people of color. Ask children to imagine each story with more diverse characters or accurate images ("Could this character be a person with dark skin instead of white skin?" "Do you think that this book tells the truth/is fair to Vietnamese people?") Invite children to dictate or write letters to authors about what they like and do not like in their stories and how they could make future stories more inclusive.

Spark children's empathy about the hurt that stereotypes can cause. As we saw in the previous example of Eric Hoffman's use of a teachable moment with a group of preschoolers, persona doll stories are especially helpful for these explorations. A doll of color can talk about being teased or excluded by her white peers because of skin color or being in a classroom where there are no images of people who look like her. As you tell the persona doll story, involve children in exploring the doll's feelings and how it feels to be the target of prejudice or discrimination. Then, ask children to help figure out what they would do to stop the discrimination described in the story. You can do many stories throughout the school year that address many types of prejudice and discrimination.

Promote children's capacity to problem-solve ways to handle incidents of prejudice and discrimination. As with the previous activities in this chapter, begin with incidents in your own classroom or in your children's lives, and then make the bridge to prejudice and discrimination directed against others. Use conflict-resolution strategies to help children resolve incidents that involve being teased or rejected because of an aspect of identity (excluding children on the basis of dress, always assigning a small child the "baby" role in dramatic play, teasing a child who wears glasses). Use these incidents to help children understand the impact of discrimination directed at people not in their immediate environment. ■

Excerpted from *What If All the Kids Are White? Anti-Bias Multicultural Education with Young Children and Families.* New York. Teachers College Press. 2006

Now retired, **Louise Derman-Sparks** was on the faculty of Pacific Oaks College in Pasadena, Calif., for more than 30 years. She has taught and directed early childhood programs and authored/co-authored several books on anti-bias and anti-racism development and learning. She speaks publicly, consults, and is an activist for peace and justice.

Patricia G. Ramsey is Professor of Psychology and Education and Director of Gorse Study Center at Mount Holyoke College in South Hadley, Mass. She is the author of *Teaching and Learning in a Diverse World* (Teachers College Press, 2004).

References

1. Ellen Wolpert. *Start Seeing Diversity: The Basic Guide to an Anti-Bias Classroom.* St. Paul, Minn. Redleaf Press. 1999.

Unwrapping the Holidays

Reflections on a Difficult First Year

By Dale Weiss

My teaching career began on the picket line.

After I was hired to teach 1st grade in a small town outside of Seattle, I spent my first month in front of the school instead of in the classroom.

After 30 days, our union settled the strike and won smaller class sizes for 1st and 2nd grade, better health benefits, and a slight raise in salary. And on a personal level, I felt that I had really bonded with my colleagues. Most of the teachers who worked at this school had been born and raised in that small town and they showed extraordinary kindness to me during the strike. My father was having major surgery and I was extremely sad and worried. Each day, teachers inquired about his health. Other teachers showed concern about my lack of income and brought me bags of food. One teacher, Joseph, even brought me several bags of plums from his tree.

But through the course of the year, many of the bonds we formed on the picket line dissolved as I became involved in a controversy over holiday curricula.

Before I became a teacher, I had spent years as a political activist. I saw my work as a teacher as important political work and wanted to create a classroom where students would learn to challenge biases and injustice and take action against unfair situations. Since this way of viewing the world seemed normal to me, I naively assumed my colleagues—with whom I experienced solidarity on the picket line—shared the same worldview. I could not have been more wrong.

Holiday Decorations

Before Thanksgiving, two 6th-grade girls approached me to ask if my 1st graders could make ornaments for the Christmas tree that had been put up in the library.

I replied, "We have been learning about four different winter celebrations: Kwanzaa, Hanukkah, Christmas in Mexico, and Winter Solstice, and we are in the process of making a book about each celebration. We could put our books in the library for other children and teachers to read as our contribution." The 6th-grade girls were persistent and still wanted to know if I would have my students make ornaments.

"I don't think so," I said, and then returned to my classroom.

I remember wondering if I would be depriving my students of something by my decision, but in my heart I felt I was doing the right thing. I was teaching them that not everyone celebrates Christmas, that there are many celebratory practices in the month of December, and that each celebration is richly marked with unique customs and beliefs. Not making Christmas ornaments would not rob my students of anything—except the belief that only Christmas occurred in December.

Thinking back to the Christmas tree in the library and feeling that holiday decorations should reflect diversity, I decided to speak with my principal, Oscar. Referring to the decorations in the library, I emphasized that I thought public areas in the school should reflect as much diversity as possible. Oscar was very supportive and agreed to discuss the issue the following day at our staff meeting. He cautioned me that many staff members might not agree with my opinions and that he found the staff to be very conservative, particularly about change.

At our staff meeting, I expressed my concern about the public Christmas displays and also mentioned the four different December celebrations we were studying in my classroom. And I shared an experience that had recently occurred in my classroom with Lindsey, a child who was a Jehovah's Witness. Her mother had expressed concern about the class study on Christmas in Mexico. After I explained that our study emphasized the cultural and not religious aspects of the celebration, the parent was relieved. I shared that as a Jew, I also did not celebrate Christmas. The next morning Lindsey ran up to me, gave me a big hug, and said, "My mom told me you don't celebrate Christmas either. Now I'm not the only one." I shared my student's reaction as an example of the pain children can experience when they don't fit in. I also felt responsibility as an educator to minimize that pain in whatever ways I could.

As the staff meeting ended, two staff members thanked me for opening their eyes to new ways of looking at things. But mostly there was silence. Later in the day I heard secondhand that Robert, the librarian, was upset about what I had said during the staff meeting.

I approached him and asked if we could talk. He responded that he usually does not decorate the library with so many Christmas items but did so this year because a few 6th-grade girls kept "hounding him." He also shared that this was the first year there had ever been a Christmas tree in the library. What bothered him most was that he felt blamed for the library decorations, despite the fact it was the 6th graders who had put up the decorations. I told him that I was not blaming him; I was merely concerned about decorations in common areas within the school.

As the day progressed, I began to notice other teachers distancing themselves from me. I visited one teacher, Linda, during our lunch hour to ask if I had inadvertently offended her. When I got there, she was speaking to another teacher and did not see me come into the room. Linda—with very large motions—was ripping the "Merry Christmas" banner off her wall, saying, "We used to be able to do anything we wanted to at Christmas time, but apparently not anymore."

I asked if she was referring to what I said at the staff meeting, and she replied, "Well, yes. Plus, I don't teach about Hanukkah because I just don't know how to pronounce all those words. Besides, I just don't feel comfortable teaching about something I don't know much about." I shared that my viewpoints were not only based in my being Jewish—though this is a part of who I am—but because I believe it is important for children to have exposure to all different kinds of people, customs, and belief systems. I also shared that I, too, have a hard time teaching something new and that one way I learn is to read books written for children. Alexis then responded, "We're used to doing the same things every year. When December rolls around, we always take out our December boxes and put on the walls whatever is in those boxes. And we really don't think about it. We prefer it that way." Just then the bell rang and our conversation ended.

As the days went on, I noticed lots of Christmas decorations coming off the walls. The library was almost barren. And, where the library Christmas tree once stood, a book was placed on Hanukkah. Though I had stated my hope that decorations should be more inclusive and had not requested all Christmas decorations to be removed—and certainly not that a book about Hanukkah take their place—what people heard was something quite different.

The following day, Friday, Oscar shared with me that my comments at the staff meeting had really stirred things up and that people had been speaking with him about the meeting all week. He said he wanted to put the issue on the agenda of the upcoming faculty committee meeting, a group that met periodically to discuss teacher concerns and was made up of representatives from each grade level. I was the representative for the 1st-grade unit.

On Monday morning, as I arrived at school, I was greeted with an anonymous letter in my mailbox. The message said, "Rights for homosexuals next?" I felt incredibly upset and scared. After showing the letter to Oscar, he said he would share the contents of the letter with the faculty committee at our meeting on the following day.

When the meeting began, one teacher suggested we start the meeting with my re-explaining what I had said and meant at the previous staff meeting. Before I could begin, she stated she felt it was important for me to understand that teachers have done things a certain way for many years at the school and that the holiday curriculum was not offensive because it was well within the district's student learning objectives. I then repeated what I had stated at the staff meeting and said that it had not been my intent to hurt or offend anyone and if I had, I was truly sorry. Another teacher piped up that she had taught for 20 years—in comparison to my two-and-a-half months—and she felt no need at all to have to explain her curriculum to me. She ended by reminding me "to check things out before jumping to conclusions about the way things are done at our school."

I thought a lot about what she said. I always had seen myself as a person with a commitment to understanding other people's views and who takes the time to talk things through. I have never been comfortable with people coming in from the outside and trying to change things immediately. I wondered if I had become that kind of person. When I first noticed the Christmas tree in the library and had thoughts that holiday decorations should reflect diversity, I shared this with Oscar prior to saying anything at the staff meeting. Should I have checked things out with other teachers as well?

A few other teachers said they wished I had brought up my concerns in October, before the holiday decorations went up. I replied that, as a new teacher, I wanted to wait and see what happened, rather than assume how things would end up. I thought I was sitting back, waiting and watching—but others saw me as a newcomer barging in, but somehow barging in too late.

Joseph (the same man who had kindly brought me plums on the picket line) then stated, "You know, several of the staff of *Germanic* background are extremely upset by the fact that the Christmas tree in the library was removed and in its place put a book on Hanukkah." I felt shocked by his comment. I said that I had no idea who removed the Christmas tree and whoever had, did so at their own discretion. I also did not know who put the book on Hanukkah in its place.

Oscar then shared the contents of the anonymous letter I had received, commenting that this was an example of how far things had gone and how ugly they had gotten. People were shocked and could not believe that "someone from a staff as kind as ours could have done something like this."

As the meeting came to a close, Oscar reiterated the importance of openly speaking with one another when differences occur and that talking behind one another's backs would only serve to divide the staff further. He said he hoped the staff could heal and move forward with understanding.

Oscar checked on me several times during the day, letting me know how offensive he found Joseph's comment about "staff of Germanic heritage." I appreciated his support since Joseph's comment really shook me up. I kept thinking it would have been one thing if Joseph had simply said "several staff," but adding "of Germanic heritage" meant something very different. It felt like a brief look into the hatred of the Nazis towards the Jews.

Misunderstandings

Prior to the faculty committee meeting, I had not realized the extent of misunderstanding and anger that existed. I felt scared and continued to search my mind for who might have put the anonymous letter in my mailbox. Up until the prior week I had looked forward to each day of teaching with great eagerness and pleasure. I now dreaded coming to school.

I felt trapped, wondering if the only way out was to join the opinion of the majority. Realizing I could not trade my beliefs for a few moments of "relief," what instead seemed to pull me through was a feeling of strong empathy for all who struggle for something that is right.

I thought about people throughout history who took the first step—and sometimes alone—to bring awareness to an injustice. I thought about people who risk so much while working to bring about a more just world, who stand on the shoulders of those who came before them and know they must keep trying. It was an empathy that forced me to keep trying as well.

In the days that followed, a few staff members offered their support, for which I was immensely appreciative. I thought back on the first days of picket duty, when relations with my co-workers seemed so promising. I was glad for these memories. They helped soften the present wounds.

At the same time, I had to acknowledge that while the strike served to unify the staff and was a way for me to become acquainted with my colleagues, sharp differences also existed. They were differences that went beyond whether or not someone was nice.

I had popped open a huge can of worms, too big to shut. My original intention was not to change others but to see more diversity reflected in the library and other common areas within the school. But what in my mind was a simple request upset the teaching foundations of many teachers, caused resistance and upheaval, and resulted in alienation among many staff members and myself.

It was a long year, that first year of teaching. I tried my best to remain cordial with my colleagues, something that was often difficult—yet important—to do. In January of that year, Oscar shared with me he would be leaving for the remainder of the school year due to poor health. He left in February and his replacement, Jeanne, offered me incredible support—both as a new teacher and as someone attempting to teach from a social justice perspective. This definitely helped me finish out the rest of the school year. Before the school year ended, Oscar died. It is to his memory and his support of, and belief in, me that first year that I have always dedicated my life as a teacher.

I remained at that school one more year, at which point I transferred to a school in Seattle.

Lessons Learned

What I have come to refer to as the "December incident" provided many valuable lessons for me. Where I believe I fell short was on several fronts.

First, I had not sufficiently assessed the staff regarding their potential reactions to being asked to be more inclusive in the school's December celebrations. I assumed I "knew" the staff because we had walked the picket line for 30 straight days. I naively equated solidarity around union issues with pedagogical agreement. Additionally, I was the first new teacher to be hired at this school in many years, and I was viewed as an outsider.

Second, I did not take into consideration that many teachers held negative attitudes toward the administration because of the strike that began our school year; although the strike was over, the administration was still viewed by many as the "enemy." Additionally, my positive rapport with Oscar was viewed by some teachers as aligning with the administration and too frequently entering "enemy territory."

Finally, what I am now able to recognize years later is that for the staff of my school, the celebration of Christmas represented much more than merely honoring a holiday that falls in December. It represented an entire belief system and something they valued and wanted to pass on to their students.

If I could turn back the wheels of time, I would definitely do things differently. I would sit through a "Christmas season" first, modeling my own beliefs within my classroom, but not pushing for change within the entire school. By allowing Christmas to happen first "as it always has," I would better be able to assess people's attachments to doing things in a particular way. I would then bring up the "Christmas issue" in the spring when the issue might not be so emotionally charged.

If I could do it again, I would start by assessing people's viewpoints and beliefs instead of assuming they would understand or desire to do anything differently. For example, my co-workers prided themselves on being nice. They heard my request for diversity as meaning they had not been nice to people who do not celebrate Christmas. While I believe that my co-workers misinterpreted my original intent, I also think that I was partially responsible for this.

I went about things in a way that did not first acknowledge the values held by most of the staff. Perhaps by first acknowledging how important the Christmas season was to the vast majority of the staff, they might have been more open to adding a bit of diversity to what to them was the "normal" way of celebrating December. Since I didn't start by acknowledging their values, people's defenses were up and they did not hear what I was trying to say. As a result, people clung more tightly to their own belief systems and my efforts essentially moved things backwards.

Introducing change into a school environment—especially one that has been firmly established for many years—is a complex process, one that I vastly underestimated. While I don't condone the reactions of many of my colleagues, I do feel I understand what precipitated their response.

I also did not fully consider that people's reactions to me might be based on the fact I was a first-year teacher. I can now see that not all veteran teachers—particularly those who have shaped the school culture and prefer things to stay a particular way—welcome new teachers with open arms.

I assumed my passionate devotion to my values could enhance the curriculum that already was in existence. I spent most of my first year of teaching trying to meld the world of my political activism with the new world I was entering as a teacher. I still believe that our best teaching occurs when we live first as authentic human beings, so I would never advocate leaving one's values at the classroom doorstep. I would, however, suggest a balance of caution and wisdom when embarking on this delicate journey. ■

Dale Weiss teaches 6- and 7-year-olds in a 1st-grade classroom at La Escuela Fratney in Milwaukee, Wis.

Part II

Make ample time for play and exploration.

"I urge you to be teachers so that you can join with children as the co-collaborators in a plot to build a little place of ecstasy and poetry and gentle joy."

Jonathan Kozol
Ordinary Resurrections

ROXANNA BIKADOROFF

The Scripted Prescription

A Cure for Childhood

BY PETER CAMPBELL

A few days before my daughter Vivian* started prekindergarten at a Portland public school, she was asked to come in and be tested. As part of the test, the teacher asked Vivian to write her name on a piece of paper. My 4-year-old daughter looked up at me with huge, puzzled eyes. I looked at the teacher with equally huge, puzzled eyes. Write her name? On the first day of prekindergarten? Vivian didn't know how to hold a pencil, much less write her name.

Traditionally, or so I've been told, the first meeting has been a time for the new student and the teacher to get to know each other. But there was no conversation about what Vivian liked to read, what she liked to do, or anything else that might have given the teacher some insight into Vivian. Her teacher appeared to believe all that she needed to know about Vivian could be discovered from this test. It saddened me to think that my daughter's first impression of school was based on taking a test and failing it.

Now, Vivian regularly brings home worksheets that she did in school—photocopies of activities like sorting, graphing, letter tracing, and letter recognition. She's very busy at school. The first 45 minutes or so of class is open, but it's surprisingly structured and fettered. The kids often work alone. There's not much in the way of spontaneous expression or originality and no time for them to engage in non-adult-supervised open-ended play situations or unstructured, whole-body activities. They have several areas set up for them—a puzzle here, a set of crayons and coloring books there.

Yet, there is little to no noise.

After the initial 45 minutes, the teacher has the students working in "centers." Each center is focused on a specific task, usually associated with a literacy skill. According to the teachers I've spoken to, these skills were the sorts of things that 6- and 7-year-olds used to do in 1st grade. Now 4- and 5-year-olds are being asked to do them in prekindergarten.

Next year, if Vivian stays at this school and attends kindergarten, she will be in school all day and she will be even busier. As a kindergartner, she will have exactly 20 minutes of recess, and then she'll get back to work.

I met with the principal and with Vivian's teacher. I expressed my concern that this practice might not be developmentally appropriate, i.e., some kids are just not ready for a heavy dose of academics and skills. The principal looked at me, rolled her eyes, and said calmly and confidently, "Well, it's not going to do them any harm."

I'm not so sure. Should we place such a heavy emphasis on academic skill development at such an early age? Is this a developmentally appropriate practice? The truth is, we don't know. That's because this heavy skills-based, academic approach has never been taken before in pre-K and kindergarten classrooms in this country. So there simply are no long-term data. Yet the lack of data on long-term effects has not stopped us from forging full steam ahead. Proponents of this approach think this emphasis on academic achievement is good for very young children. But we don't actually know what effect it's having, nor do we know what effect it will have five, 10, or 15 years from now.

Where I'm from, we call this "driving with your eyes closed." Others call it hoping. Call it what you will, but the fact of the matter is that our children in public schools—my daughter included—are participating in a giant experiment that none of us agreed to. Our children are guinea pigs, to put it nicely. Others might call them lab rats.

My daughter came home the other day in an incredibly grumpy mood.

"How was school today?" I asked.

"Terrible," she answered.

"Why? What happened?"

"I want to play with my friends," she said.

"Don't you get a chance to play with your friends?"

"No," she replied.

To be honest, it's not so much the addition of academics that worries me, as it is the subtraction of everything else. We seem to have lost the balance here. What are we getting rid of to make more time for all this skill building? Art, music, foreign languages, and—yes—recess are being cut to make more time for skills, specifically math and reading skills. Starting in pre-K.

So I met with a district administrator at the Office of Teaching and Learning. I said to her: "Ideally for me, pre-K can be about play, socialization, and fun. I think we can introduce some early literacy and numeracy in kindergarten, but let's wait until 1st grade to get into formal instruction."

She replied, "Oh, no. That would be too late."

"Too late?" I asked. "Too late for what?"

The truth is, I'm not in a hurry. Neither is my daughter. But kids are being pushed to be super-achievers at earlier and earlier ages. The rush to make adequate yearly progress (AYP) under No Child Left Behind has only exacerbated this trend that David Elkind chronicled in his 1981 book, *The Hurried Child.*

Elkind argues that in blurring the boundaries of what is age-appropriate by expecting—or imposing—too much too soon, we force our kids to grow up far too fast. He referred to it as nothing less than an assault on childhood.

I'm worried that we're setting kids up to fail. We may succeed in getting some of them to read, write, and complete math equations precociously. But we may also be creating a cohort of 4- and 5-year-old children who look at school as a place where they simply don't belong. As a place that is devoid of fun. I'm concerned that children like my daughter are forming a negative self-image when asked to perform cognitive tasks that they are clearly not able to do or not comfortable doing. Children may not only form negative self-images and develop negative self-esteem, but they may also form negative impressions about school, e.g., it's too competitive, too stressful.

Competition and stress may or may not be something we want kids to learn to deal with. And I'm not one of those parents who wants to shield my little shnoogums from nasty people who don't think she's as marvelous as I do. But do we really want 4-year-olds to deal with these things in pre-K, in the grade before the beginning grade of elementary school? When are children ever allowed to be beginners? Surely prekindergarten is a good place for kids to be beginners. Or so we used to think.

The notion of children being "kindergarten ready" is a bizarre oxymoron. It's like saying you have to know how to play the piano before you can learn how to play the piano. But if you are not "kindergarten ready," then you are considered behind. How odd that a policy called "No Child Left Behind" can define children as "behind" on their very first day of school.

Children learn to play together by playing together. They learn how take turns by taking turns, how to share by sharing, how to resolve conflicts that come up by resolving conflicts that come up. In order to learn how to do these things, children need to experience them firsthand. They need to do these things. But if they are not being given the time to do them, then how are they supposed to learn them?

In the context of the educational assessments that children like Vivian are subject to, we see a diagnostic model that specializes in both quantifying educational deficiencies in very young children and providing an antidote that meets the needs of the diagnosis. We see the emergence of large publishing companies that control the definition of the symptoms as well as prescribe and furnish the cure—for a hefty price. We see the emergence of the scripted curriculum, where "scripted" means an explicit formula to cure what ails them, as in "prescription." The prescription goes by various names, but they all have this in common: invent, identify, and remediate deficiencies, all in one slick package.

So what do I want? I want what Vivian wants: for her to be able to spend time with her friends, playing and being a little kid. She doesn't have any kids to play with on her block, so school is the only place she has any chance to socialize and interact with her peers. I want her to have the chance to make friends. I want her to be given the opportunity to play. I want her to learn how to share and solve problems with her peers. I want this more than I want her to be phonemically aware. There will be time for such academic pursuits when she's a bit older. But there's only so much time she's allowed to be a little girl.

Lest you think this sounds a bit touchy-feely and out of synch with today's calls for accountability, let me remind you of this: A 2004 study by the Paris-based Organization of Economic Cooperation and Development looked at literacy and reading skills for 15-year-olds. Finland was the top-ranked producer of readers. The United States was 15th out of 30 countries surveyed.

So what does Finland do? Children in Finland start learning to read in the 1st grade. The Finns believe that play is a crucial component of early childhood education and view playing as indistinguishable from learning.

I want this for all young children, not just my daughter. I want all children to have the opportunity to develop intellectually, socially, and emotionally. But most importantly, I want children to be allowed to have childhoods. ■

* Names have been changed.

Peter Campbell is a parent, educator, and activist who served in a volunteer role for four years as the Missouri State Coordinator for FairTest before moving to Portland, Ore. He has taught multiple subjects and grade levels for more than 20 years. He blogs at transformeducation.blogspot.com.

JEAN-CLAUDE LEJEUNE

What About Play?

BY SHARNA OLFMAN

Creative, open-ended play is rapidly vanishing from our homes, outdoor spaces, and schools. Today instead, children consume 40 hours of media each week (mostly on screens), surpassing the time given to every activity but sleep. As media moguls compete for their market share, these entertainments are increasingly rapid-paced, violent, and sexualized, jolting children out of their age-appropriate activities and encroaching on not only the time available to play but on children's very capacity for deeply imaginative play.

Economic and cultural constraints force parents to work longer days and weeks, and increasingly, parents rely on "electronic babysitters" to keep kids inside, or alternatively in structured after-school programs. And, with the intense escalation of standardized testing and curricula in the public school system, many preschools and most kindergartens are emphasizing structured academic work in lieu of play.

Upon rereading several classic children's novels to my own children recently, I was struck by a common feature among them. The children who populate *Little Women, The Secret Garden, All of a Kind Family, The Railway Children,* and *National Velvet,* to name a few, play make-believe games well into mid-adolescence. Today, Barbies are passé by preschool, 5-year-olds are playing with edgy, streetwise Bratz dolls while grooving to Britney, and preteens have long since moved on to electronic games, TV shows, movies, and music with ultra-violent and explicitly sexual content.

Is it really so problematic for children to adopt the outward trappings of adulthood in their dress, activities, and talk? Should we care about the loss of innocence and make-believe when so many dire matters—war, terrorism, environmental decay, poverty—weigh heavily on our collective consciousness? Perhaps—as those who have spearheaded the most recent set of educational reforms believe—it is wise to direct children's attention rapidly away from play and toward the body of facts deemed necessary to be a competent citizen in our technologically advanced society. I believe the demise of play is cause for profound concern and part and parcel of the myriad of other stressors in children's lives.

Thousands of studies spanning four decades have established incontrovertibly that creative play is a catalyst for social, emotional, moral, motoric, perceptual, intellectual, linguistic, and neurological development. Across socio-economic, ethnic, and cultural divides, play is a constant in childhood. It is a central feature in the lives of all young primates and most young mammals, underscoring its lengthy evolutionary history and adaptive value.

JEAN-CLAUDE LEJEUNE

Academic Success Is Predicated on Play

According to psychologist Erik Erikson's theory of psychosocial stages, the central challenge for young children is the development of initiative through fantasy play. Children the world over engage in vivid fantasy play between the ages of 3 and 5. These activities are not mere diversions, but vital exercises that spark creative potential.

When we force children to foreclose on the stage of initiative, and then prematurely push them into the stage of industry, we may indeed succeed in getting some children to read, write, and complete math equations precociously. But we may also be creating a cohort of children who lack spontaneity, creativity, and a love of learning. Children who are not emotionally engaged with the material they are learning and by the teachers who instruct them, cannot grow intellectually. Teachers who facilitate healthy play in the early childhood classroom provide an ideal means of integrating social, emotional, and intellectual growth. But in the wake of the No Child Left Behind Act, there is a growing disconnect between what education majors learn about optimal child development and what they are told to do in the classroom, which, increasingly, is to follow prescribed curricula and to sideline play in preparation for standardized testing.

School reforms did not just drop out of the sky. Over the past few decades, children in the United States have not been performing well in international tests comparing children's math, reading, and science competency. Like others, I believe that our public school system should undergo reform. However, the creation of standards and accountability must be grounded in principles of child development and humane pedagogy. If the mandate of the public school system is to support children's capacity to become thoughtful, caring, creative citizens capable of exercising independent judgment and free will, then treating age-appropriate, play-based curricula as expendable diversions in preschool and kindergarten is not the answer.

Perhaps, though, it is a quintessentially American answer, in a culture where "faster is better." There is a well-known anecdote about Jean Piaget—the famous Swiss cognitive psychologist—that he did not like to speak to American audiences because after he had described the natural pattern of children's development, Americans would invariably ask, "Yes, but how can we get them to do things faster?"

Piaget taught us that development unfolds over time in recognizable stages that nonetheless allow for considerable individual variation. In each of these stages, a child's understanding of her world is qualitatively different, and in the preschool and kindergarten years, children think and learn optimally through play. We embrace stage theories that pertain to our children's physical development: they must be able to sit before they can stand, stand before they can walk, and so on. At the same time, we understand that the child who enters puberty at 16 as opposed to 12 is nonetheless normal, and may tower over us five years hence. However, we have no such patience with respect to cognitive abilities. Woe to the American child who reads and writes at 7, rather than 5! She will almost certainly be subject to at least one diagnostic label, even though 7 is the normative age for beginning reading instruction in a majority of European countries.

Learning Through Play

If this seems to be an idealistic or romantic notion—that 4-, 5- and 6-year-olds should be learning through play—let's consider the following research comparing education among industrialized nations. It was, after all, international comparisons that catalyzed our most recent educational reforms. In a highly respected international survey conducted in 2004 by the Organization of Economic Cooperation and Development, Finland came in first in literacy and placed in the top five in math and science among 31 industrialized nations. The rankings were based on reading, math, and science tests given to a sample of 15-year-olds attending both public and private schools. U.S. students placed in the middle of the pack.

Finland's recipe for success? Children start learning to read in grade one at 7 years of age on the theory that play is the most effective learning tool in the early years and sets the stage for a lifelong love of learning. Preschool for 6-year-olds in Finland is optional. At first, the 7-year-olds lag behind their peers in other countries in reading, but they catch up almost immediately and then excel. Also, from grades 1 through 9, after every 45-minute lesson, students are let loose outside for 15 minutes so they can burn off steam with physical or musical activities. Art, music, physical education, woodwork, and crafts—subjects increasingly deemed expendable in U.S. public schools—are required subjects throughout the grades. (How much Ritalin might be spared if all school children in the United States had the freedom to "burn off steam" every 45 minutes and participate in physical education, art, music, and crafts on a regular basis?) Although there is a standard national curriculum, teachers in Finland are held in very high regard, and have considerable authority to devise and revise curricula suitable to individual students.

While the United States continues to slash play from its preschool and kindergarten curricula, several European nations, including those in the United Kingdom, are reforming their school systems in ways that echo Finland's choices: increasing the age at which children begin formal academic subjects, utilizing play-based curricula in the early years, and eliminating standardized testing in the early grades. The catalyst for these changes is a growing, research-based recognition of the success of developmentally appropriate curricula that do not arbitrarily divide children's cognitive, social, and emotional needs.

In December 2000, the British House of Commons Education Select Committee issued a report stating that there was "no conclusive evidence that children gained from being taught the three Rs before the age of 6." Creative play and small class size were deemed essential in early childhood education. The report expressed the following concerns about early academics:

> The current focus on targets for older children in reading and writing inevitably tends to limit the vision and confidence of early childhood educators. Such downward pressure risks undermining children's motivation and their disposition to learn, thus lowering rather than raising levels of achievement in the long term. … Inappropriate formalized assessment of children at an early age currently results in too many children being labeled as failures, when the failure in fact, lies with the system.

It is unfathomable that the United States is moving its approach to education further and further away from that of the very countries whose academic achievements it strives to emulate, and in a manner that ignores decades of child development research.

Screen Nation

The inordinate amount of time children spend consuming media not only robs them of valuable opportunities that could be devoted to quiet contemplative play or social play, it also undermines their ability to play. In her book *Failure to Connect*, Jane Healy articulates how both the content and the process of watching and interacting with screens "short circuits" brain development, in ways that undermine the acquisition of impulse control, imagination, higher order thinking, and the ability to generate visual imagery. (An excerpt from Healy's book is included in this book.) A vicious cycle is set in motion. The capacities needed to initiate play are undermined by screen culture, and the subsequent loss of playtime undermines these same capacities even further.

Preschool and kindergarten teachers report that many children today literally don't know how to "make-believe" and have to be taught to play. Grade school teachers are finding that some of their students don't spontaneously visualize the characters they are reading about—and so reading becomes a colossal bore. Increasingly, the "play" that children are bringing to the preschool and kindergarten classroom is a repetitive mimicry of violent sequences that aired on their television or video game screen the night before, not tempered by the impulse control and judgment necessary to avoid inflicting injury or pain on other "players." Small wonder that parents and educators sometimes lose sight of the value of play, if this is what is now construed as play.

Time Crunch

Healthy play is facilitated by adults, not so much as "play partners," but rather as models of emotionally centered human beings, engaged in activities that become the raw materials for play. Whether mother or father is raking the lawn, cooking a meal, or doing a craft, these activities are woven into healthy play. But increasingly, parents aren't home much with their children. In the wake of "welfare reform" our government has failed to provide women re-entering the work force with regulated, high quality, affordable child care. As the minimum wage continues to stagnate, the ranks of "working poor" parents continue to swell. Wage freezes are becoming ubiquitous among the working and middle classes, even as their workweeks lengthen. And so, parents are burning out. When we add the cult of individualism and the rampant consumerism in the United States, which prompts us to place our own needs first, the results are fairly predictable. Already-exhausted parents may elect to abandon their children to screens, structured activities, or the streets, while they "tune out" with the aid of their own screen entertainments.

When my daughter was 5, after visiting a conservatory, she told me that "flower fairies" had brushed against her legs. "Did the leaves of the plants touch your legs?" I offered. "No, Mommy, they were flower fairies," she reiterated with quiet resolve before drifting off to sleep.

What would my daughter's inner life be like if she had never been visited by "flower fairies"? Despite decades of empirical research on play, there is much that we still do not understand—that we may never fully understand—and yet must respect and honor. Perhaps in children's imaginative play lie the seeds of the sense of wonder that we feel when we gaze at a sunset or a starry sky whose secrets will never fully be revealed to us, filling us with a deep reverence for the splendors and mysteries of the universe, and our place within it. ■

Sharna Olfman is a professor of clinical and developmental psychology at Point Park University in Pittsburgh and the editor/author of the Childhood in America book series for Praeger Publishers. She is the author of *Childhood Lost: How American Culture Is Failing Our Kids* (Praeger Press, 2005).

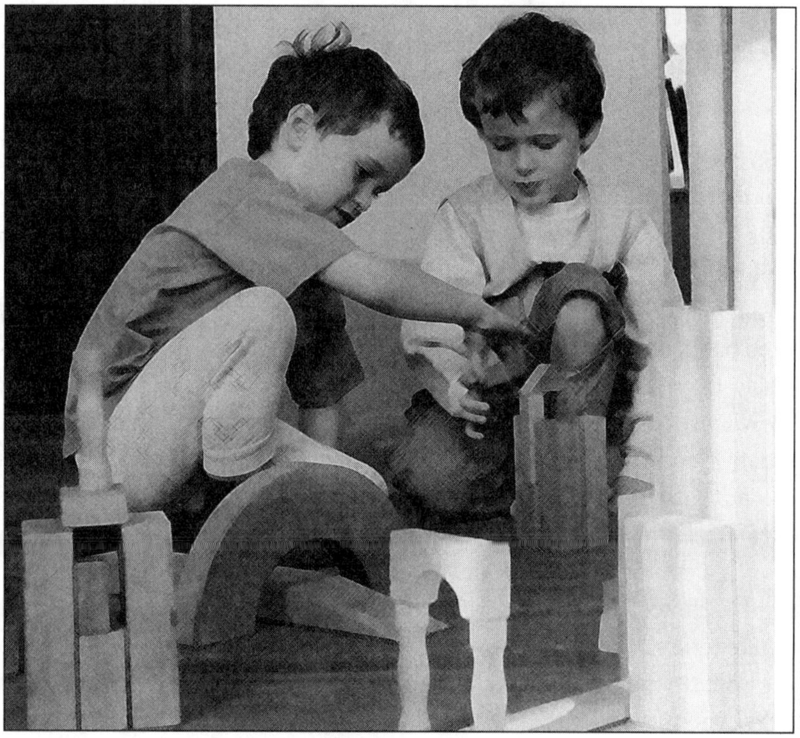

JOSEPH BLOUGH

Confession

My Students Play in the Classroom—and It's Good for Them

BY SETH SHTEIR

I confess: My students play with blocks.

Despite the current obsession with standards and standardized testing, some of us are still letting children play in our classrooms.

Those of us with intimate views of child development experience the physical, social, and intellectual benefits of play. Our opinions contradict a widely accepted view of play as a whimsical activity that contrasts sharply with the disciplined nature of work. But play can be a purposeful, intellectual activity that is hard work.

Block building, with proper guidance, has a great deal of educational value. It can help children acquire literacy, develop social skills, gain experience problem-solving, and enhance spatial sense.

I work at a progressive elementary school called Children's Community School, where block building is an important part of the curriculum from kindergarten through 2nd grade.

My 1st- and 2nd-grade class's experience with block building began after a field trip to a local butterfly garden. We had participated in an extensive tour of the garden, compost heap, and cages, where we viewed different stages of the monarch life cycle. Afterward, I wanted the children to build with blocks so I could assess what they had learned on our field trip. It was a way to allow them to process their knowledge while having fun.

"We could build the compost heap!" Ari* volunteered.

"Let's make the cages where we saw the monarch caterpillars and chrysalises," added Stacy. The children demonstrated their knowledge of the field trip by working with me to construct a map of the garden grounds. I wrote their ideas onto a chart, which served as a reading lesson. The students signed up to construct the butterfly garden, compost heap, cages, chrysalises and cocoons, and even bathrooms. The vocabulary words the children generated connected to our earlier study of bugs.

JOSEPH BLOUGH

Teachers can observe children's social interactions by having them participate in block building. When children work together to decide which size of blocks to use, where to build, and who should do what, they are practicing skills they will use throughout their adult lives. They are negotiating and resolving conflicts.

Although some educators say it's predominantly boys who gravitate toward blocks, at our school block building is a fundamental part of the curriculum instead of a choice. As a result, many girls become passionate builders and players.

Like any other lesson, teachers need to facilitate building activities. When my students encounter problems, I stop the activity and initiate a discussion. I ask the children to come up with solutions to the problems. Over the course of the school year there's less discord. The students develop better social skills due to my facilitation and the process of problem-solving.

The possibilities for problem-solving in block building are limitless. Sometimes the children identify problems, and other times I do. I believe my role as a facilitator is not only to take advantage of "teachable moments," but also to help my students discuss their interests and concerns.

One teachable moment occurred when we were studying animals that live in and around water. When the class built a community on a river, I noticed that structures blocked the river. I realized this was an excellent opportunity to explore the concept of life cycles. I gathered the children in an open section of the room to discuss this problem.

"The salmon won't be able to swim upstream!" shouted Billy, when I asked how our building would affect the salmon. The children discussed possible solutions and eventually agreed on raising the bridges above the water. During community block building, two students noticed that our market had run out of food. Several industrious children immediately began coloring and cutting out miniature hams, tomatoes, and carrots for the market.

Constructing buildings is a disciplined activity that requires planning, geometry, and spatial sense. Unlike paper and pencil, blocks require a different mode of thinking. The graphite line of a pencil is easily manipulated and erased, while blocks retain their form and need to be reconfigured. Yet this rigidity of form doesn't constrain creativity. I'm continually impressed with the way my students stack and balance the blocks.

I've observed students who clearly had mental templates of their buildings before they began construction, like Timothy, who meticulously selected and placed the blocks for the steps of our nature center. Children become very concerned with symmetry, shapes, and the heights of their buildings. Still others seem to improvise, adding and subtracting blocks to their edifices as needed. Throughout the year, their block building becomes more detailed.

Sadly, regimentation of school schedules makes it difficult for teachers to support alternative ways of learning. I believe blocks are a medium and an assessment tool that haven't gained the recognition they deserve. My students' participation in this playful yet disciplined activity enhances their language skills, social skills, problem-solving, and spatial sense. It's an important foundation upon which their education is built. ■

* Names have been changed.

Seth Shteir is a teacher at Children's Community School in Van Nuys, Calif.

Playing with Gender

BY ANN PELO

Three 4-year-old boys sat in a circle, each with a doll tucked under his shirt.

"It's time to have our babies!" Nicholas* declared. One by one, the boys pulled their babies from their shirts and cradled them tenderly for a moment before they leaped into action, cutting the babies' umbilical cords, wrapping them snugly in small cotton blankets, and holding their babies to their chests to nurse.

"You gotta feed your baby some milk," Jon instructed. "When your baby cries, that means he wants some milk."

"Or he might have a poopy diaper," Sam added. "Then you gotta change the diaper or the baby gets a rash."

"We're the dads of these babies," Nicholas said.

"But dads can't have babies," Sam objected. After a brief pause, he found a way to resolve the conundrum: "We're human sea horses!"

The boys tended to their babies gently and deliberately, alternating between nursing and diapering their newborns. Their game stretched until lunchtime, when they carefully tucked their babies into little improvised bassinets—dress-up clothes bundled into soft nests.

At the beginning of the school year, teachers at Hilltop Children's Center, the full-day childcare program where I worked in Seattle, took up a research question: How are the children exploring and expressing their identities through their dramatic play?

This was the second year we had explored a yearlong research question as a way to make our teaching more intellectually engaging for ourselves as well as for the children. Working with a research question helped us with detailed observation of children's play, and our observations were the foundation for our curriculum planning.

We chose the research question because we wanted to bring an intentional focus to our learning about anti-bias principles and practices. We'd said for a long time that anti-bias, culturally relevant practices were integral to our program. But we hadn't invested institutional energy to explore what this meant or to reshape our pedagogy. The research question helped us do that.

Hilltop is located in an affluent Seattle neighborhood, and, with only a few exceptions, the staff and families are mainly white. They are also, for the most part, politically and socially liberal and highly educated. While many of the teachers live paycheck to paycheck, as most childcare workers do, the families at Hilltop are from upper-income brackets. With our research question, we began to look directly at the issues of culture and class that shape our program. We wanted to deepen our understanding of what it means to do anti-bias work in a privileged community.

When we began our work with the research question, our goal was to learn about how the children understood gender, race, class, and other core elements of cultural identity, so that we could either reinforce their understandings or challenge them. We wanted to get better at responding to the subtle "teachable moments" that children create. And we wanted to plan a curriculum that counters racist, sexist, and classist understandings. We didn't anticipate the ways our study would lead us right to the heart of anti-bias teaching and learning.

Our Research Begins

That year there were 55 preschool-aged children at Hilltop, in four classroom groupings of various sizes, each with two, three, or four teachers (we had 12 teachers in our preschool classrooms). Once a week, each team came together for collaborative curriculum planning for an hour and a half. As the mentor teacher at Hilltop, I facilitated each team's meetings. Teachers would bring detailed notes about children's play and conversations to the team meetings. We studied teachers' observations and asked ourselves the following questions: What questions are the children expressing in their play? What understandings or experiences are they drawing on? What theories are they testing? How does this present an opportunity for us to strengthen the values we want to pass on to the children?

From our study and reflection, we planned one or two concrete next steps the teachers would take in the classroom and in communications with the children's families. These steps were intended to extend, deepen, or challenge children's thinking about identity, difference, and issues of culture. These next steps, in turn, launched us into another round of observation and study.

Early in the year, Sandra brought to her team meeting the notes she'd made as Nicholas, Jon, and Sam played about birthing and caring for babies. As we looked beneath the surface details of the game, teachers began to tease out elements of identity and culture.

"Sam clearly understands that men don't birth babies, but he wanted to be in that 'maternal' role and found a way to do that by being a sea horse," Megan said.

"I was curious about why they wanted to play this game at all," Sandra added. The teachers shared hypotheses. One teacher pointed out that Sam's mom had recently had a baby: "Maybe this game is a way for Sam to stay connected to his mom." Another teacher called attention to the boys' knowledge of the tasks of caring for babies, and the mastery they demonstrated with diapers and nursing; clearly, they'd been watching adults take care of babies. A third teacher commented on Sam's leadership role in the game: "That's new for Sam, to give direction to a game. I see this game as a way for him to try on this new role, now that there are younger kids in the group and some of the older kids have gone on to kindergarten."

I nudged the teachers to turn their attention back to the elements of gender identity in this game: "The boys acknowledged that men don't give birth or nurse babies, but they weren't willing to let go of the maternal role. Instead, they let go of being human and became sea horses, which allowed them to stay male and keep doing the maternal work that's associated with being female. They seem to be wrestling with how to be both male and maternal. What can we learn about their understandings of masculinity? Of moms and dads?"

I wanted to move us away from individualistic explanations. While these factors are important, they don't give us the full picture of children's identities. In our discussion about the three boys' play, I hoped to focus us on gender identity, through their internalized understandings of masculinity, caregiving work, and the distinctions between motherhood and fatherhood.

It took a lot of effort continually to refocus the discussion on the social and political contexts shaping this play—and my efforts weren't particularly successful. At the time, I attributed the struggle to the newness of our work with the research question; we were still training ourselves to look through the lens offered by the question. I expected that this would soon become a regular, familiar practice. I underestimated the work we had in front of us.

Unexpected Challenges

Week by week, our teams' collections of observations expanded.

Claudia, a 3-year-old, emphatically refused the role of princess in a game with three other girls. "I hate princesses, and that's why I'm a boy!" she exclaimed fiercely.

Two-year-old Juliet chose a mask to wear. It was a mask with long braids and with freckles. "This is a girl mask," she explained, "because it has freckles." She noticed the mask that Molly was wearing, a mask with short hair: "You look like a boy in that mask, Molly."

Matthew and Joshua, 4-year-old buddies, slipped capes over their shoulders. "We're rescue heroes and our job is to save babies who are in danger!" Joshua called out, as he and Matthew raced across the room.

Kathryn, a 3-year-old, initiated a game with John. She draped a piece of silky fabric over his shoulders, shawl-like, exclaiming delightedly, "You're Cinderella!" Then she shifted the fabric onto his shoulders to be more like a cape: "Now you're the prince." Back and forth, from shawl to cape, Cinderella to prince, Kathryn transformed John again and again.

As fall slipped into winter, a couple things became increasingly apparent to me. Within the context of our research question, children's exploration of gender identity had become teachers' primary focus. When we launched our research question in the fall, we'd started out with a bigger frame. We naively expected that we'd be looking at race, class, and gender, all lumped together under the vague heading of "culture." As the fall progressed, our focus narrowed as gender became the lens through which we explored the idea of cultural identity.

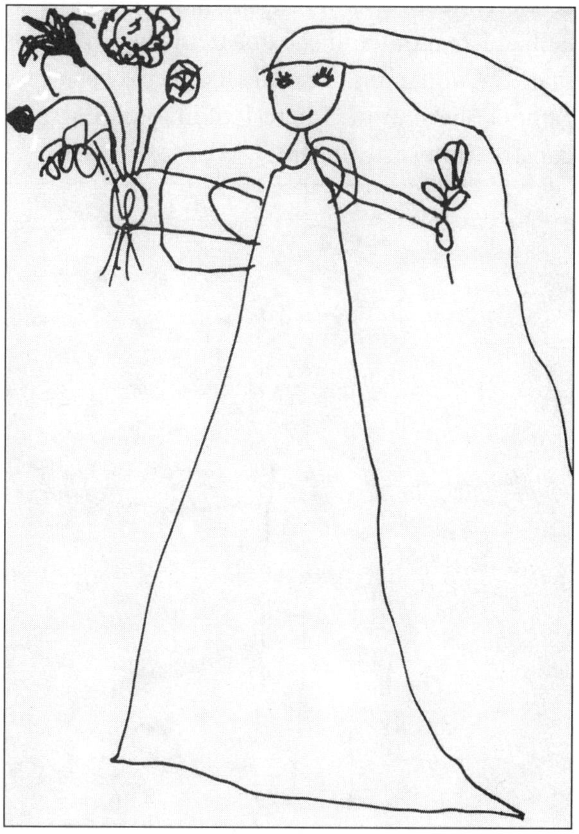

Certainly, the children's play provided us with many opportunities to pay attention to gender. But, more significantly, gender was comfortable terrain for our staff of predominantly white women. We were familiar with considering the impact of sexism on our lives. We assumed that we shared values and goals about what we want children to learn about gender identity. Gender seemed a safe starting place for our staff as we stepped into more conscious and intentional anti-bias work.

The other striking aspect of our work with the research question was that, even within the fairly comfortable arena of gender identity exploration, teachers continued to struggle to stay focused on the social and political aspects of children's play. In their discussions about their observations, teachers emphasized children's individual developmental and family stories. For example, reflecting on Claudia's assertion that she hates princesses and that's why she's a boy, teachers made the following observations: "Claudia's mom is athletic and strong, and not very 'princessy.' Maybe she's trying to figure out how to be like her mom and she doesn't have words for that." "Claudia doesn't really like to play princess games. She's more interested in building and construction sorts of games."

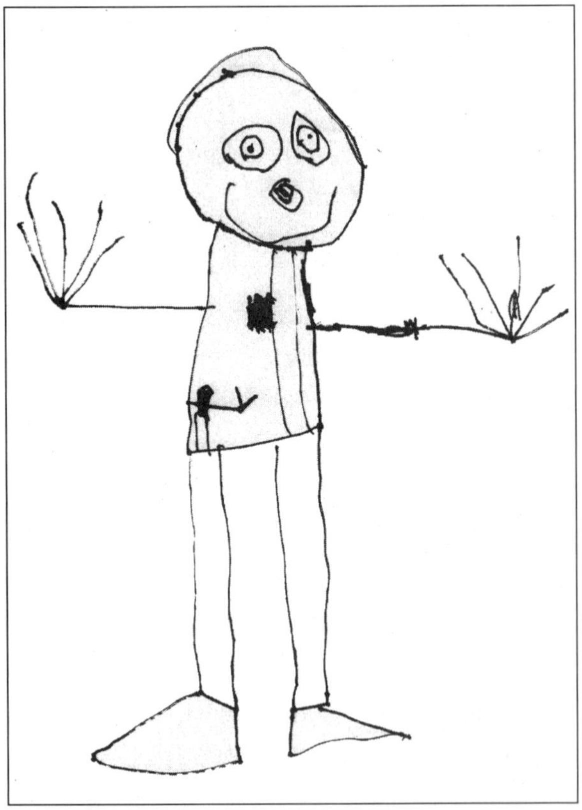

I asked, "What if Claudia's comment isn't really about princesses at all? What if she's trying to find words for questions about what it means to be a girl or a boy? What if she's asking, 'To be a girl, do I have to wear dresses and play games about being rescued and feasting and dancing? If I don't do that stuff, does that make me a boy? What is possible for me as a girl?'"

With our research question we wanted to develop the habit of paying attention to the ways children's play reflects their understandings of their political and social contexts. We wanted to strengthen this practice in ourselves until it became as easy and instinctive for us as paying attention to children's individual circumstances like their family relationships, their play and learning styles, their skills with literacy or math. But this effort was much more difficult than we'd imagined.

Why was this so challenging?

Claiming Our Cultural Perspectives

Four months into our work with the research question, I experienced a dramatic moment of understanding. During one week's team meeting, Lisa brought an observation of 5-year-old Jamie's play with his younger friend, 3-year-old Laura:

> Jamie ran to greet Laura at the door as soon as she arrived. He swept her into his arms, exclaiming, "Let's play baby and dad!" Laura grinned her agreement, and Jamie picked her up, carrying her to the drama area. As their game unfolded, Jamie told Laura what to do: "Now cry, baby." "Now go to sleep." "Now eat, baby." Laura cheerfully followed Jamie's directions. Jamie picked her up, set her down, rolled her over, changed her diaper, put her to bed, woke her up; Laura didn't move her body on her own, but waited for Jamie to instruct her or physically to move her.

Lisa's co-teacher, Kirstin, had an immediate and strong reaction: "I see Jamie and Laura play this game just about every morning that they're both here, and I've been putting a stop to it. I tell Laura that she's a powerful girl, that she can move her own body. And I tell Jamie to let Laura walk, that he's not to carry her anymore."

Lisa quickly echoed Kirstin's passionate words: "I absolutely agree with your decision.

This game really bugs me, and I'm not sure why—but I don't like it."

Jamie and Laura's baby game was in itself fairly innocuous in the context of our program; we tend to be quite comfortable with kids' physicality and with affectionate, informal touch between children. However, Lisa and Kirstin had stepped away from the usual perspectives that shape discussions at Hilltop about this sort of game. They began their conversation by focusing on aspects of Jamie's and Laura's personal circumstances: Jamie's much older than Laura, he's an only child and just beginning to develop the flexibility in his play that makes room for other children's contributions; Laura is young and is just beginning to move into collaborative play. But Kirstin and Lisa quickly left this terrain of individual psychology and circumstances and stepped emphatically into the terrain of gender identity.

"As a woman, I hate seeing a girl being so passive," said Kirstin, startling me with the force behind her words.

"I see Jamie telling Laura what to do and even moving her body for her and all my protectiveness for Laura as a 16-year-old girl on a date comes out," Lisa continued. "I want Laura to tell Jamie, 'No!' and I want Jamie to hear it!"

Lisa and Kirstin were responding to the children's play as women, reflecting on Jamie and Laura's play through their own experiences. They responded to their students' play with their hearts as well as from a more considered, measured place of intellectual reflection.

As I listened to Kirstin and Lisa talk, I experienced a sudden clarifying of what we'd been working with (and against) all fall. We'd been paying attention to children's gender identities but not paying attention to our own understandings and identities. We'd failed genuinely to acknowledge our own lenses, our own experiences, values, questions, and tensions related to gender. In order to see children as cultural beings, we must see ourselves as cultural beings, and we hadn't tended to that work.

We weren't asking central questions of ourselves: What does each of us know about gender? How have we each experienced the meaning and impact of gender in our lives? What values and goals do we each hold for children's learning about gender identity? With the research question, we'd challenged ourselves to pay attention to gender identity as the children experience and understand it. Now, we needed to investigate the ways in which we adults express and explore our gender identities.

I brought this new awareness to Claudia's teachers, eager to examine her comments about hating princesses and being a boy through the lens of the teachers' experiences of gender. "We've been trying to understand what's going on for Claudia," I said. "But we haven't talked about what each of us has experienced about gender. I think that could help us understand Claudia's experience. When you think about Claudia rejecting princesses and claiming to be a boy, do you see any connection to what you've experienced in your life?"

Sandra started talking before I finished my question: "Yes! When I was a little girl, growing up with two sisters, I knew early on that I wasn't like them. It wasn't about being lesbian or straight or anything like that, but I knew I didn't like to play dolls and dress up like they did. I wanted to be outside riding my bike or playing tag."

Sonja nodded in eager understanding. "I remember really clearly my feeling of relief when I learned the word 'tomboy.' There was a word to describe how I was in the world! There were other people like me!"

Megan listened intently, adding, "I think of 'tomboy' as a little insulting. Why do girls who are athletic have to be called anything other than girls? Why some cute word that refers to boys?"

We talked for a while about how our early experiences shaped who we are now, as teachers and as women. We considered the ways these early experiences could help us understand Claudia's comment.

"It helps me think about Claudia being like I was as a kid," said Sandra. "She's not necessarily trying to figure out if she's a girl or a boy, but what it means to be someone who's not a girlie girl. Maybe the only language she has for 'not a girlie girl' is 'boy.'"

"When I remember my own girlhood, trying to reconcile what I felt excited by and what I knew I was supposed to be excited by as a girl, it helps me think about Claudia," said Sonja.

"I wonder if Claudia knows the word 'tomboy'" I asked. "I wonder what it would mean to her to hear your stories about growing up as girls."

The teachers made plans to share their stories with Claudia and the rest of the group, as well as to bring in photos of themselves from childhood soccer games and tree-climbing adventures. Their planning was anchored by an explicit awareness of their political and social experiences and perspectives, and by their goals for children. These teachers, all of whom are female, knew how it feels to be a girl growing up in a sexist culture, and they wanted to support Claudia as she claimed her identity as a girl who rejects princess play and embraces full-bodied adventure.

Our Journey Continues

Once a month, all four preschool teaching teams would come together for a two-hour meeting for reflection and study. At this meeting, after my conversations with Kirstin, Lisa, Sonja, Sandra, and Megan, I shared my new awareness and questions.

"I've noticed that, in our team meeting discussions about our research question, we've struggled to stay connected to the political and social contexts of children's play," I said. "We're really good at seeing kids as individuals with individual life stories, but we're not as good at seeing them as political, cultural beings. When we fail to recognize children's social identities, we erase fundamental aspects of who they are and who their families are. And when we fail to give voice to our cultural identities or to acknowledge our co-teachers' cultural perspectives, we erase fundamental aspects of ourselves," I added.

I posed several questions for discussion during our full-staff meeting:

- Why is it an effort for us at Hilltop to address the political and social context that shapes children's identities?
- What are the societal values and belief systems that focus us on individual circumstances rather than broader cultural identities?
- What do we gain when we emphasize political and social identity—both the children's and our own?

The discussion that unfolded was rich with insight and with contradiction.

Lisa described her sense of not wanting to emphasize what could divide people: "I want to bring us closer together, not make us feel different and separated."

Susan said, "Our society's storyline is that we achieve or fail as individuals. When we emphasize being women, or people of color, or white, we either are held back or we get unfair advantages—according to society's storyline."

"We haven't had to look at these issues as teachers at Hilltop because of our cultural privilege on many fronts," I added. "It's an aspect of white privilege not to think about race, for example. We need to keep asking ourselves: How have we each experienced the meaning and impact of gender—or race, or class—in our lives? What values and goals do we each hold for children's learning?"

During the rest of that staff meeting, we took the first steps toward explicitly naming the cultural lenses that shape how each of us experiences our teaching and learning. First, Lisa and Kirstin recapped our discussion about Jamie and Laura's game. And Sonja, Sandra, and Megan told the story of their conversation about Claudia and tomboys. Then, we practiced doing what these teachers had done, acknowledging our cultural perspectives as we studied children's play. Teachers

> **Trying to Be a Boy**
>
> Makely: "I'm trying hard to be a boy."
>
> Megan: "Why?"
>
> Makely: "They have cooler bikes."
>
> Jamice: "They're stronger than us girls."
>
> Makely: "No, actually girls can do more sooner than boys."
>
> Jamice: "Well, they can pee standing up."
>
> Makely: "But that's not why I want to be one. They get treated better! They get to watch more violent things like Pokemon and Yu-Gi-Oh. Plus their clothes are really cool—like I have old clothes from my brothers and they're so cool."

worked in small groups with one of several observations of children's play that I provided. A typical example focused on a conversation I'd overheard among several children as they tried to figure out why their buddy (a girl) had commented that "she's trying hard to be a boy" (see sidebar, p. 72).

I asked teachers to read and talk about each observation "not as teachers trying to understand the children's points of view, but as who you are: a lesbian, or a person from a working-class background, or a Filipina, or a European American, or a woman." I posed several questions to guide their discussion of the observation:

What caught your attention right away? What was your first reaction or judgment?

What experiences in your life are you tapping into?

What values come to the surface for you? Can you trace those values back to their roots in the political and social context of your life?

With this activity, I introduced what I hoped would become a regular element in our team meetings: I wanted us to make explicit the social and political contexts and assumptions that shape our thinking and planning as teachers, so that we bring clarity and awareness to our planning for the children's learning. I wanted us to acknowledge and claim our work as political work—seeing teaching as not only about supporting children's individual development and learning, but also about cultivating particular values and practices that counter oppression and enhance justice.

This staff meeting launched us into a new stage of our journey. Our practice with the research question unearthed our collective discomfort with talking about culture—and talking about culture is essential if we are to take up the work of anti-bias, culturally relevant teaching and learning. Probably at the beginning of the year we could have said that we needed to examine our own political and social identities at the same time as we pay attention to children's political and social identities. But without our observations of the children's interactions and our deeply felt reactions, our inquiry would have remained abstract.

For too long, our anti-bias efforts at Hilltop had been standard-issue: brown play dough, books with characters from a range of families, dolls with different skin colors. The new work we were aiming to do was much less comfortable and easy; it made us squirm and stammer and get angry and defensive to look at the ways in which our cultural privileges had been knit together to form the fabric of our program.

As we continued to do this work, we looked more closely at race, building on the work described above. And we added a step to our curriculum planning process. In addition to reflecting on the possible meanings of the children's play, staff committed to considering the personal social-political experiences and identities that they bring to their observations before planning next steps and curriculum investigations to take up with the children. Our encounter with the research question initiated a slow-but-sure transformation of practice. ■

* Names have been changed.

Ann Pelo is an early childhood teacher and teacher mentor in Seattle, Wash.

JOSEPH BLOUGH

Cybertots

Technology and the Preschool Child

BY *JANE HEALY*

Debate rages among parents and educators as to whether and how computers should be used with young children. Thus far, however, public discussion of technology has skirted important questions of age-appropriate use, with marketers cheering when someone opines: "The earlier the better. Let's prepare these kids for the future!" Yet, as we have seen, preparation for the future involves a far different set of abilities. Time spent with computers in the early years not only subtracts from important developmental tasks but may also entrench bad learning habits, leading to poor motivation and even symptoms of learning disability.

Children in different stages of brain development have different needs. Just as in shoes, mathematics, or sports, there is no one-size-fits-all in electronic learning. I have come to believe that computers—at least as they are currently being used—are not necessary or even desirable in the lives of most children under 7 (with the exception, of course, of children suffering from certain handicaps). I realize this opinion is not a popular one, especially with parents who have invested money, time, pride, and faith in an electronic tutor. It will be even more vocally scorned by those who stand to make substantial profits from those parents' good—if misplaced—intentions.

Research supporting preschool computer use is almost nonexistent; what is available has mainly been promulgated by those who stand to gain in some ways from their advocacy. And there's plenty to gain. Software for toddlers is a rapidly growing market niche, and computer "classes" have parents enrolling their children as young as 2½—and many arrive already familiar with the machine. A favorite cartoon in my file shows a young boy entering his mother's kitchen with a downcast expression. "I got sent home from computer camp because I couldn't button my shirt," he announces.

I believe we need a reality check. Because some parents and teachers will rush to new technology anyway, I will also mention a few applications for tots that may prove useful or at least benign, along with realistic guidelines for those who insist on believing that digital technology can improve on nature's program for childhood.

A Busy Time for the Brain

> Buy my 4-year-old a computer? What nonsense! She needs first to build up her own mind, to learn writing, math. You must realize the computer can do only what the human mind tells it to. Our children need good minds so they'll be able to run the computers.
>
> —INDUSTRIAL SOFTWARE ENGINEER, FRANKFURT, GERMANY

During the early years, the brain has a staggering number of developmental tasks to accomplish, and environments influence its formation. If the environment is a poor one, final sculpting of neuronal connections will bypass or distort important aspects of development. During these critical periods when the brain is changing rapidly, we may see relatively sudden growth (interspersed with needed regressions, or "rest periods") in a child's ability to perform certain types of mental operations. Since virtually all parts of the brain are active during these years, anything that limits appropriate experiences or sets up undesirable emotional/motivational patterns will have profound and lasting effects.

In the first two years of life, networks of connections are forming for social, emotional, and cognitive abilities—with emotional and language interaction from human caregivers the main impetus. Eighteen months is an extremely important juncture when a mental growth spurt opens new windows for conceptual understanding of natural laws governing both human behavior and the physical world. This age is also a turning point in sociability and for organizing the child's senses around movement. Putting normally developing babies on computers for any amount of time is so ridiculous that it hardly bears further comment. In fact, animal studies looking at "augmented sensory experience," or abnormal overstimulation of more than one sense too early in life, have shown it has lasting negative effects on attention and learning. Scientists can't ethically do this type of research on humans, but some parents seem to be trying!

From ages 2 to 7, profound developmental tasks to be mastered include the following seven types of learning that may be distorted by too much electronic stimulation:

1. Learning in a Social Context

> "Can a computer cheat at tic-tac-toe?"
> "Yes, it's alive, it cheats, but it doesn't know it's cheating." —ROBERT, A 7-YEAR-OLD[1]

Since even older children and adults have trouble sorting out the "humanness" of electronic brains, young children may be profoundly affected by the social and emotional relationship they develop with their machines. Computers must never supplant supportive human environments. In a large study of day care, researchers at 14 universities found that children's intelligence, academic success, and emotional stability were determined primarily by the personal and language interaction they had with adults. Optimally, the brain does its important work in a context of relaxed exploration guided primarily by the child and supported by helpful and emotionally responsive but not overly intrusive adults.

Digi-tykes may be especially at risk if certain types of software induce overactivation of the right hemisphere and concurrent underactivation of the left. In one provocative study, 4-year-old children with greater amounts of left frontal activation displayed more social competence, while children who showed more right activation displayed social withdrawal. Whether computer use will prove to be related to similar electrophysiological changes is an interesting question.

2. **Learning to Use All the Senses**

From birth, sensory areas in the back of the brain refine their ability to perform basic functions effortlessly: listening, looking, touching, and moving. These systems should become automatic so that around age 7 children can integrate them smoothly (e.g., watch a guitarist and move to the beat; think about story content while writing words; look at the chalkboard and listen to a teacher). This "intersensory integration" is critical for good learning, and it takes a lot of progress.

Open-ended computer use—such as a drawing program—offers some combining of sensory abilities but differs qualitatively from nature's programming of whole-body, three-dimensional sensory experience. A time may come when specially designed software can "teach" intersensory integration, but I haven't seen any yet that I would trust to do the job.

3. **Learning to Be a Powerful Learner**

Early years are a time for learning one's "stance" toward the world. Children are wrestling with important personal issues: (1) Should I trust or mistrust others—or myself? (2) How does the world really work? (3) How powerful am I as an independent learner?

Autonomous control of play materials by the child (as with nonelectronic toys or materials) is very important because the child is laying the groundwork to be either an internally motivated or a weak learner. Young children naturally tend to disbelieve their own power as compared with a computer, which is "opaque"—that is, one can't really understand or see what makes it work. Even though youngsters become adept at running programs, they can't ultimately control the computer's behavior (with the possible exception of LOGO programming). On the contrary, good play materials (paints, empty boxes, nonanimated dolls, toy tools, Tinkertoys, and playing cards, for example) are fully under the child's control (in accordance with natural scientific laws, such as gravity). They not only empower the young learner/problem solver, but subtly convey major principles of how the world works. For example, cause and effect—as well as self-control—are easy to learn when you're trying to hammer a nail into a board (if I miss, then I might hurt my finger), but hard to learn when a system crashes for no apparent reason or things jump around on the screen without a visible source of propulsion.

As frontal lobe development sets up the basis for executive control systems, the preschooler needs experiences in managing his own mind—not having it distracted or programmed from outside. Among other skills, children of this age should develop:

- Ability to regulate one's own emotions
- Problem-solving skills, flexibility, originality
- Motivation and persistence
- Attention
- Social skills
- Body rhythm and coordination of movement
- Imagination

If these foundations are neglected during a critical period, they may be difficult—or even impossible—to regain.

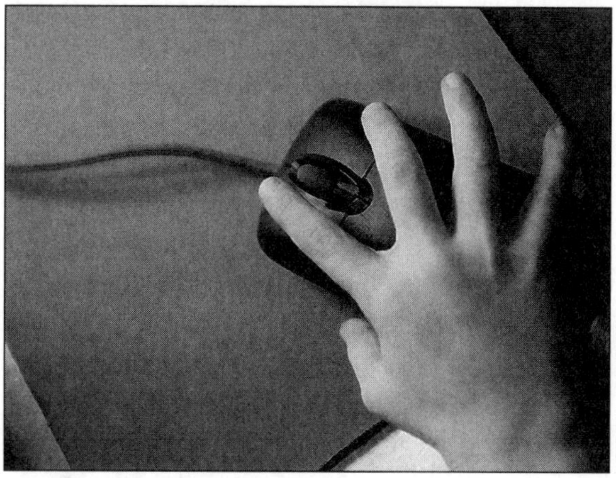

JOSEPH BLOUGH

4. **Learning to Pay Attention**

One of the most important learning skills threatened by electronic stimulation is selective attention: the ability to direct one's own attention and focus clearly on what is to be learned without succumbing to distraction. Children who can't resist touching anything that comes into sight or whose mental focus shifts every time something happens are said to be "stimulus bound."

Little children's attention naturally jumps from thing to thing, but some forms of electronic media may prolong this immaturity. Distracting graphics and special effects, coupled with the temptation to click impulsively, encourage stimulus-bound behavior that, in turn, contributes to attention problems.

JOSEPH BLOUGH

I believe it is possible to develop software to improve attention skills. A few programs are in the works, and we may hope for some good research on this issue.

The crowded computer lab in one elementary school has been carved out of a spare room next to the front office. In it, a veteran kindergarten teacher is attempting to demonstrate to a group of eight students at one machine how to make alphabet cards with a hyperstack she has developed. Later they will learn to illustrate them with an electronic drawing program. She is shouting a little to hold their attention, since 16 5-year-olds and a teaching aide are arrayed around the other machines in the room. Most are playing with edutainment software, including "reading" and "writing" programs, and their choices consist mainly of flashy graphics and noise. The entire room sounds like the video arcade of an amusement park.

The alphabet card group moves to computers to work in pairs. They need to follow a fairly complex sequence of steps to complete the assignment, but they set to work diligently. Gretchen McFarland, my host for the day, agrees with my observation that this activity incorporates some worthy educational goals (as it would, of course, if they were making illustrated alphabet cards by hand). As I circulate around the room, however, I find myself wondering how much mental energy these young brains must expend to keep focused on a complex task in the middle of this electronic cacophony. While most youngsters eventually learn to screen out background noise (an ability called "auditory figure-ground perception"), it takes an unconscious toll on a child's resources and may result in subtle overstimulation and accumulating stress. A young child stressed by such sensory overload usually reacts in one of two ways: either he shuts down, or he gets "hyper"—both physically and mentally. A child genetically at risk for learning or attention problems may be particularly affected. Many of today's youngsters have grown up in these taxing environments—television, videos, loud music, and now the beep, beep, beep of computer games—so they almost need stressful background noise to feel "normal."

The period ends, and the children line up to file out. Their teacher looks tired, although it is only 10:00 a.m.

"These kids get more hyper every year!" she comments to me, as she tries to establish order in the line.

No kidding.

5. Learning Visual Imagery and Memory

Frontal lobe maturation throughout childhood and adolescence gradually enables better "working memory," the ability to juggle a number of ideas or thoughts at one time. For example, preschoolers naturally have difficulty visualizing a story while paying attention to the plot and the characters' names all at the same time; they are not terribly efficient in their thinking because they can't hold many alternatives in mind. With maturation and practice, the brain learns to visualize and hold alternatives. Children with weak visualization skills may always be plagued by inefficient memory and difficulty with more formal symbol systems (e.g., reading, math).

Research suggests that the way adults help children learn to practice these skills makes a clear difference in their thinking abilities. For example, suggesting such exercises as, "Can you make a 'movie' in your mind of how Cinderella looks in the story?" can aid kids in expanding their abilities. For youngsters on a computer, no such spur is available, as the computer simply makes their pictures for them.

6. **Learning to Think Logically: If-Then (Causal) Reasoning**

Children between the ages of 3 and 4 years are beginning to make logical inferences with "if-then"—or causal—reasoning. It is difficult for adults to understand just how elementary their reasoning really is. For example, when 3-year-old Paul sees two balls hitting each other and then one rolling off, he is likely to view these as two unrelated incidents.

By age 5, Paul will be able to infer that the second ball rolled away as a result of being hit by the first. Very young children like to play around with causality (Paul used to drop cookies off his high-chair tray, then look up at his mom with an anticipatory grin: If I drop the cookie, then Mom will ...), but this form of reasoning takes a significant jump between ages 3 and 4.

How do children learn to reason about these abstract relationships? Psychologists have concluded that, along with requisite brain changes, they need physical experience of action sequences that they themselves control (e.g., first I do x, then as a result y happens—and I can change that if I do x differently). Thus, the years between 3 and 4 may be a particularly bad time to introduce an opaque and arbitrary electronic "toy" into the child's world. Better quality children's software tries to address this problem, but there is no evidence it can do the job.

If we confuse children of this age about cause and effect by giving them too many things to select and watch, as opposed to doing, will we jeopardize their causal reasoning? Teachers today tell us a surprising number of older children don't seem to "get it" in the realm of "if-then" logic; they struggle with math and science concepts as well as with social relations, strategy use, and ethical choices.

Social causal reasoning—the ability to infer how someone else might be feeling ("If I don't come when Dad calls me, he might feel worried.")—is also important. Progress requires interaction with human beings and human emotions (e.g., "I took Jimmy's toy and [as a result] he got so mad he hit me!"). Physical and social experiences are intricately tied to the younger child's mental development. Barbara Bowman of the Erikson Institute in Chicago worries that too many children learn to use computers without understanding their "social contexts." Three- and 4-year-olds cannot fully understand that real people with particular points of view produced what is on the screen, she points out, and they need human mediators to help them make sense of what they see. "Even in the age of technology, it is through relationships with others—through joint activities, language, and shared feelings with other human beings—that children grasp meaning."

In addition, children under age 5 have a tendency to confuse appearance with reality. If something moves, for example, they may believe it is really alive. They tend to have difficulty taking another's perspective; they are a bit hazy on "theory of mind," understanding what it means to have a mind containing thoughts or being a discriminating judge of another person's motives and point of view. Thus their gullibility to Internet advertising or implicit messages in children's computer games.

By ages 5 to 7, children start to move outside their own perspectives. They begin to discriminate fact from fiction in television viewing. By age 7 most understand that fictional characters do not retain their roles in real life and that fictional shows are scripted and rehearsed. But this development is inversely related to the child's viewing experience—the more TV, the less he tends to understand the difference between fact and fiction. For children unable to discriminate what is real from what is not, electronic playmates may be more confusing than we think. Even older children have trouble deciding whether computers are alive or not and tend to place too much trust in them.

7. **Learning New Symbol Systems**

"The importance of embedding educational technology in other instructional activities has grown out of a disadvantage of technological media: that they always 'disrupt' reality to some extent and put demands on symbolization capacities that younger learners might lack."

—Heinz Mandl, University of Munich, Germany

Between ages 4 and 7, children begin mastering formal symbols of adult reasoning (written words, numerals), and it's a tempting time to introduce software for phonics or early math skills. Yet the 4-, 5-, and even 6-year-old brain is not necessarily ready for this disembodied learning. A symbol is not really useful until it has been internalized: a young child may be able to count to 10 or recognize numerals, but until he really understands what "3" represents in the real world (e.g., he can give you three objects when you show him the numeral, or understand that "3" is less than "4"), he has not connected the real number concept to the symbol.

If you want your child to be good at reading, you should contextualize the learning, that is, read with him, talk with him about stories and daily events, expand vocabulary, listen to him, and provide him with open-ended manipulative materials (e.g., aids for pretend play, rocks or button collections, building or sewing materials, puppets, costume box) to encourage concepts and problem-solving skills. If you want him to be good at math, you should talk about number concepts (e.g., "We need two more place settings when your aunt and uncle come to dinner") and play board and card games with him. Such games, by the way, constitute the strongest predictor of math ability that researchers have yet found, and thus far even well-constructed computer programs can't achieve the same result.

One experiment cited by psychologist Robbie Case compared young children's math learning from board games played on computers with the same games played by a child with an adult. Although the researchers thought they had developed a software package to duplicate the benefits of real-life experience, the one-on-one contact with an adult still produced far greater gains. What was the difference? It was the spontaneous language interaction when the adult played with the child. Older children, ages 10 and 11, on the other hand, learned some difficult concepts (e.g., inventing a function) more readily from carefully designed math software than from classroom experiences.

Another reason young children don't profit as much from computer simulations as from real activities is something developmental psychologist Irving Siegel calls "representational distance." Children who understand "representational distance" do better in school because they can separate themselves from the "here and now." They understand a thing or name can stand for something else (like a flag representing a country) and that something happening in one place can represent something happening in another (like reading about Alaska when you're sitting in Brussels).

Children under age 7 are only beginning to learn representational competence; computer simulations may confuse them. Even the physical distance between the mouse and the screen (or the two-dimensional touch screen) makes the simulation less powerful than physically holding and moving a piece on a three-dimensional game board. Siegel also found that a big boost in representational competence comes from close conversations with parents and caregivers ("Let's talk about what we did at the park today.").

Why Age 7?

Most thoughtful professionals I have interviewed agree on one particular philosophy about computer use. It is, simply: If the computer can accomplish the task better than other materials or experiences, we will use it. If it doesn't clearly do the job better, we will save the money and use methods that have already proven their worth. In the case of the child under 7, there are few things that can be done better on a computer and many that fail miserably by comparison.

Because age 6 to 7 represents such an important developmental milestone for the human brain, I believe it is a realistic stepping-stone into constructive computer use. In fact, for children above age 7, combining computer and manipulative activities may result in better learning. Younger children, however, are better off spending this valuable time in a physically and linguistically enriched environment. Even for children who lack this type of privileged experience, there is no evidence that today's computer applications will make up the inevitable gaps. Spend the money on better early childhood programs.

If You Must

The reality, of course, is that many parents, teachers, and childcare providers will continue to believe they must propel their young charges into the electronic future. The powerful National Association for the Education of Young Children has reversed its previous stance and squeezed out a limited endorsement of "developmentally appropriate" computer use for children in preschools. Many parents and teachers firmly disagree, and it should be noted that the caveats in this report are so stringent as to make "appropriate" use difficult or even unlikely in most schools. NAEYC recommends that teachers take much more training, spend more time observing children for computer-related problems, make an effort to avoid the flood of bad software, take responsibility to guarantee that computers serve the curriculum in appropriate ways, and participate more in technology decision-making. Appropriate use also guarantees that the cost of new technologies will not subtract from other learning materials. In other words, if you already have an exemplary program, it's OK to add a little computer experience if you have time to plan and supervise extra activities that will dovetail with your regular instruction.

JEAN-CLAUDE LEJEUNE

With young children it is even more important than with older ones to determine what we want them to learn before choosing the technology to do the job. Purchase equipment because it fits a specified need, not because it's "cute" or novel. In fact, if we define "technology" more broadly as "any tool that extends the senses," such as hand lenses, magnifying bug boxes, string telephones, compasses, thermometers, creative art materials, rulers, and audiotapes, computers become only one of many options for early learning. Moreover, because young children require 30 to 50 minutes of free play or independent exploration to become fully engaged in learning materials, occasional large blocks of time with adult supervision—not superficial jabs at software—should be scheduled.

As technology and software progress, we will doubtless see increasing numbers of worthwhile applications. In the meanwhile, if you must plunge your preschooler into an artificial world, you might review the following suggestions for computer use:

Guidelines for Young Children Using Computers

- Starting children on computers too early is far worse than starting them too late.
- A child should be able to understand the cause-effect relationship of moving a mouse or touching the screen to get a reaction before she starts to use a computer.
- Look for software that makes the child feel independent, e.g., being able to navigate in and out of activities, hear spoken directions, or access understandable help screens.
- Downplay skill-and-drill math and phonics activities in favor of interactive problem-solving or more open-ended uses where the child is free to explore and discover ways to use the materials.
- Discourage impulsive clicking. Stop the program occasionally to encourage the child to talk about what is happening, what he is doing, and why. You may need to turn off the visual distractors at this time. Describe what he has done and ask questions about how he accomplished something. If there is an icon or image on the screen, make sure the child understands its relationship to real-life objects and events.
- Supplement "eyes-on" with "hands-on." Find real-life experiences that extend and complement the virtual ones.
- Help the child understand how the computer works and what is going on as he manipulates a program. Let him see how you physically connect computer, printer, and other components. Keep emphasizing that people control the computer, not the other way around.
- Don't let screen time substitute for lap time and don't expect books on CD-ROM to substitute for interactive reading with loving adults. Be sure to take the time for questions about and personal discussion of the story you are reading. Encourage children to dictate stories. Young children tell more complex stories, using more mature language, when they dictate rather than type them.
- Consider eliminating the use of clip art if you decide to let your child use digital drawing tools.
- Evaluate the aesthetic qualities of software, including, of course, CD-ROMs.
- If your child goes on the Internet, closely supervise him.
- Whenever possible, make computer use a social experience by putting two chairs at the machine and encouraging conversation and collaboration with peers, siblings, or adults.
- If your young child begins to show signs of computer addiction, cut down on or eliminate screen time and make sure plenty of alternative activities are available.
- Don't ever forget that the best multimedia, interactive environment is the real world.

Conclusion

> Children do not have to be amused, cajoled, or tricked into learning. This is only an American problem and it's disrespectful of children.
>
> —Lillian Katz

The immature human brain neither needs nor profits from attempts to "jump start" it. The fact that this phrase is being successfully used to sell technology for toddlers illustrates our ignorance of early childhood development. Our wish to rush young children willy-nilly into the electronic grip of an unproven medium also reflects a belief that learning is something the young must be enticed into, whereas it is, in fact, the driving force of their existence. Unfortunately, many adults don't recognize real learning when they see it.

The brain tends to seek what it needs at each age of development, and it doesn't need the blandishments of software programmers to distract it. Why, after all, are we so unwilling to trust the wisdom of the young child's brain to seek out the stimulation it needs from a naturally enriched environment? The minute we introduce an artificially engaging stimulus with fast-paced visuals, startling noises, silly scenarios, and easy excitement, the brain is diverted away from its natural developmental tasks. Kids will be enthusiastic about any novelty, but their enthusiasm is uncritical. It's up to the mature minds in the situation to discriminate and select what is truly valuable.

"Yes, we get a lot of pressure from parents, but we believe the gains from working with computers do not outweigh the losses for 4- and 5-year-olds," states Mary Ucci of the Wellesley Child Study Center. "At this age they need to be pushing playdough, not buttons."

David Elkind, child development authority, laments our failure to respect the unique qualities of childhood learning. It has become fashionable to try to bring children into many aspects of the adult world too soon, he points out, "collapsing" the stages of childhood and thus depriving youngsters—and their brains—of the opportunity to complete necessary developmental tasks. To enter school successfully, Elkind suggests, children don't need technological expertise. Instead they should be able to:

- Express themselves, listen, and follow directions
- Start a task and bring it to completion themselves before jumping off to another project
- Cooperate with other children

As we have all seen, all of these qualities may be eroded by the wrong kind of computer exposure.

MIT's Joseph Weizenbaum was once a booster for everything digital but now offers articulate warnings about its use. Do we want, he asks, to expose our young children to artificial minds that possess no human values or even common sense? The physical world, not the two-dimensional screen, is where they will learn the real skills for the future and become complex "systems thinkers"—able to relate things to each other, to see real-life connections, patterns, and context.

One preschool teacher says it eloquently: "Let us not let our adult excitement with what computers can do in the adult workplace deter us from offering to children the squishiness of making mud pies, the scent of peppermint extract when making cookies, and the feel of balancing a block at the top of a tower. ... The adult world of the plastic workplace comes all too soon." ■

Jane Healy has been an educational psychologist and professional educator for more than 35 years as a classroom teacher, college professor, reading and learning specialist, and elementary school administrator. She is the author of three books about early childhood learning and works as a lecturer and consultant to public and private schools and parent groups.

References

1. Sherry Turkle. *The Second Self.* Cambridge, Mass. The MIT Press. 2005.

Part III

Use curriculum approaches that are responsive to children's developmental and intellectual pursuits.

"We want to know what the children think, feel, and wonder. We believe that the children will have things to tell each other and us that we have never heard before. We are always listening for a surprise and the birth of a new idea. This practice supports a mutual quest for understanding. It is a practice of searching together for new meaning. Together, we become a community of seekers."

Louise Boyd Cadwell
Bringing Learning to Life

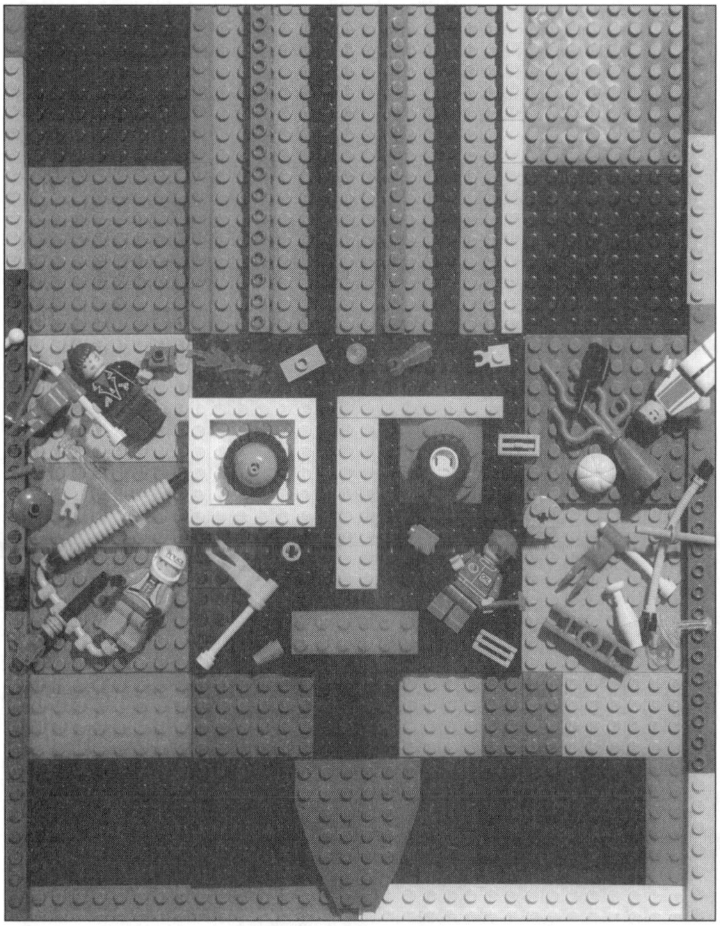

DAVID MCLIMANS

Why We Banned Legos

Exploring Power, Ownership, and Equity in the Classroom

BY ANN PELO AND KENDRA PELOJOAQUIN

Carl and Oliver, both 8-year-olds in our after-school program, huddled over piles of Legos.* They carefully assembled them to add to a sprawling collection of Lego houses, grocery stores, fish-and-chips stands, fire stations, and coffee shops. They were particularly keen to find and use "cool pieces," the translucent bricks and specialty pieces that complement the standard-issue red, yellow, blue, and green Lego bricks.

"I'm making an airport and landing strip for my guy's house. He has his own airplane," said Oliver.

"That's not fair!" said Carl. "That takes too many cool pieces and leaves not enough for me."

"Well, I can let other people use the landing strip, if they have airplanes," said Oliver. "Then it's fair for me to use more cool pieces, because it's for public use."

Discussions like this led to children collaborating on a massive series of Lego structures we named Legotown. Children dug through hefty-sized bins of Legos, sought "cool pieces," and bartered and exchanged until they established a collection of homes, shops, public facilities, and community meeting places. We carefully protected Legotown from errant balls and jump ropes, and watched it grow day by day.

After nearly two months of observing the children's Legotown construction, we decided to ban the Legos.

The Investigation Begins

Our school-age childcare program—the "Big Kids"—included 25 children and their families. The children, ages 5 through 9, came to Hilltop after their days in elementary school, arriving around 3:30 and staying until 5:30 or 6:00. Hilltop is located in an affluent Seattle neighborhood, and, with only a few exceptions, the staff and families are white; the families are upper-middle-class and socially liberal. Kendra was the lead teacher for the Big Kid program; two additional teachers, Erik and Harmony, staffed the program. Ann was the mentor teacher at Hilltop, working closely with teachers to study and plan curricula from children's play and interactions.

A group of about eight children conceived and launched Legotown. Other children were eager to join the project, but as the city grew—and space and raw materials became more precious—the builders began excluding other children.

Occasionally, Legotown leaders explicitly rebuffed children, telling them that they couldn't play. Typically the exclusion was more subtle, growing from a climate in which Legotown was seen as the turf of particular kids. The other children didn't complain much about this; when asked about Legos, they'd often comment vaguely that they just weren't interested in playing with Legos anymore. As they closed doors to other children, the Legotown builders turned their attention to complex negotiations among themselves about what sorts of structures to build, whether these ought to be primarily privately owned or collectively used, and how "cool pieces" would be distributed and protected. These negotiations gave rise to heated conflict and to insightful conversation. Into their coffee shops and houses, the children were building their assumptions about ownership and the social power it conveys—assumptions that mirrored those of a class-based, capitalist society. As we watched the children build, we became increasingly concerned.

Then, tragedy struck Legotown and we saw an opportunity to take strong action.

Hilltop is housed in a church, and over a long weekend, some children in the congregation who were playing in our space accidentally demolished Legotown.

When the children discovered the decimated Legotown, they reacted with shock and grief. Children moaned and fell to their knees to inspect the damage; many were near tears. The builders were devastated, and the other children were deeply sympathetic. We gathered as a full group to talk about what had happened; at one point in the conversation, Kendra suggested a big cleanup of the loose Legos on the floor. The Legotown builders were fierce in their opposition. They explained that particular children "owned" those pieces and it would be unfair to put them back in the bins where other children might use them. As we talked, the issues of ownership and power that had been hidden became explicit to the whole group.

We met as a teaching staff later that day. We saw the decimation of Legotown as an opportunity to launch a critical evaluation of Legotown and the inequities of private ownership and hierarchical authority on which it was founded. Our intention was to promote a contrasting set of values: collectivity, collaboration, resource-sharing, and full democratic participation. We knew that the examination would have the most impact if it was based in engaged exploration and reflection rather than in lots of talking. We didn't want simply to step in as teachers with a new set of rules about how the children could use Legos, exchanging one authoritarian order with another. Ann suggested removing the Legos from the classroom. This bold decision would demonstrate our discomfort with the issues we saw at play in Legotown. And it posed a challenge to the children: How might we create a "community of fairness" about Legos?

Out with the Legos

Taking the Legos out of the classroom was both a commitment and a risk. We expected that looking frankly at the issues of power and inequity that had shaped Legotown would hold conflict and discomfort for us all. We teachers talked long and hard about the decision.

We shared our own perspectives on issues of private ownership, wealth, and limited resources. One teacher described her childhood experience of growing up without much money and her instinctive critical judgments about people who have wealth and financial ease. Another teacher shared her allegiance to the children who had been on the fringes of Legotown, wanting more resources but not sure how to get them without upsetting the power structure. We knew that our personal experiences and beliefs would shape our decision-making and planning for the children, and we wanted to be as aware as we could about them.

We also discussed our beliefs about our role as teachers in raising political issues with young children. We recognized that children are political beings, actively shaping their social and political understandings of ownership and economic equity—whether we interceded or not. We agreed that we want to take part in shaping the children's understandings from a perspective of social justice. So we decided to take the Legos out of the classroom.

We had an initial conversation with the children about our decision. "We're concerned about what was happening in Legotown, with some kids feeling left out and other kids feeling in charge," Kendra explained. "We don't want to rebuild Legotown and go back to how things were. Instead, we want to figure out with you a way to build a Legotown that's fair to all the kids."

The children had big feelings and strong opinions to share. During that first day's discussion, they laid out the big issues that we would pursue over the months to come.

Several times in the discussion, children made reference to "giving" Lego pieces to other children. Kendra pointed out the understanding behind this language: "When you say that some kids 'gave' pieces to other kids, that sounds like there are some kids who have most of the power in Legotown—power to decide what pieces kids can use and where they can build." Kendra's comment sparked an outcry by Lukas and Carl, two central figures in Legotown:

> Carl: "We didn't 'give' the pieces, we found and shared them."
>
> Lukas: "It's like giving to charity."
>
> Carl: "I don't agree with using words like 'gave.' Because when someone wants to move in, we find them a platform and bricks and we build them a house and find them windows and a door."

These children seemed to squirm at the implications of privilege, wealth, and power that "giving" holds. The children denied their power, framing it as benign and neutral, not something actively sought out and maintained. This early conversation helped us see more clearly the children's contradictory thinking about power and authority, laying the groundwork for later exploration.

Issues of fairness and equity also bubbled to the surface during the animated discussion about the removal of the Legos:

> Lukas: "I think every house should be average, and not over-average like Drew's, which is huge."
>
> Aidan: "But Drew is special."
>
> Drew: "I'm the fire station, so I have to have room for four people."
>
> Lukas: "I think that houses should only be as big as 16 bumps one way, and 16 bumps the other way. That would be fair." ["Bumps" are the small circles on top of Lego bricks.]

This brief exchange raised issues that we would revisit often in the weeks ahead. What is a fair distribution of resources? Does fairness mean that everyone has the same number of pieces? What about special rights: Who might deserve extra resources, and how are those extra resources allotted?

After nearly an hour of passionate exchange, we brought the conversation to a close, reminding the children that we teachers didn't have an answer already figured out about Legotown. We assured them that we were right there with them in this process of getting clearer about what hadn't worked well in Legotown, and understanding how we could create a community of fairness about Legos.

We'd audiotaped the discussion so that we'd be able to revisit it during our weekly teaching team meeting to tease out important themes and threads. The children's thoughts, questions, and tensions would guide us as we planned our next steps. We weren't working from carefully sequenced lessons on ownership, resource sharing, and equity. Instead, we committed to growing an investigation into these issues, one step at a time. Our planning was guided by our goals for social justice learning, and by the pedagogy our school embraces, inspired by schools in Reggio Emilia, Italy. In this approach, teachers offer children a provocation and listen carefully to the children's responses. These responses help teachers plan the next provocation to challenge or expand the children's theories, questions, and cognitive challenges

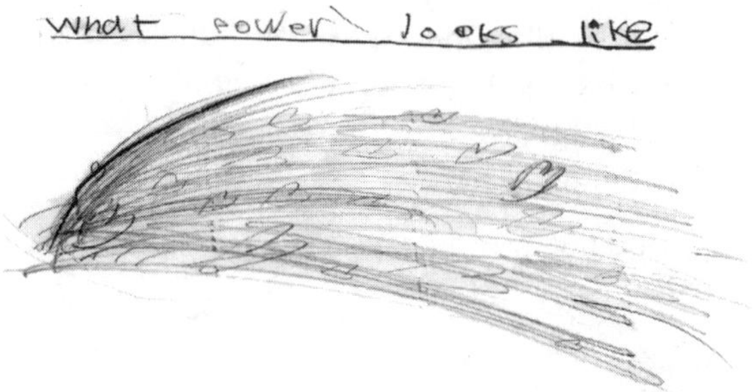

What Does Power Look Like?

A few days after we'd removed the Legos, we turned our attention to the meaning of power. During the boom days of Legotown, we'd suggested to the key Lego players that the unequal distribution of power gave rise to conflict and tension. Our suggestion was met with deep resistance. Children denied any explicit or unfair power, making comments like, "Somebody's got to be in charge or there would be chaos," and "The little kids ask me because I'm good at Legos." They viewed their power as passive leadership, benignly granted, arising from mastery and long experience with Legos, as well as from their social status in the group.

Now, with Legotown dismantled and the issues of equity and power squarely in front of us, we took up the idea of power and its multiple meanings. We began by inviting the children to draw pictures of power, knowing that when children represent an idea in a range of "languages," or art media, their understandings deepen and expand. "Think about power," said Kendra. "What do you think 'power' means? What does power look like? Take a few minutes to make a drawing that shows what power is."

As children finished their drawings, we gathered for a meeting to look at the drawings together. The drawings represented a range of understandings of power: a tornado, love spilling over as hearts, forceful and fierce individuals, exclusion, cartoon superheroes, political power.

During our meeting, children gave voice to the thinking behind their drawings.

> Marlowe: "If your parents say you have to eat pasta, then that's power."
>
> Lukas: "You can say no."
>
> Carl: "Power is ownership of something."
>
> Drew: "Sometimes I like power and sometimes I don't. I like to be in power because I feel free. Most people like to do it, you can tell people what to do and it feels good."

Drew's comment startled us with its raw truth. He was a member of the Legotown inner circle, and had been quite resistant to acknowledging the power he held in that role. During this discussion, though, he laid his cards on the table. Would Drew's insight break open new understandings among the other members of the inner circle?

Exploring Power

To build on Drew's breakthrough comment about the pleasure and unease that comes with wielding power, and to highlight the experience of those who are excluded from power, we designed a Lego trading game with built-in inequities. We developed a point system for Legos, then skewed the system so that it would be quite hard to get lots of points. And we established just one rule: Get as many points as possible. The person with the most points would create the rules for the rest of the game. Our intention was to create a situation in which a few children would receive unearned power from sheer good luck in choosing Lego bricks with high point values, and then would wield that power with their peers. We hoped that the game would be removed enough from the particulars and personalities of Legotown that we could look at the central Legotown issues from a fresh perspective.

This was a simple game about complicated issues.

We introduced the Lego trading game to the children by passing a bin of Legos around the circle, asking each child to choose 10 Legos; we didn't say anything about point values or how we'd use the bricks. Most children chose a mix of colored Lego bricks, though a few chose 10 of one color. Liam took all eight green Legos, explaining that green is his favorite color; this seemingly straightforward choice altered the outcome of the game.

When everyone had their Legos, the teachers announced that each color had a point value. The more common the brick color, the fewer the points it was worth, while the scarcest brick color, green, was worth a whopping five points.

Right away, there were big reactions.

> Liam: "I have all the green! I have 40 points because I have all the green!"
>
> Drew: "This isn't fair! Liam won't trade any green, I bet, so what's the point? What if you just want to quit?"
>
> Carl: "I don't want to play this game. I'll just wait for Liam to give me a green. If he doesn't, it's hopeless."

We didn't linger with the children's reactions, but carried on with the game, explaining that the object of the game was to trade Lego pieces in an effort to get the most points. Kids immediately began to calculate how they'd trade their pieces, and dove into trading. Several children shadowed Liam, pleading with him to give them a green—but he refused.

After a few minutes of trading, we rang a bell and children added up their scores. Liam and Kyla had scores that far out-totaled those of the other children. Kendra asked them each to create a rule, explaining that we'd play another round of the game, following the new rules and aiming for the same goal: to get the most points possible.

We expected that the winners would make rules to ensure that they would win the next round—for instance, "All greens are worth 50 points," or, "You can only win if your name starts with a K." We were surprised at what happened.

Liam instituted this rule: "You have to trade at least one piece. That's a good rule because if you have a high score at the beginning, you wouldn't have to trade, and that's not fair."

Kyla added this rule to the game: "If you have more than one green, you have to trade one of them."

With these new rules on the books, we held a second short round of trading, then rang the bell and added up points. Liam, Kyla, and Lukas won this round. The three winners grinned at each other as we gathered in a circle to debrief the game. Before we could launch a conversation as teachers, the children's raw emotion carried us into a passionate exchange.

> Drew: "Liam, you don't have to brag in people's faces."
>
> Carl: "The winner would stomp his feet and go 'Yes' in the face of people. It felt kind of mean."
>
> Liam: "I was happy! I wasn't trying to stomp in people's faces."
>
> Carl: "I don't like that winners make new rules. People make rules that are only in their advantage. They could have written it simpler that said, 'Only I win.'"
>
> Juliet: "Because they wanted to win and make other people feel bad."
>
> Kyla: "I wasn't trying to make other people feel bad. I felt bad when people felt bad, so I tried to make a rule that would make them feel better. It was fun to make up the rule—like a treat, to be one of only three people out of the whole group."

When the teaching staff met to reflect on the Lego trading game, we were struck by the ways the children had come face-to-face with the frustration, anger, and hopelessness that come with being on the outside of power and privilege. During the trading game, a couple of children simply gave up, while others waited passively for someone to give them valuable pieces. Drew said, "I stopped trading because the same people were winning. I just gave up." In the game, the children could experience what they'd not been able to acknowledge in Legotown: When people are shut out of participation in the power structure, they are disenfranchised—and angry, discouraged, and hurt.

To make sense of the sting of this disenfranchisement, most of the children cast Liam and Kyla as "mean," trying to "make people feel bad." They were unable or unwilling to see that the rules of the game—which mirrored the rules of our capitalist meritocracy—were a setup for winning and losing. Playing by the rules led to a few folks winning big and most folks falling further and further behind. The game created a classic case of cognitive disequilibrium: Either the system is skewed and unfair, or the winners played unfairly. To resolve this by deciding that the system is unfair would call everything into question; young children are committed to rules and rule-making as a way to organize a community, and it is wildly unsettling to acknowledge that rules can have built-in inequities. So most of the children resolved their disequilibrium by clinging to the belief that the winners were ruthless—despite clear evidence of Liam and Kyla's compassionate generosity.

In Legotown, the children had constructed a social system of power where a few people made the important decisions and the rest of the participants did the grunt work—much like the system in the trading game. We wanted children to critique the system at work in Legotown, not to critique the children at the top of the Legotown hierarchy. At the same time, we wanted them to see that the Legotown system was created by people, and, as such, could be challenged and reformulated. The children's reaction to the winners of the trading game was a big warning flag for us: We clearly had some repair work to do around relationships, as well as some overt teaching about systemic fallibility. The Lego trading game presented core issues that would be our focus for the months to come. Our analysis of the game, as teachers, guided our planning for the investigation into the issues of power, privilege, and authority that spanned the rest of the year.

Rules and Ownership

In the weeks after the trading game, we explored questions about how rules are made and enforced, and when they ought to be followed or broken. We aimed to help children see that all rules (including social structures and systems) are made by people with particular perspectives, interests, and experiences that shape their rule-making. And we wanted to encourage them to consider that there are times when rules ought to be questioned or even broken—sharing stories of people who refused to "play by the rules" when the rules were unjust, people like Rosa Parks and Cesar Chavez.

We added another thread to our investigation of power, as well, by turning our attention to issues related to ownership. In Legotown, the builders "owned" sections of Legotown and protected them fiercely from encroachment. We were curious to explore with the children their beliefs about how ownership happens: How does a person come to own something? How is ownership maintained or transferred? Are there situations in which ownership ought to be challenged or denied? What are the distinctions between private and public ownership?

We looked at ownership through several lenses. With the children, we created an "ownership museum," where children displayed possessions they brought from home—a Gameboy, a special blanket, a bike helmet, a baseball card, jewelry, dolls—and described how they came to own them. And we visited Pike Place Market, the farmers and artisans market in downtown Seattle, and asked questions to provoke kids to think about ownership, like: Does a farmer own her produce? Or does the consumer own it?

In their reflections during these explorations, the children articulated several shared theories about how ownership is conferred.

- **If I buy it, I own it:**
  Sophia: "She owns the lavender balls because she makes them, but if I buy it, then it's mine."
- **If I receive it as a gift, I own it:**
  Marlowe: "My mom bought this book for me because she thought it would be a good reading book for me. I know I own it because my mom bought it and she's my mom and she gave it to me."
- **If I make it myself, I own it:**
  Sophie: "I sewed this pillow myself with things that my teacher gave me, like stuffing and fabric. I sewed it and it turned into my pillow because it's something I made instead of something I got at the store."
- **If it has my name on it, I own it:**
  Alex: "My teacher made this pillow for me and it has my name on it."
  Kendra: "If I put my name on it, would I own it?"
  Alex: "Well, Miss S. made it for me … but if your name was on it, then you would own it."
  Sophie: "Kendra, don't put your name on it, OK?"
- **If I own it, I make the rules about it:**
  Alejandro: "I own this computer, because my grandpa gave it to me. I lend it to my friends so that they can play with it. But I make the rules about it."

The Return of the Legos

Throughout the investigation, the staff continued to meet weekly to study our notes about the activities we took up with the children, watching for moments when children identified contradictions in their own thinking, took on new perspectives, or questioned their own assumptions. In late spring, we decided it was time to challenge the children to wrestle their theoretical understandings into practical shape and apply their analysis of individual and collective ownership to a concrete project. After five months of naming and investigating the issues of power, rules, ownership, and authority, we were ready to reconstruct Legotown in a new way.

We invited the children to work in small, collaborative teams to build Pike Place Market with Legos. We set up this work to emphasize negotiated decision-making, collaboration, and collectivity. We wanted the children to practice the big ideas we'd been exploring. We wanted Lego Pike Place Market to be an experience of group effort and shared ownership: If Legotown was an embodiment of individualism, Lego Pike Place Market would be an experiment in collectivity and consensus.

We offered the children some guidelines to steer them into a new way of interacting with each other and with the Legos: "Create teams of two or three people, decide as a team on some element of Pike Place Market that you'll build, and then start constructing." The first day or two, children created signs warning the other teams "Do Not Touch" their collaboratively constructed vegetable, fruit, and crafts stands. As they settled into this construction project, though, the teams softened the rigid boundaries around their work and began to leave notes for each other describing their work and proposing next steps for Pike Place Market. We celebrated this shift, seeing it as a sign that the children were beginning to integrate the thinking of the last months into their interactions.

A New Ethics for Legotown

This "practice" round of Lego construction served as a foundation for a full-fledged return of Legos to their front-and-center place in the classroom, but with a new location in the consciousness of the group. In preparation for bringing Legos back, we held several meetings with the children to generate a set of key principles for Lego play. We met with small groups of children over snack or as we walked to and from the park, posing questions like "If you were going to play with Legos, what would be important to you?" "What would be different if we bring the Legos back to the classroom? How could we make it different?" "What could we do if we fall into old habits with the Legos?" From our conversations, several themes emerged.

- **Collectivity is a good thing:**

  "You get to build and you have a lot of fun and people get to build onto your structure with you, and it doesn't have to be the same way as when you left it. … A house is good because it is a community house."

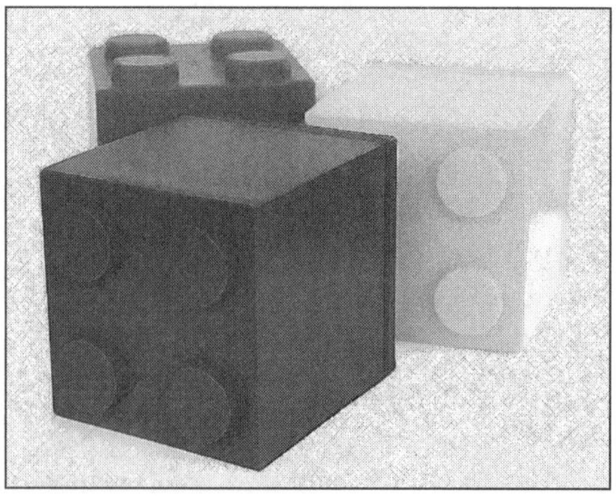

- **Personal expression matters:**

  "It's important that the little Lego plastic person has some identity. Lego houses might be all the same except for the people. A kid should have their own Lego character to live in the house so it makes the house different."

- **Shared power is a valued goal:**

  "It's important to have the same amount of power as other people over your building. And it's important to have the same priorities."

  "Before, it was the older kids who had the power because they used Legos most. Little kids have more rights now than they used to and older kids have half the rights."

- **Moderation and equal access to resources are things to strive for:**

  "We should have equal houses. They should be standard sizes. … We should all just have the same number of pieces, like 15 or 28 pieces."

As teachers, we were excited by these comments. The children gave voice to the value that collectivity is a solid, energizing way to organize a community—and that it requires power-sharing, equal access to resources, and trust in the other participants. They expressed the need, within collectivity, for personal expression, for being acknowledged as an individual within the group. And finally, they named the deep satisfaction of shared engagement and investment, and the ways in which the participation of many people deepens the experience of membership in community for everyone.

From this framework, the children made a number of specific proposals for rules about Legos, engaged in some collegial debate about those proposals, and worked through their differing suggestions until they reached consensus about three core agreements:

- All structures are public structures. Everyone can use all the Lego structures. But only the builder or people who have her or his permission are allowed to change a structure.
- Lego people can be saved only by a "team" of kids, not by individuals.
- All structures will be standard sizes. Kids won't build structures that are dramatically bigger than most folks' structures.

With these three agreements—which distilled months of social justice exploration into a few simple tenets of community use of resources—we returned the Legos to their place of honor in the classroom.

Children absorb political, social, and economic worldviews from an early age. Those worldviews show up in their play, which is the terrain that young children use to make meaning about their world and to test and solidify their understandings. We believe that educators have a responsibility to pay close attention to the themes, theories, and values that children use to anchor their play. Then we can interact with those worldviews, using play to instill the values of equality and democracy. ■

* This piece resulted in a great deal of media coverage and reader correspondence after it appeared in *Rethinking Schools* magazine (vol. 21, no. 2) in 2006. To read a response written and published by the editors, see page 95.

Ann Pelo is an early childhood teacher and teacher mentor in Seattle, Wash.

Kendra PeloJoaquin has worked with children for most of her life. She spent four years as the coordinator of the school-age program at Hilltop Children's Center.

RANDALL ENOS

'Lego Fascists' (That's Us) Vs. Fox News

RETHINKING SCHOOLS MAGAZINE PUBLISHED THE FOLLOWING LETTER FROM ITS EDITORS IN SUMMER 2007

It's been a while since we've been called fascists. But this has been a strange couple of months.

The winter 2006-07 issue of *Rethinking Schools* featured "Why We Banned Legos" by Ann Pelo and Kendra PeloJoaquin, teachers at Hilltop Children's Center in Seattle. We had intentionally given the article a provocative title, and knew that many people's first reaction would be: No, not Legos! What could possibly be wrong with Legos? We also knew that those readers who probed beyond the playful headline would be rewarded with an extraordinary piece that recounted how a group of teachers investigated children's play in order to discover the lessons children were absorbing about power, ownership, authority, and cooperation—and how those teachers responded. And by the way, Legos are not banned at Hilltop and never were; Hilltop teachers simply removed them temporarily to help focus students' attention on issues of fairness.

Then the email began to pour in:

> "You Teachers Are Fascists!!! To Ban Legos and Brainwash Them Like This!"

> "You don't want us to defend ourselves against the Islam-o-fascist Terrorists you

just want us to roll over and die or convert to Islam."

"If this does NOT prove once and for all that the Teachers Unions are full of Socialist S.O.B's! Nothing will! Break Up the Damn Teachers Unions!!!"

A woman writing from Augusta, Ga., offered her opinion more economically:

"Ya'll are just plain NUTS!"

Right-wing bloggers, evidently taking a break from defending the Iraq war, began the "Legos" assault. Rush Limbaugh and other AM radio talk show hosts picked up the story. And finally, Fox television ran a segment on an evening newscast, "Big Story, Big Outrage." (A Google search of "Why We Banned Legos" in late April 2007, pulled up over 17,000 entries.)

Many of the critics appeared to read no further than the winter issue's headline and offered passionate testimonials on the benefits of Legos. But others, like John J. Miller writing in the *National Review Online*, inferred deeper implications. In a March 27 posting, Miller expressed outrage that youngsters at Hilltop sometimes use Legos to construct "community meeting places." Miller declared that his kids would never dream of something so "rotten," as he put it. "Instead, they make monster trucks, space ships, and war machines. These little creations are usually loaded with ion guns, nuclear missiles, bunker-busting bombs, force-field projectors, and death-ray cannons. Alien empires have risen and fallen in epic conflicts waged in the upstairs bedrooms of my home." If children don't play war and empire then evidently the "latte-sipping guardians" in Seattle have led kids astray.

Common to Miller et al.'s critiques is an aversion to the notion that everything that goes on in school—including play—teaches values. Our critics appear content to let children absorb without reflection the values from the broader society—competition, militarism, consumerism, aggression, selfishness. By contrast, "Why We Banned Legos" tells the story of the Hilltop teachers who seek opportunities to help children reflect about "the meaning of power and ways to organize communities which are equitable and just."

Critics also derided Pelo and PeloJoaquin's insistence that children can be encouraged to question inequality in the worlds they create in their play and consider alternatives. One blogger was indignant: "What happens when [children] grow up and not everyone wins?"—i.e., injustice happens, deal with it; children should not be taught to question it, to think of democratic alternatives, but should simply see unfairness as a natural state of affairs. Another blogger at a site called "The Sixth Column" wrote: "[C]hildren will not be prepared to face brutal competition which makes up real life outside of the carefully constructed feel-good environment found in many of today's classrooms. ... In the real world, not everyone will be able to participate in 'the power structure.'" Like these attacks on the article, many writers insisted that injustice was eternal and that questioning it was not merely futile, but misled children about human nature and the world that they would inherit.

Underlying much of the blog and email commentary was a profound disregard for children's capacities to reflect together about their own interactions and to thoughtfully discuss notions of fairness. As one blogger wrote, the conversations among children described in "Why We Banned Legos" revealed "willful manipulation of young minds"—presumably because in the real world, kids could never think like this on their own. This was a revealing criticism. Because what if kids are indeed always making meaning about their world and, with good teaching, are more and more able to express their insights with sophistication? Then we need a curriculum that honors children's potential, rather than the scripted lessons of memorization and correct answers favored by so many conservatives.

If these right-wing attacks were confined to the Lego article then we might dismiss them as mere annoyances, reminders of the tenacity of conservative views of schooling. But they seem to be part of a pattern—an emerging attack on social justice teaching itself. For example, when Fox News went after the Legos issue, they turned to Jim Copland of the Manhattan Institute as the sole outside "expert." (Fox: "How ridiculous is this?" Copland: "Preposterous.") The Manhattan Institute is a free-market-oriented think tank whose education mission is to promote vouchers, charter schools, and more testing—in public schools only, of course, not private schools. Sol Stern, a Manhattan Institute senior fellow, is waging a smear campaign against social justice education work, most recently attacking the El Puente Academy for Peace and Justice in Brooklyn, Eric Gutstein (University of Illinois-Chicago professor and co-editor of the Rethinking Schools book *Rethinking Mathematics*), the New York Collective of Radical Educators, and the math and social justice conference held in New York City called "Creating Balance in an Unjust World." Writing in the Rupert Murdoch- owned *New York Post*, ("Math and Marxism: NYC's Wack-Job Teachers," March 20, 2007), Stern first caricatures social justice teaching and then complains that it "violates every commonly accepted standard of ethical and professional responsibility for public school teachers," and laments that "the city's Department of Education has so far turned a blind eye."

Some of these attacks represent nothing new. They are simply part of the right wing's ongoing attempt to discredit public schools and push more "accountability" (read "testing"), vouchers, and school privatization. (Even though Hilltop Children's Center is not a public school and its teachers are in the Service Employees International Union, not one of the two teacher unions, neither fact deterred critics, who used the Legos article to attack both public schools and teacher unions—as exemplified in the excerpt from our antifascist friend, above.)

But there may be something else afoot. It's become increasingly difficult to ignore social and environmental ills—whether it's the climate change crisis, the Iraq war, or growing global inequality. More and more educators now talk about "social justice teaching"—albeit not always with clarity around what this means. With greater frequency, educators seem to recognize that at this crucial juncture in world history, schools need to address the issues of our time; and that at all educational levels, we need a conversation and literature describing how educators can respond effectively.

Inevitably, this curricular exploration calls into question existing cultural patterns and systems of ownership and control that are at the root of today's crises. And this will step on some powerful toes. This teaching may take the form of early childhood programs encouraging children to reflect on the implications of their play. Or it may take the form of high school math teachers analyzing the concept of "peak oil" in algebra class, or 5th-grade teachers prompting students to evaluate the manifold costs of the Iraq war.

This is important and exciting work. Rethinking Schools is committed to helping nurture a grassroots literature of social justice teaching. And we're committed to defend this teaching wherever and whenever it comes under attack. This is no time to be meek. The world is becoming more perilous by the day. Schools can either be part of the problem or part of the solution. ■

STEPHEN KRONINGER

'I Just Want to Read *Frog and Toad*'

BY MELANIE QUINN

One mid-September night, when I was tucking my 5-year-old son Eamonn in bed, the standardization madness came home to roost. With quivering lip and tear-filled eyes, Eamonn told me he hated school. He said he had to read baby books that didn't make sense and that he was in the "dummy group."

Then he looked up at me and said, "I just want to read *Frog and Toad.*"

I am an experienced elementary teacher and college professor, with a long-standing disdain for "ability" grouping, dummied-down curricula, and stupid, phonics-driven stories that make no sense. And yet here I was, seemingly unable to prevent my own child from being crushed by a scripted reading program of the type so beloved by No Child Left Behind (NCLB).

What's So Bad?

Eamonn had left kindergarten happy and confident, even requesting his own library card that summer. His older brother and sister were wonderful role models who had enjoyed sitting at the kitchen table on dreary Northwest days writing and illustrating their own books and, when they were older, reading chapter books in bed before they fell asleep.

But then the desire to quickly "fix" struggling readers and standardize curricula descended on the primary grades at his school.

When my son had been in kindergarten, the 1st- and 2nd-grade classroom teachers, with the principal's strong urging, had looked at two scripted programs: SRA/McGraw-Hill's "Open Court Reading" and "Houghton Mifflin Reading." When I heard about this, I spoke to the Site Council, principal, and teachers in an effort to persuade them to instead focus on improved teaching using authentic literature. The principal assured me that a decision to buy either program was on hold.

That fall, however, I opened the Welcome Back to School Newsletter and read that the Houghton Mifflin program would be used for the 1st and 2nd grades. Mixed in with feelings of dismay and anger, I felt guilty that I had not fought harder to ensure that the scripted curriculum was not adopted.

After Eamonn's lament about *Frog and Toad*, I decided to do further investigation. I grabbed Eamonn's backpack and found a wad of photocopied "books" and a 20-page chunk of stapled-together workbook pages.

Limiting Vocabulary

One of the photocopied "books" was *The Big Pig's Bib*. I'd give a synopsis of the tale, but it makes no sense and is little more than a collection of unrelated words. The story begins by introducing the human characters and saying, "It is Tim and it is Mim." In standard English, the word "this" would be used to introduce Tim and Mim—i.e., "This is Tim and this is Mim." Unfortunately, the program has not yet presented the word "this," so instead it introduces the characters using clumsy, nonstandard English: "It is Tim and it is Mim."

At one point, the story says the pig is not big but then at the end, Tim and Mim fit it with a "big pig's bib"—even though there are no events or clues as to how the pig, who was not big, can now wear a "big pig's bib."

Then there's the story of *Can Pat Nap?* The simplistic line drawings show a child sitting down under a tree. In the tree is a bird that one assumes is a woodpecker. The text reads, "Pat can nap. Tap, tap, tap. Pat can not nap. Tap, Tap, Tap. Sap on the cap. Can Pat nap? Not here, Pat!"

I am confused. Can Pat nap or can't he? Better still, who cares?

A Waste of Resources

The workbook pages, meanwhile, are supposed to coincide with the books but are little more than simplified skills. One asks the student to circle short "I" sounds; another asks the children to draw a diagonal line from one part of a compound word to another. All of the writing and thinking is done by the publisher, and the children merely fill in disjointed blanks. Once they identify the pattern, there is no need to even read the surrounding text.

There are a few pages that ask for some sort of thought process, for example to write an alternate ending for a story. Unfortunately, those exercises have been crossed out. Apparently, having children actually think and write takes up too much time.

After a few days, I cooled down enough to approach the principal, classroom teacher, and reading teacher. I asked that Eamonn be allowed to read real books and during workbook time, to write his own stories in a journal. I was assured accommodations would be made. (It turns out, however, that they weren't.)

Life continued at its hectic pace. Eamonn stopped crying about reading, and he seemed relatively happy with school. Weeks, then months, passed.

Capitalizing on Students' Interests—or Not

The following spring, as we sat on the couch one afternoon, Eamonn offered that reading was beginning to be fun. I asked why. "Well, since it is the end of the year, we are getting to read words like 'about' and our reading workbook and worksheet packets ask us to fill in the blanks with bigger words," he explained. "All year until now the blanks have been for little words like, 'I,' 'I,' 'I.'"

Eamonn hopped up excitedly and ran to his backpack to show me a book he had just gotten. He pulled out a photocopied book, Number 71, entitled *White Knight.* On the cover was a whimsical knight dressed in armor with a large "W" on his shirt and a banner with WK on it. Then Eamonn said, "See, it is a knight!"

Eamonn explained that the students were also excited because the teacher had handed out the book to the class a while earlier, but then taken it back. "She goofed up," he said. "See, she had all these books copied and ready and she passed out the wrong number. We had other ones we had to read first before we could get to this number. We had not read numbers 69 and 70 yet."

While the Houghton Mifflin program boasts of quality stories from well-known children's authors, those apparently are sparingly dispersed in the classroom. The photocopied books sent home for children to read and add to their "library" are boring both textually and visually, filled with black-lined drawings of androgynous human characters.

And then there is the case of the "White Knight" with the large W on his chest, perpetuating stereotypes of the damsel in distress being rescued by the white knight who "always does what is right."

Eamonn opened up the four-page book and read:

> (Page 1) White Knight said,
>
> "I am brave. I fight for what is right!"
>
> (Page 2) Miss Moll was up high. She called, "White Knight! White Knight!"
>
> (Page 3) White Knight climbed high to get Miss Moll, but he did not hang on tight. He fell on his thigh.
>
> (Page 4) Miss Moll came down to White Knight. She said, "You might like some pie." White Knight sighed.

At the end of the reading, Eamonn's head dropped and he looked up with disappointment. "Well, that wasn't very good," he admitted.

But then he proceeded to tell his own story:

> It could have been that the White Knight is going by a dragon and he pulls out his sword—this might be bad but there could be blood—and he kills the dragon and then he goes to the castle and battles the guards. Then he runs up a bunch of stairs, and he rescues Miss Moll. When they are running down the stairs, there are new guards and he battles them. Then they get on horses and ride past the dead dragon, ride off down the road and get to their castle and live happily every after.

"That could be a good story," he says prou dly.

What could I say? I affirmed what he already knew: that stories need to be complete, not exercises in the "long i spelled igh." And Eamonn's story actually had a plot. It had a beginning, middle, and end, a problem and a solution, a protagonist and an antagonist. Unfortunately, the main lesson he took from *White Knight* was the reinforcement of the damsel in distress stereotype.

I am angry that Eamonn did not get to write his own knight story, and that he and his classmates were denied the opportunity to critically think about the stereotype being perpetuated in *White Knight.* Instead he had his time wasted by filling in "about" on a workbook page while the teacher tried to distribute the next book in chronological order.

When Eamonn started 2nd grade, his teacher granted my request that he be allowed to read actual books during reading time, not photocopied nonsense. He has become an avid reader and falls asleep every night with a book in his hand. He prefers reading real books with real stories—the kind you find in public libraries and bookstores but, increasingly, not in our nation's elementary classrooms. ■

Melanie Quinn is an assistant professor at Lewis & Clark College in Portland, Ore., and the program director for the Elementary Preservice Program.

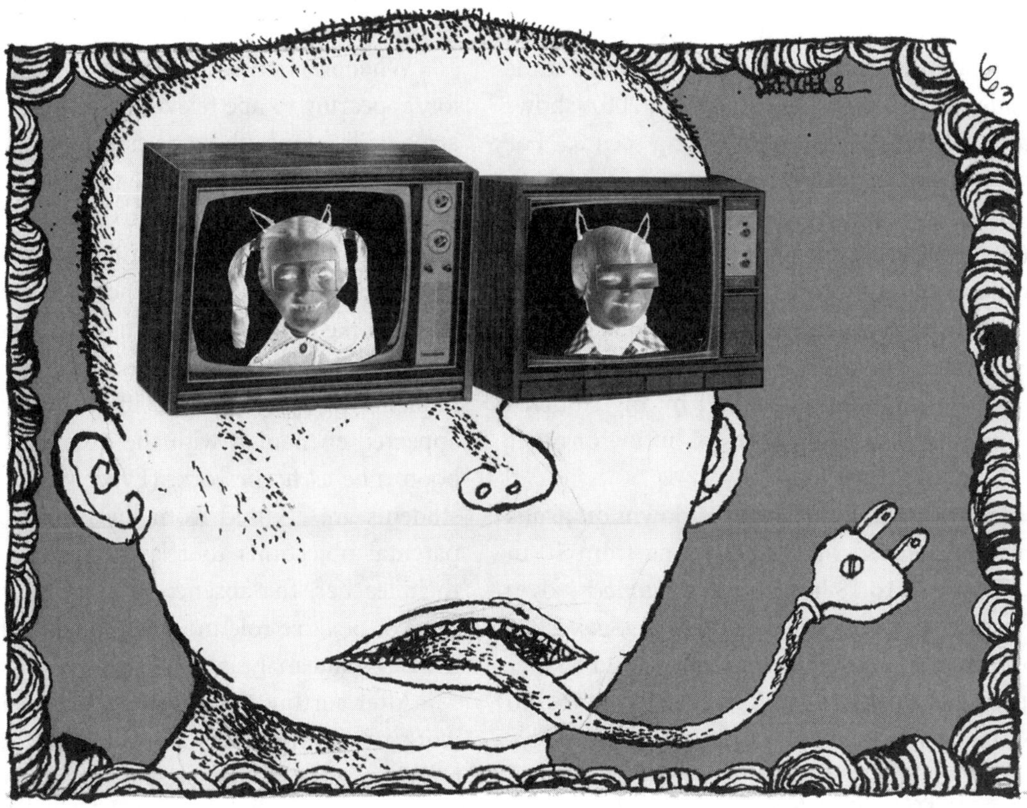

Tuning In to Violence

Students Use Math to Analyze What TV Is Teaching Them

BY MARGOT PEPPER

Six years into the "War on Terror," my 2nd-grade Spanish immersion students found that aggression, selfishness, and insults had exploded on national television.

Since the late 1990s, I've had my students at Rosa Parks Elementary School in Berkeley, California, analyze television shows preceding National TV-Turnoff Week, organized by the TV-Turnoff Network. I ask the 7- and 8-year-old students to collect all the data themselves. For seven days, students study a random sampling of about 35 English- and Spanish-language children's television shows—and one or two soap operas or reality shows.

The first day of the study, as homework, students shade in a square on a special graph sheet each time they see hitting, hurting, or killing on half-hour segments of the shows they regularly watch, viewed from beginning to end. The second day, they focus on acts of selfishness; the third day, on instances of put-downs; and the fourth day, on the number of times a typical class rule is broken. Finally, in class, four groups of students compile the data produced by the homework, each focusing on one of the four variables in the study. In April 2007, when I pulled out model graphs compiled by a class in April 2002—year one of President Bush's "war on terror"—the contrasts between their graphs and those produced five years prior shocked my students.

"In a half-hour of [the cartoon] *Jackie Chan* in 2002 you would see hitting 10 times at most," wrote 7-year-old Flynn in the essay I assigned summarizing the findings of our study. "In 2007, shows of *Jackie Chan* had [up to] 34 hitting scenes." For the 2001–02 season, nearly one-fourth of the television shows my students watched had one or no acts of violence at all in one half-hour. In 2007, only *That's So Raven* continued to have no violence, and all other shows have at least three instances of hitting or violence in one half-hour. That year, nearly half the shows randomly viewed by my students contained seven to 34 instances of hitting or other violent acts each half-hour.

The maximum number of put-downs or insults had nearly doubled since 2002, going from 10 in *That's So Raven* to 18 in *Dumb and Dumber*—over one put-down every two minutes. In *SpongeBob SquarePants*, Flynn pointed out, one would hear at most two put-downs in 2002. In 2007 it was 16. No shows had more than 10 put-downs in 2002. Five years later, three shows did—*SpongeBob*: 16; *Dumb and Dumber*: 18; *Betty la fea*: 13. Very few shows had no insults at all.

All the shows my students watched in 2007 showed people or characters being selfish at least once per half-hour segment. From our class rule to "be considerate and cooperative," my students interpreted "selfish" to mean any time a character did something that put himself or herself first at the expense of someone else. In 2002, only three shows had more than three acts of selfishness in a half-hour. In 2007, 10 did. Half of the 2007 shows contained five to nine instances of selfishness in each episode.

Students also found that in April 2002, only one show depicted the violation of ordinary class rules—making good decisions, no hitting, put-downs, being unsafe, etc.—12 or more times. In April 2007, the number of such programs rose to six. In 2002, the maximum times class rules were broken on a given half-hour show was 17. In 2007 the number of such shows quadrupled with the maximum number of rules broken on a given show doubling or reaching over 35. The worst offenders, with 18 or more broken rules, were *SpongeBob*, *Dumb and Dumber*, *Jackie Chan*, and *Phil of the Future*—the latter two topping the hitting and selfishness categories as well.

Whenever students exhibit disruptive behavior, appearing to ape television—pretend shooting, arms flailing, mouth ceaselessly chattering gibberish, etc.—I ask them to please turn off the television in their head if they happen to have left it running. Students often chuckle and, following my lead, turn off an imaginary knob around their ear. Now, as we embarked on our study, many of these students seemed eager to learn more about the television implants I implied existed in their brains; others appeared enchanted with the excuse to watch the boob tube as homework. (Every year, one or two students are excused from the homework due to parental objections to television viewing or, like their teacher, the absence of a set at home. They serve as positive role models and still participate in the class data analysis.)

After sorting the completed television homework graphs into four piles, I assigned one variable or "change" (e.g., "violence") to student groups to compile into one of four large rainbow-colored graphs like the 2001–02 model I had on the board in front of them.

"Which homework graph sheet recorded the highest number of hitting or hurting instances?" I asked the "blue group" in Spanish. Students sifted through to find the greatest number of shaded-in squares.

"¡Mira! ¡*Jackie Chan* tiene 34! (Look! *Jackie Chan* has 34!") Leah voiced her discovery in perfect Spanish, though her multi-ethnic roots, which include African American and Jewish, do not include Latina.

For the sake of easy comparison, I wrote "Jackie Chan" on our Violence Graph in the same color and position relative to its appearance on the 2002 graph. Then I had a student take a turn to color in 34 squares.

"Let's put a check by every 'Jackie Chan' you see on other homework sheets because we're done looking at that program," I reminded them. "Now which homework has the next largest number to 34 of violent acts?"

Just as my students had in 2002, the students proceeded through the pile recording the top 16 violent shows, assigning each a particular color. Regardless of discrepancies in student perceptions of violence of up to three instances for the same program, date, and variable (the margin of error over the years), just as in 2002, students recorded the highest number of aggressive acts for each of these shows. After each group of five students completed its specific group bar graph of findings, and students saw it next to the colorful 2002 graph of the same variable, they were visibly horrified. Gisell clasped hands over her mouth to refrain from completing an exclamation of "Oh my," while others gasped, "Ieeew!"

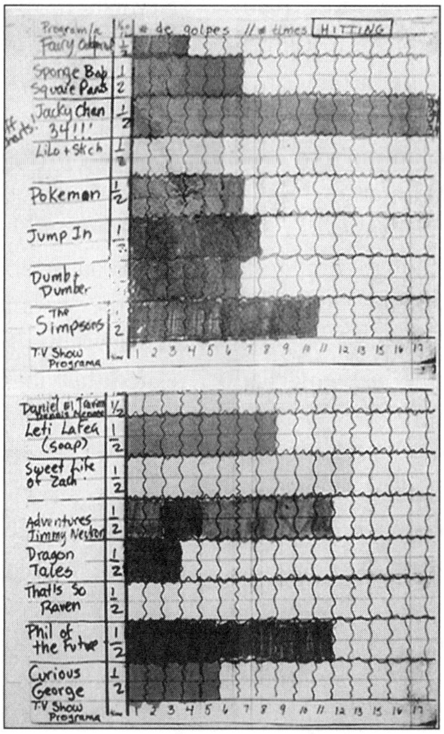

Ever since the first month of school when we studied opposing points of view about the so-called discovery (or not) of the Americas, I've encouraged my students to turn to other sources like library books and the internet to answer questions or prove social studies and science hypotheses and, for the most skilled, to question the sources of their answers. So when I proposed searching the internet to support our findings, many were delighted.

The next day, I rotated each group of five through my English internet research station around a large computer. The class had decided on the preliminary Google search terms: "television violence increase." Though students controlled the mouse and keyboard, I helped weed out irrelevant sites and urged them to explore promising ones. We'd scroll through these until we found something which either the students or I thought related to our hypothesis about increased violence. Next, I'd give them time to read paragraphs on the screen to each other. "Puppies" (native standard-English speakers) would read the material to the "Kittens" (standard-English language learners), explaining if necessary. When they got to a finding, they would let me know so I could record it on chart paper in the color corresponding to their group.

Traditionally, in this way, virtually all students have been able to discover something to share with their group. Usually two students in each group alight on juicy, complex information and, perhaps because of the immersion program's need for translation, are able to simplify explanations for the rest. The overall quality of research and writing vocabulary has been extraordinary in part, I think, because of each group's heterogeneous composition ranging from one to two high-skilled students to one or two who are currently performing well below grade level. Typically, my two-way Spanish immersion classes have been composed of one third children of college-educated professionals, while half qualify for free lunches. About a third are native Spanish speakers or Latino children; up to one fifth African American children, and the rest Euro American and other minorities.

I had the "green group" explore the TV-Turnoff Network site. The students clicked on the Real Vision study. "Wow! Kids will have seen '200,000 violent acts on television by age 18 … and 16,000 murders,'" Maeve was shocked. Some wondered if the increase in television violence highlighted on the site had led to more real-life killing.

"What words do you think you might see in a report that says killing is related to television?"

They decided on "television + violence + killing."

"Oh my gosh! 'TV shows and Video Games Teach Children to Kill!' Look, down there!" Ceilidh was pointing to the screen of search results. The note turned out to be a footnote in a report from the Parents Television Council (PTC). I showed the group how important it was to trace primary sources and helped them type in the name of the author of the study, which turned up in a Senate Judiciary Report.

"This is a report by our own government!" Now I was excited, too. We typed in the report's title and got the full report entitled "Children, Violence and the Media."

"Video Games and TV are 'teaching kids to kill,' and 'teaching them to like it!'" Maeve read aloud for us from the report.

"Violence on TV is over 300 times more than before the war!" Students in the yellow group were jumping up and down. Well, not exactly. I darted to the board and shaded parts of pizzas to explain percentages. This made the concept more understandable to some, but for most, I had to translate. Using both the internet and fact sheets, children in the "yellow group" found that according to a 2007 study by the PTC called "Dying to Entertain," since 1998, violence on ABC TV has quadrupled (a 309 percent increase—a huge rise, though not quite the "300 times" increase students had mistakenly proclaimed).

They found that in 1998 the network had about one act of violence per hour (.93). By 2007, it was almost four (3.8) on average. CBS, according to the PTC study, which can be found at www.parents.org, had the highest percentage of deaths during 2005-06, with over 66 percent of violent scenes after 8 p.m. depicting death. Incidentally, the study points out that, in general, violence in all television shows has shifted to being more central to the story—with more graphic autopsy or torture scenes—than it was over five years ago. It indicates that the 2005-06 season was one of the most violent ever recorded by the PTC.

After each group read its findings aloud, facts discovered by students in the red group persuaded the rest of the class, through a show of hands, to agree to limit their television viewing, turning it off completely during the TV-Turnoff Network's TV-Turnoff Week—something they were reluctant to do when our television unit began. What this group had discovered, thanks largely to the TV-Turnoff Network's website (www.tvturnoff.org) is that there are more televisions (2.73) in the average home than people (2.55) according to *USA Today*. The average home keeps a television turned on eight hours a day, according to the 2006 Nielsen report. Children who watch six or more hours a day perform worse on reading tests than do those who watch one hour a day or don't play video games, reports the Center for Screentime Awareness, on-line at www.screentime.org. And by the time they finish high school, children will have spent more hours watching TV than in school.

I knew students would brainstorm both absurd and frighteningly astute reasons to justify the increase of violence and selfishness on television. My aim was to get these young philosopher-scientists in the habit of asking "why" about their world instead of merely consuming it—of making educated hypotheses then requiring multiple sources of supporting evidence.

During the group discussion, I learned that they were most troubled by the Senate report statement that television was teaching them to "like killing." The Senate report also claimed that 10 percent of crimes committed are caused by violence seen on television. The study, though predating ours, related the violence they saw on television directly to their present world.

I asked students if they had noticed an increase in violence in their world with the increase in television violence. Jacobo and several others fiercely nodded: "Three years ago, I'd only see one or two kids in trouble in the office now and then; now there's up to six or seven," Jaboco commented. I, too, have noticed an increase in behavior problems at the school since 2001, despite better leadership and more effective intervention. However, increasing poverty and less spending on social services leading to a rise in domestic or neighborhood violence could be as equally valid contributors.

"What do you think the reason is behind the increase in television violence?" I asked.

"For brainwashing. TV advertises or sells violence. It influences us to vote for a president who uses war to solve problems," Flynn said.

"I suspect the increase in television violence has something to do with the war on terror," English-learner Andres emulated his classmate Sebastian's elevated vocabulary in his summarizing essay. "By scaring kids and parents and pushing violence, people are more likely to vote for war. The TV makes you dumb because if you see a lot, it makes you forget things. It makes parents forget how things were when they were kids."

One of the most shocking facts my students found was that according to the TV-Turnoff Network's Real Vision project, parents spend only 38.5 minutes a day with their children in meaningful conversation. And more than half of 4- to 6-year olds (54 percent) would rather watch TV than spend time with their parents.

This finding inspired Alejandro's conclusion: "I think George Bush wants to make people more scared. We know George Bush likes war. And TV makes you like more war. What's scary is kids spend more time seeing TV than being with their dad. Since our study, I turn off the TV more and go play with my dad. Maybe the president used to watch more TV than being with his dad."

"And if Bush isn't responsible? Why would television stations or their advertisers want us to like war?" I asked after reading Alejandro's essay aloud.

"To make money, to sell things and make rich people richer like the people selling guns," Ceilidh said.

"To steal stuff from other countries to make our own country the richest!" Jacobo asserted.

What impact did the students think this increase in television violence and selfishness was having on the world around them?

"TV makes people want violence by making it seem cool," Ceilidh said.

Sebastian added, "Then they want to be part of the army. It's a cycle. TV affects the world, then the world affects the TV, which affects world violence. It's a 'chain reaction of evil,'" Sebastian said, borrowing from a Martin Luther King Jr. quote I had them memorize for Dr. King's birthday.

"Yeah, TV leads to more fighting. Fighting leads to war," added Jacobo. He evoked Dr. King to finish his thought: "'Hate begetting hate. Wars producing more wars. …' We need to stop or 'we shall all be plunged into the dark abyss of annihilation.'"

It was a peak teaching moment. Students were assimilating valuable things they had learned earlier in the year to shape their thinking about the world. While some of the conclusions tended toward hyperbole, I can't argue with the soundness of my students' hypothesis that television selfishness and violence are part of a propaganda campaign to foment war and enrich certain sectors. But more importantly, my students are learning to think for themselves, to question the sources of their information.

One of my former students, Daniel, once commented that "watching television replaces your imagination with television thinking and there's not much space left after that." Now my current students had begun to turn off the televisions in their own brains and turn on their imagination and curiosity. At last, they had begun to internalize the insight contained in Maeve's essay—"If you watch too much TV, you lose the kid that is inside you"—wherein lies our higher inner wisdom. ■

Mexican-born journalist and educator **Margot Pepper** has worked as a Two-Way Spanish Immersion (TWI) teacher and poet with California Poets in the Schools for more than a decade. Her memoir, *Through the Wall: A Year in Havana* (Freedom Voices, 2005), was a top nomination for the 2006 American Book Award. She is on the Web at www.margotpepper.com and freedomvoices.org/new/node/93.

Talking with Children About War and Peace

BY ANN PELO

"TV makes people want violence by making it seem cool."
—Ceilidh

"TV leads to more fighting. Fighting leads to war."
—Jacobo

"By scaring kids and parents and pushing violence, people are more likely to vote for war. The TV makes you dumb because if you see a lot, it makes you forget things."
—Andres

The 2nd graders in Margot Pepper's class are eloquent in their analysis of the links between TV violence and war, and passionate in their conviction to resist TV's "brainwashing." Alejandro says, simply and beautifully, "Since our study, I turn off the TV more and go play with my dad."

As teachers and parents, we can stand with these children in their resistance to violence and war. Often, young children have only vague understandings of "war" and "peace," describing "peace," for example, as "quietness." We can give children something more solid to work with, understandings that invite them to see beyond the glamorized violence of war and the imagined hush of peace.

During the Persian Gulf War, I collaborated with Dr. Judy Myers-Walls at Purdue University on a research project aimed at understanding how parents talk about war and peace to their children. From that research, we crafted descriptions of war and peace that emphasize the concrete work of peace, as well as the grief of war. These descriptions give children firm ground to stand on, as they work to make sense of war and peace.

What Is War?

War is when people in countries fight with people in other countries, or when groups of people inside countries fight each other. They may fight because one group has things or land that the other group wants, or because one group wants to be in charge of the other group, or because the groups have different ideas about how people should live and each group wants to change the other group's ideas. The people who are doing the fighting don't usually think about the other side as "people"; they think about them as "the enemy."

Leaders in the countries or leaders of the groups usually make the decision to go to war and sometimes they teach the people in their groups to hate the people in the other group. People who are asked to fight need to decide whether to follow the leaders, not get involved at all, or try to stop the fighting.

During wars people are killed. They are fathers, mothers, brothers, sisters, sons, daughters, and friends. Their friends and families are very sad and sometimes very angry. Even the people who are not killed cannot live normal lives during war. Schools, stores, and work places are destroyed or closed down.

What Is Peace?

Peace is when countries, groups of people, and individual people solve their problems without hurting each other. They try to understand their own and other people's problems. They try to talk about their feelings and listen to other people's feelings. And they find ways to make sure everyone has what she or he needs, things like healthy food, clean water, safe places to live, schools, community centers, and parks.

When people are acting peacefully, they learn about how all people are the same and they learn about how each group of people and every person is different. It's the same as in a family: there are some ways that the people in a family are the same and some ways that they are different. When people are at peace with each other, they learn that the things we all share help us to understand each other, and the things that are different make each person or group special and make life interesting.

Being at peace does not mean you never have problems or you are never angry. Instead, peace means understanding that everyone gets angry sometimes, and that disagreements will happen when people live together and share the things they need. Peace means working out those problems so that everyone feels included and loved, and feels good about the solutions.

Ann Pelo is an early childhood teacher and teacher mentor in Seattle, Wash.

ROXANNA BIKADOROFF

Testing Tots

Why We Need a Better Means of Evaluating Our Nation's Children

BY RICHARD ROTHSTEIN

Since 2003, the government has administered standardized literacy and math tests to all children in the Head Start program.* Four-year-olds are asked to count objects, name alphabet letters and simple geometrical shapes, understand directions, characterize facial expressions, and identify animals, body parts, and other objects in pictures.

It is hard to discern why the Bush administration insisted on the test over the objections of most leading early childhood experts and even members of its own Head Start advisory panel.

Perhaps it is nothing more than a reflexive decision of administration ideologues who see tests and more tests as the solution to every conceivable educational problem—or worse, a way to expose the academic failures they fundamentally believe to plague the public school system in America.

There are certainly some legitimate issues to address. One is that the government spends nearly $7 billion annually on Head Start, and we should know what we're getting for our money.

From national studies, it appears that Head Start graduates have better adolescent and adult outcomes than low-income children who weren't in the program; they are more likely to graduate from high school and attend college, they have higher earnings, and they are less likely to commit crimes. But it also appears that Head Start children, especially blacks, may get an initial cognitive boost that soon fades away, so by 4th grade their reading and math scores may be no higher than their peers.'

Another challenge for the program is a growing consensus among early childhood experts that 4-year-olds are capable of better literacy and mathematics performance than was previously thought. Contrary to experts' thinking a generation ago, preschoolers can begin to read and do math, as any parent of a literate, middle-class 4-year-old knows.

But a standardized test, like that now administered by Head Start, is a poor way to address these challenges. Indeed, it can make things worse.

President Bush has assured educators that he considers it "absurd" for 4-year-olds to take tests like those given in elementary schools; yet in important respects, the flaws of the Head Start test are similar to—and perhaps more severe than—those of standardized tests for older children. As yet, nobody knows what the consequences of doing poorly on the test could be, because the federal Head Start Bureau, though determinedly pushing ahead, still can't say how results might be used. But the fear of adverse consequences alone must create incentives to "teach to the test," as high-stakes exams must do.

Administration officials like to say that if the test assesses appropriate literacy skills, teaching to it can't be bad. But this fails to consider that a 20-minute test (that's the length of the Head Start exam) can't possibly reflect fairly the full breadth of an adequate curriculum. It must inevitably change program emphases.

Consider the items calling for identification of alphabet letters, in matched upper- and lower-case pairs, like "Aa" or "Nn." Research shows that young children who can recognize and name letters are more likely to read later on. So why shouldn't a test give Head Start teachers incentives to teach the alphabet? The reason is that research showing that letter recognition predicts reading success is based on assessing children who learned letters through natural literacy activities, like having stories read to them or playing with picture books. There is no evidence that memorizing alphabet letters out of context predicts later reading skill. But the test will lead teachers to spend more time on alphabet drills and less on reading—just the opposite of what Head Start needs.

Head Start was never intended to be primarily an academic program, but one that prepares low-income children for school by developing their health and their social, emotional, and physical skills, as well as math and reading readiness. The Bush administration claims to support this broad definition of Head Start's goals, and denies it intends to make the program academic. Yet just as rational teachers will shift their instruction to drilling letters and numbers if those are mostly what are tested, so Head Start programs will shift their focus if academics are emphasized in a test-based accountability system. "The administration says it supports all the goals of Head Start, but this test, in its present form, is sending a very different message," said Jacqueline Jones, who knows something about standardized tests. She heads early childhood and literacy initiatives at the Educational Testing Service and was a member of the Head Start advisory panel.

In response to such criticism, Head Start officials claimed they were trying to standardize measures of 4-year-olds' social and emotional development, but didn't want to include such items on a test until they had been "validated"—i.e., proven to predict later school success. This claim is consistent with the administration's proclivity to invoke "scientific" standards in support of favored programs but to ignore science when it contradicts policy preferences.

After all, the literacy items in the Head Start test have not themselves been validated for the manner in which they are being used. In general, very little (only 25 percent) of the variance in 1st- or 2nd-grade academic performance can be predicted by tests in preschool. For the Head Start test in particular, some items have been borrowed from tests for older children, and some were validated only in combination with other items in a larger test. Early childhood educators do have test items that assess social and emotional development or fine and gross motor skills. For example, a child's ability to control impulses, a good predictor of whether a 4-year-old will benefit from elementary school academic instruction, can be assessed by items like asking a child to delay opening a wrapped gift when the tester leaves the room. Motor skills can be assessed by seeing if a child can move a toy turtle (slowly) or toy rabbit (rapidly) along a meandering path sketched out on a piece of paper.

These haven't been scientifically validated either, but that makes them little different from the reading items. Including social and emotional items on the Head Start test would at least signal to Head Start teachers that the government was not trying to get them to make academic drills their only priority.

An even better signal would be given if each child's assessment had to include a teacher's report of whether the child was up-to-date on regular pediatric and dental visits and had been given comprehensive vision and hearing screening—measures that are among Head Start's legislated objectives and that have at least as much to do with 4-year-olds' later school success as alphabet recognition.

If, as officials sometimes insist, the goal is to assess Head Start program quality and not to evaluate individual children, there is a better system already in place—one ignored by the administration in its compulsion to test first and wonder why later. Currently, federal officials evaluate the quality of every Head Start program in the nation triennially, sending teams of as many as 25 monitors—experts in management and finance, early childhood pedagogy, social-emotional development, health, and nutrition—for a full week to Head Start centers. Results of their investigations are forwarded to the government. Programs must develop plans to correct deficiencies in any area and submit to remonitoring to verify that flaws have been corrected. If the deficiencies are severe, or remain uncorrected, the government ends its contract with the Head Start operator and seeks bids for other organizations to run the community's program—a regular enough occurrence to ensure that Head Start programs take the reviews quite seriously.

Among the standards that Head Start programs must meet to satisfy these review teams is whether each child has been individually evaluated at least three times during the year in all the domains that Head Start should cover, including knowing alphabet letters and one-digit numbers, but also other important school-readiness skills like whether the child knows how to take turns or how to handle disappointments. Head Start teachers are required to show what kind of progress children are making by keeping samples of their work, notes of conversations and observations that document students' skill in each of the academic, social, and emotional areas in which children are expected to grow. Records must indicate whether the child has had regular medical and dental checkups. The one thing the review teams do not demand of teachers is that they give children a sit-down test, inappropriate for 4-year-olds, of decontextualized math and reading skills.

There are ways this accountability system could be improved. Policy makers could join the expert teams, for example, to familiarize themselves with the challenges faced by early childhood programs. The monitoring standards could be revised to require that Head Start programs, consistent with what is now known about children's development, have somewhat higher expectations for academic skills without needlessly downgrading other important goals. And the system could require a higher level of skills in instruction and assessment from Head Start teachers—an elusive goal so long as funding for Head Start is so sparse that many teachers have no more than a high school education and are paid accordingly.

Yet even with their flaws, Head Start program reviews comprise the most comprehensive and high-quality accountability system in American education today. Rather than asking Head Start to ape the standardized testing regime of the No Child Left Behind law for K-12 education, we'd be better advised to ask elementary and secondary schools to submit to the kind of accountability already characteristic of the Head Start program. ■

* This piece originally was published 2004. While some of its references are dated, the trends in early-childhood testing that it identifies unfortunately have not changed.

Reprinted with permission from Richard Rothstein, "Too Young to Test." *The American Prospect*, www.prospect.org. Vol. 15, No. 11: Nov. 1, 2004. The American Prospect, 2000 L Street NW, Suite 717, Washington, D.C., 20036.

Richard Rothstein is a senior correspondent at *The American Prospect*, a research associate of the Economic Policy Institute, and a visiting professor at Teachers College, Columbia University, in New York. He is the author of *Class and Schools*.

JOSEPH BLOUGH

Testing Lang

BY AMY GUTOWSKI

Lang* was a student of mine, an 8-year-old with big brown eyes and a shy, quiet nature. He hated writing; putting pencil to paper was a brutal task for him. Yet he wrote, sharpened lead pressing hard onto the paper, forehead wrinkled in concentration and pain.

Lang taught our class how to say "hello" and "goodbye" in his first language, Hmong. He loved math and could spot an equivalent fraction a mile away. He would add numbers into the hundreds of thousands and stun the class.

During morning work I would often have the kids try to find as many words as they could from a larger word—like finding the word "leap" within the word "apple." Lang would discover the word "nectar" in "concentration" and wow his fellow 3rd graders. He spelled the word "hypothesis" in our heated classroom game of spelling hoops, which allowed him the chance to make the final, winning shot. I said a small prayer before the orange-sized Nerf basketball left Lang's hands—he so deserved to experience the glory. When the ball swished through the mini-basket, the class went wild and sprung to their feet, cheering. Lang went back to his seat, hands warm from high-fives, cheeks red from excitement, smiling.

Lang also devoured *Captain Underpants* books, checking them out weekly from the classroom library. His excitement for reading increased with each new adventure.

In March, we had to give the 3rd-grade standardized reading test, a thick booklet brimming with multiple-choice questions and treacherous reading passages. The kids knew it was coming;

we had prepared, worked in practice booklets, and perfected the art of filling in the bubbles.

But as the other kids finished their tests, my heart grew heavy. Lang still sat there, forehead wrinkled in pain. His pencil filled in perfect, lead-heavy circles. He was almost finished when I noticed his bloody lip, bitten from anxiety. I told him that he did his best, and that was definitely enough.

He smiled, wiped his lip with a wet tissue and asked if he could go to music.

Months later, I sat at my desk after school reading the test scores that had just been shipped back to us. I sat in silence, lights off, while sun streamed through the window. According to the test, Lang wasn't "advanced," he wasn't "proficient." He was "basic," which couldn't have been further from the truth.

How many other students and teachers have this same experience when the test scores come back? Lang and I will survive this, of course, but as the tests approach this year I wonder which of my students will find themselves explaining test scores to parents, who thought no child was going to be left behind. ■

* Names have been changed.

Amy Gutowski is a 3rd-grade teacher in the Milwaukee, Wis., public schools.

JORDIN ISIP

Think Less Benchmarks

A Flawed Test Does More Harm than Good

BY AMY GUTOWSKI

I'm staring at this bulging envelope on my desk. It's a big envelope, much larger than your typical letter-sized envelope, you know, a big one, one that could fit about 15 test booklets and answer sheets. It was just dropped off by our school's "literacy coach." I put quotes around these two words because I often wonder why she was given that title. Much of what she does has nothing to do with literacy. I think we should just call her the "test passer-outer" or something like that, because that is really the bulk of what she does throughout the school year. Positions like these have been hijacked by testing crusaders in schools and districts around the country. Originally, our district adopted these ThinkLink benchmark assessments for schools identified as not making adequate yearly progress (AYP). As if that weren't disturbing enough ("Our kids are failing, so let's make them take more tests"), later, virtually all schools were forced to participate regardless of AYP status.

ThinkLink tests are designed to mirror the format of our state assessments. According to the district—and to the salespeople at ThinkLink—the ThinkLink "formative" assessments would help our district better predict student performance on our state's high-stakes exams. These high-stakes tests are aligned with our state's arbitrary set of standards for each grade level, standards that tend to be incredibly unrealistic and developmentally inappropriate.

There are four benchmark tests a year. Thanks to the folks at the Discovery Channel, that TV channel with the nifty little logo of the earth spinning, my 8-year-old students have four more opportunities to stop learning and fill in the bubbles. The folks at Discovery Education have added an extension to their suite of services. They've branched into the assessment market and now produce ThinkLink formative assessments for districts across the country.

According to the catchy little press release from Discovery Education: "Discovery Education acquired ThinkLink Learning in April 2006, expanding the business unit's high-quality products and services to include formative assessment. ThinkLink pioneered a unique approach to formative assessment that uses a scientifically research-based continuous improvement model that maps diagnostic assessment to state high-stakes tests." So essentially, it's an expensive assessment program—

They Call This Data?

Oscar Wilde, Svab, and My Students

According to the "data" collected on our fourth and final ThinkLink benchmark of this school year, most of my 3rd-graders had a hard time reading a paraphrased excerpt from Oscar Wilde's *The Importance of Being Earnest.* I was shocked. I mean, why would 8- and 9-year-olds in Milwaukee (or anywhere else for that matter) have trouble reading Oscar Wilde? The questions were so simple for a beginning reader to decode.

For example: **Read this sentence from the passage.** *He laid particular stress on your German, as he was leaving for town yesterday.* **Now look at the dictionary entry.**

stress *noun*

1 worries caused by difficulties in life

2 saying a word or part of a word more strongly than another

3 force of weight caused by something heavy

verb

4 to give importance to something

Which meaning of stress is used in the sentence above?

(A.1, B.2, C.3, D.4)

But wait. What *is* the correct answer anyway? I'm confused. I guess I'm going to have to dust off my AP anthologies from high school if I'm going to teach to this test.

According to the "formative" assessment "data," my 3rd-graders also had trouble reading a story called "The Broken Pot." In this paraphrased tale—what is it with all the paraphrasing on these tests anyway? Would it be too much to ask that my students read a whole story, written for children?—there's a Brahman by the name of Svab. He has to beg for food. One day he receives a large pot of rice gruel, eats a bit, then hangs the leftovers on a nail above his bed. While full in his bed, his mind gets away with him, and he has greedy thoughts of selling the rice gruel, then buying goats, then trading goats for cattle, then trading calves for horses, horses have foals, he can sell the foals, etc. Then eventually he will meet a beautiful girl with a dowry. (And how many 3rd-graders know what a dowry is? Just curious.) Anyway, Svab gets carried away with his thoughts, startles himself, and knocks the pot of rice gruel on his own head. Now, this is the part that kills me—the moral: "He who makes foolish plans for the future will be white all over, like Svab." Huh? Most of my students are children of color. Imagine their surprise at the ending. Some of my students laughed out loud. They didn't get it. I didn't get it either.

I don't think any of us will "get it" until this obsession with prepackaged testing ends. It's so absurd, it's almost funny, like straight out of an *Onion* article. But I'm not laughing when during a staff meeting, after a long day of working with kids in the classroom, I'm staring at a projection of a large, fancy, color-coded, computer-generated bar graph showing the dismal results of our last reading benchmark, being told my students don't know how to analyze text. I'm not laughing when we spend hours drafting our ed plan, discussing how we can bring up our test scores. I'm so very tired of wasting my valuable time discussing this so-called data. Instead, I'll continue to tell tales of the insanity of it all. Hoping that one day, my 3rd-graders will no longer be subjected to such nonsense.

—Amy Gutowski

our district spent roughly $400,000 on it in one year—built on the assumption that repeated testing of children will help them to do better on tests. Forget about reading specialists, art, music, school psychologists, nurses, social workers, or support staff. It's ThinkLink to the rescue!

This is why the overstuffed envelope has landed on my desk. My first impulse is to chuck it in the trash. I'm sure this is the impulse of any teacher who has actually read these assessments. The first time I saw a ThinkLink benchmark I was shocked and dismayed. It was poorly written (e.g., "There was once a little peasant girl. She was pretty as a star in its season. Her real name was Blanchette. She was called Little Goldenhood because of a wonderful little coat with a hood she always wore."); riddled with errors (e.g., "I th ink of my summers on Grandpa's farm."); and developmentally inappropriate (e.g., "Reread the title of the story: The Armadillo: A Shelled Mammal. What happens when –ed is added to the word shell in the title?

A. it becomes a word that tells when the mammal was shelled

B. it becomes a word that tells how armadillos move

C. it becomes a word that describes the word mammal

D. it becomes a word that is the present tense of the verb shell").

It was all completely disconnected from the curriculum I was teaching.

I decided to call our district's director of assessment in December 2006, after our first round of benchmarks, to ask about them. It amazed me that this program was implemented so quickly. After all, hadn't Discovery Education just rolled out this new suite of assessments in April 2006? Teachers in the district were never asked if we wanted to use such testing in our classrooms; the tests were just bought and then mandated, without any discussion. I was upset because my 3rd graders had just finished the weeklong state assessment in November (and all of the preparation preceding), and then we had to stop reading *Charlotte's Web* for two days and instead fill in more bubbles. The phone conversation was interesting.

According to the assessment director, teachers around the district loved the ThinkLink assessments. She said that I was the only one who complained, and that teachers were amazed at the quick return of test results and data. She said that teachers told her they were learning so much about their students and their learning from these assessments. I was surprised by this response. I had just spoken to a teacher at another elementary school who told me that the entire staff had written a letter protesting the district-wide adoption of these additional tests. The assessment director even claimed that some principals were requesting benchmark assessments for their 1st- and 2nd-grade classrooms. (In our district, these tests start at 3rd grade and continue all the way through 10th grade. No classroom is left unscathed except kindergarten, 1st, and 2nd grades—which may very well change if this madness continues.) I could not believe what I was hearing.

The benchmark testing questions were all over the place. Most of them were not at all related to what I was teaching in the classroom. For example, after reading a confusing passage about edible insects—in which there was no explanation of what "edible" means, nor any obvious context clues to help children figure out the meaning of "edible"—my students were asked:

"Which of the following is nearly the opposite of edible?

A. antiedible

B. preedible

C. anedible

D. inedible."

Is this not insane?

I teach about prefixes and suffixes in my classroom, but come on, people. The questioning is so convoluted. My students are 8-year-olds who just started reading two years ago. I want my children to become independent learners and lovers of books. These tests make reading seem awful and tedious. An equally upsetting question asks children to identify an author's purpose (one of our 3rd-grade reading "standards" in Wisconsin). My 3rd-graders are often asked if a passage was written to entertain, persuade, or inform. Much of what we read in our lives does all of these. We recently finished reading *Turtle Bay*. It's a story about friends cleaning a beach so sea turtles will come and lay their eggs. The story was definitely entertaining, it persuaded my students to think about their actions (e.g., littering hurts animals), and we were informed about turtles. So, in the name of "standards," my students are expected to answer these horribly misleading questions. Why has reading been reduced to this?

At the end of our conversation, the director of assessment asked me if I wanted to participate in making the tests better. I agreed to go over the initial assessment, highlighting grammatical errors and misplaced questions. I sent the offending booklet to her office with red marks and comments. I was then asked if I would be interested in going over future ThinkLink assessments, and at the time, I agreed. But then I began to think about it. I was never asked my opinion about these lame assessments in the first place, and now here I was agreeing to spend my valuable time working to make them better? These tests were mandated in our district without critical discussion and questioning. I was also told that the district would survey teachers about these assessments at the end of the school year. I have yet to see a survey.

Needless to say, I did not spend more of my time working to improve the flawed benchmarks. I have, instead, decided to advocate for my students and their learning. I have been sending opinion pieces to local newspapers and magazines. I have testified at school board meetings. I stand up at staff meetings (often alone), and express my concerns. I will not be apathetic. I'm not buying into this random adoption of mandated assessments. I am tired of this anti-child, for-profit agenda in our schools and classrooms. Teachers must come together and speak out against the foolishness and absurdity of it all. Our students deserve more than this. The huge sums paid to Discovery Education could be put to much better use.

So here I sit, staring at the envelope full of ThinkLink tests. The envelope conjures up conflict within me. I don't want to subject my students to this nonsense. I want to resist. I want to shred each booklet page by page, especially the top page with the cute little earth logo. But I can't. I have to pass out these tests or risk my job. Tomorrow, when I pass out the booklets and scantron sheets, I'll explain to my students that some of the questions were confusing even to me, their teacher. I'll ask them not to worry. I'll ask them to do their best. NCLB puts pressure on districts to gather more data, and testing companies get richer producing tests which guarantee large amounts of failure, thus ensuring future customers. It's a vicious, mean-spirited cycle. The way we educate our children is being driven by these test scores. We spend hours at staff meetings looking at the "data" gathered from these mass produced assessments instead of sharing ideas about meaningful learning and what really works in the classroom.

Who needs the arts? Screw recess. Let them eat tests. I'll think about this tomorrow as my 3rd graders fill in perfect little circles on their benchmark score sheets—3rd graders, who are most definitely being left behind. ■

Amy Gutowski is a 3rd-grade teacher in the Milwaukee, Wis., public schools.

LAURA DESANTIS

From Critique to Possibility

New Zealand's Radical Approach to Assessment

BY *MARGIE CARTER*

Critical conversations about standards and assessments in the United States can be discouraging. Current formulations reduce teaching and learning to their most superficial forms. We're challenged to find examples of assessment that align with progressive values about children's learning and about the purpose of education.

The work of educators and government officials in New Zealand can reinvigorate our efforts to reshape assessments in our country, carrying us from critique to possibility.

In the mid-1990s, the early childhood community in New Zealand mobilized to influence the development of a national curriculum, *Te Whariki*. They worked closely with their Ministry of Education to create a curriculum built around four core principles integral to the indigenous Maori culture: empowerment, holistic development, family and community, and relationships. In conjunction with that curriculum and its values, early childhood educators and Ministry officials crafted an assessment system called "Learning Stories."

What outcomes are assessed in this system?

- Belonging/Mana Whenua: Expressed in children's lives as taking an interest
- Well-being/Mana Atua: Expressed in children's lives as being involved
- Exploration/Mana Aoturoa: Expressed in children's lives as persisting with difficulty

- Communication/Manu Reo: Expressed in children's lives as expressing an idea or a feeling
- Contribution/Mana Tangata: Expressed in children's lives as taking responsibility

The first step in the Learning Stories assessment protocol asks teachers to record, in narrative form, their observation of a child's work. The next step asks teachers to analyze that narrative in relation to the outcomes listed above. Another step in the assessment asks teachers to plan from their analysis: what might they offer to encourage the child's interest, ability, or disposition?

Learning Stories offers a dramatic contrast to most U.S. assessment systems, even those that include anecdotal records alongside the typical checklists and tests. Some of the striking differences:

- Learning Stories prioritize narrative as a valuable approach to recording children's learning. Narrative makes learning visible, offering families a window into the often invisible life of the classroom and offering children a way to revisit and reflect on their experiences and to set new goals for their learning.
- Teachers observe, document and tell stories using a strength-based, rather than deficit, approach to describing children's learning.
- Dispositional learning is a focus as much as skill development. It adds inclination to skills; dispositions turn skills into action.
- Learning Stories contribute to shared culture, history, and literacy experiences in the classroom; they become a lively part of the community—not a piece of paper filed away out of view.
- In preparing Learning Stories, teachers make their reflections and perspectives visible as they write and analyze the narrative. They are thinkers and researchers, not merely technicians administering tests.
- Learning Stories invite families to participate in their children's early childhood experience. Families often contribute stories from home which in turn can shape the curriculum.

As we work to change the shape of assessment in the United States, we can learn from our colleagues in New Zealand. Another world is possible—another approach to assessment, one that is guided not by narrow academic outcomes, but by aspirations for children's development as thinkers engaged in a joyful community of learners.

To learn more about the work of educators in New Zealand and their inspiring efforts to create a meaningful assessment system, take a look at these books and articles:

- Margaret Carr. *Assessment in Early Childhood Settings: Learning Stories.* London. Paul Chapman Publishing. 2001.
- Margaret Carr, Wendy Lee, and Carolyn Jones. *Kei Tua o te Pae: Assessment for Learning: Early Childhood Exemplars.* Wellington, New Zealand. Learning Media. 2008.
- Mary Jane Drummond. *Assessing Children's Learning (Second Edition).* London. David Fulton Publishers. 2003.
- Ann Hatherly and Lorraine Sands. "So What Is Different about Learning Stories?" In *The First Years: Nga Tou Tuahati: New Zealand Journal of Infant and Toddler Education.* 4 (1). pp. 133–135. 2002.
- Wendy Lee. "ELP: Empowering the Leadership in Professional Development Communities." In *European Early Childhood Education Research Journal.* 16 (1). pp. 95-106. 2008. ■

Margie Carter began her work in early childhood education as a teacher of 1st grade, kindergarten, and preschool children and has gone on to direct childcare programs, create staff development videos, and co-author seven books. She travels widely to speak and consult, and she is on the web at ecetrainers.com.

Part IV

Cultivate a sense of place—of belonging to a particular patch of earth and sky—and a connection to the earth and its creatures.

"Being with a child is largely a matter of becoming receptive to what lies all around you. It is learning again to use your eyes, ears, nostrils, and fingertips, opening up the disused channels of sensory impression. For most of us, knowledge comes largely through sight, yet we look about with such unseeing eyes that we are partially blind. One way to open your eyes to unnoticed beauty is to ask yourself, 'What if I had never seen this before? What if I knew I would never see it again?'"

Rachel Carson
The Sense of Wonder

DAVID McLIMANS

A Pedagogy for Ecology

BY ANN PELO

The year I turned 40, I found my way home. That year, in Utah's red rock desert for the first time, I wept as I climbed across the slickrock, wound along canyon floors, balanced my way up and over canyon walls. This wildly unfamiliar place moved me more than I'd expected. I'd thought it would be beautiful and that the challenge of backpacking there would be energizing—but I hadn't expected my heart to break open. My visit to Utah awakened me to a passionate love, born in my childhood, that I'd forgotten, or never consciously acknowledged: love for a spacious, uncluttered horizon, love for dirt, rock, and sage, for heat and dust and stars, for open sky. In the red rock desert, I felt a hunger for place that I hadn't recognized until it began to be sated by the vast sky and expansive rock.

I grew up in arid eastern Washington, near Idaho, and spent my childhood outdoors, digging tunnels into the sage-scrub gully across from my house, running across the open fields to flush pheasants and quail from the tall grass, piling pine needles into nests and curling into them like an animal into a den. When I left home, I moved west, to the "wet side" of the state, and my sense of place was unsettled. I continued to spend long stretches of time outdoors, trekking through the rain-drenched mountains or along the wild and rugged coast, and felt glad to be there. But I didn't let the place seep into me and become part of me; shoulders hunched against the wet, I held myself at some distance from the Pacific Northwest. In Utah, I remembered, with a child's open-hearted joy, how it feels to give over to a place, to be swept into an intimate embrace with the earth. In Utah, I understood that place is part of our identity—that place shapes our identity.

This is what I want for children: a sensual, emotional, and *conscious* connection to place; the sure, sweet knowledge of earth, air, sky. As a teacher, I want to foster in children an ecological identity, one that shapes them as surely as their cultural and social identities. I believe that this ecological identity, born in a particular place, opens children to a broader connection with the earth; love for a specific place makes possible love for other places. An ecological identity allows us to experience the earth as our home ground, and leaves us determined to live in honorable relationship with our planet.

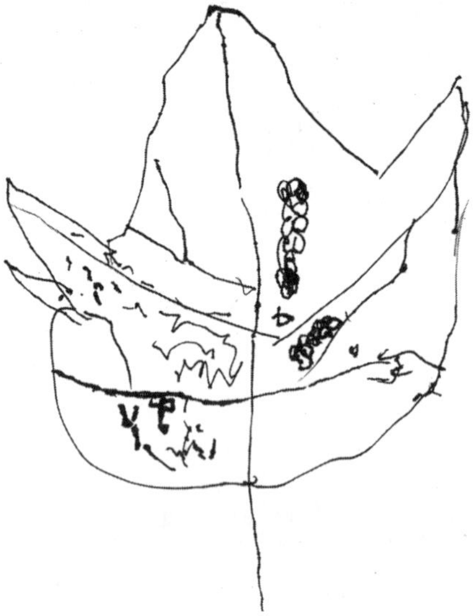

We live in a culture that dismisses the significance of an ecological identity, a culture that encourages us to move around from place to place and that posits that we make home by the simple fact of habitation, rather than by intimate connection to the land, the sky, the air. Any place can become home, we're told. Which means, really, that no place is home.

This is a dangerous view. It leads to a way of living on the earth that is exploitative and destructive. When no place is home, we don't mind so much when roads are bulldozed into wilderness forests to make logging easy. When no place is home, a dammed river is regrettable, but not a devastating blow to the heart. When no place is home, eating food grown thousands of miles away is normal, and the cost to the planet of processing and shipping it is easy to ignore.

Finding a Place

Our work as teachers is to give children a sense of place—to invite children to braid their identities together with the place where they live by calling their attention to the air, the sky, the cracks in the sidewalk where the earth busts out of its cement cage. For me, teaching in a childcare program in Seattle located next to a canal that links Lake Union and Puget Sound, "place" means the smell of just-fallen cedar boughs and salty, piquant air, the sweet tartness of blackberries (and the scratch of blackberry thorns), the light grey of near-constant clouds, the rough-voiced call of seagulls and the rumble of boat engines. It is exhilarating to offer children this place as home ground.

Other places are less compelling as home ground. What does it mean to do this work of connecting children to place when the immediate environment numbs rather than delights the senses? What can be embraced in a school neighborhood dominated by concrete, cars, and convenience stores?

Children's worlds are small, detailed places—the crack in the sidewalk receives their full attention, as does the earthworm flipping over and over on the pavement after rainfall. They have access to elements of the natural world that many adults don't acknowledge. When we, like the children, tune ourselves more finely, we find the natural world waiting for us: cycles of light and dark, the feel and scent of the air, the particularities of the sky—these are elements of the natural world and can begin to anchor us in a place.

Rather than contribute to a sense of disconnection from place by writing off the environments around our most urban schools as unsalvageable or not worth knowing, teachers can instill in children an attitude of attention to what exists of the natural world in their neighborhoods. The sense of care for and connection to place, then, can become the foundation for a critical examination of how that place has been degraded. Rick Bass, in *The Book of Yaak*, describes his experience of the interplay between love of place and willingness to see the human damage done to that place: "As it became my home, the wounds that were being inflicted upon it—the insults—became my own."[1]

Every child lives someplace. And that someplace begins to matter when children are invited to know where they are and to participate in the unfolding life of that place—coming to know the changes in the light and in the feel of the air, and participating in a community of people who speak of such things to each other.

Cultivating an Ecological Identity

Children know how to live intimately in place; they allow themselves to be imprinted by place. They give themselves over to the natural world, throwing endless rocks into a river, digging holes that go on forever, poking sticks into slivers of dirt in pavement, finding their way up the orneriest tree. They learn about place with their bodies and hearts. We can underscore that intuited, sensual, experiential knowledge by fostering a conscious knowledge of place in children.

Kathleen Dean Moore, director of the Spring Creek Project for Ideas, Nature, and the Written Word at Oregon State University, writes that, "To love—a person and a place—means at least this: 1. To want to be near it, physically. 2. To want to know everything about it—its story, its moods, what it looks like by moonlight. 3. To rejoice in the fact of it. 4. To fear its loss, and grieve for its injuries. 5. To protect it—fiercely, mindlessly, futilely, and maybe tragically, but to be helpless to do otherwise. 6. To be transformed in its presence—lifted, lighter on your feet, transparent, open to everything beautiful and new. 7. To want to be joined with it, taken in by it, lost in it. 8. To want the best for it. 9. Desperately."[2]

How do we cultivate this love of place in young children's hearts and minds, moving beyond the tenets of recycling to intimate connection with their home ground? From my experiences as a childcare teacher, I've distilled a handful of principles.

- Walk the land.
- Learn the names.
- Embrace sensuality.
- Explore new perspectives.
- Learn the stories.
- Tell the stories.

My primary work is as a teacher in a full-day, year-round childcare program in an urban Seattle neighborhood that serves families privileged by race, class, and education. I've also worked closely with teachers and children in urban Head Start programs. The principles I suggest resonate in these widely varying contexts; all children deserve home ground.

Walk the Land

Contemporary U.S. culture is about novelty and fast-moving entertainment: a million television channels to surf, and news stories that flash bright and burn out fast. This disposition to move quickly and look superficially translates to a lack of authentic engagement with the earth: Get to as many national parks as we can in a two-week vacation, drive to a scenic view, take some photos, and drive to the next place. D. H. Lawrence critiques these shallow encounters: "The more we know superficially, the less we penetrate, vertically. It's all very well skimming across the surface of the ocean and saying you know all about the sea. Underneath is everything we don't know and are afraid of knowing."[3]

As teachers, we must be mindful of this cultural disposition to superficial knowledge. It's easy to fall into the habit of aiming for novelty, offering children many brief encounters with places, too-short experiences that leave them familiar with the surface, but not the depths. Instead, we ought to invite children to look below the surface, to move slowly, to know a place deeply.

For many years, my emphasis in planning summer field trips was to get to as many city parks and beaches as I could. Each week, we'd head out to two or three different places, so that by the end of the summer we'd taken a grand tour of the city. I thought that, by visiting a range of places in Seattle, the children would come to know their city. We had a hoot on those trips, but each place was a first encounter, and offered novelty rather than intimacy. The children came away from those summers not so much with a sense of place as with confusion about how these various places fit together to make up their home ground. We'd skimmed the surface of Seattle, but didn't know its depths.

Now, my emphasis has shifted. I plan regular visits to the same two or three places over the course of a year. Spending time at the same park and the same beach, we see it change over a year. I point out landmarks on the beach to help the children track the tide's movement up and down the beach. At the park, the children and I choose a couple trees that we visit regularly; we take photos and sketch those trees to help us notice the nuances of their seasonal cycles. From the top of a big rock at the park, the children play with their shadows on the ground below, noticing how shadow and light changes over the year. The children greet the rhododendron bushes like dear old friends, and know the best places to find beetles and slugs.

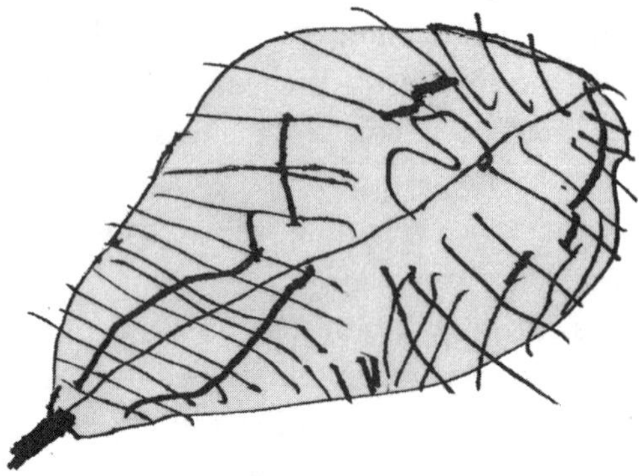

My commitment to walking the land consciously with children has changed how I walk with them to the park in our neighborhood. I used to focus our walk on getting there efficiently and safely, and chose our route accordingly. Now, I've charted a longer route, one that takes us past a neighbor's yard full of rosemary and lavender and tall wild grasses. We take our time walking past this plot of earth, and I coach the children to point out what they notice about this very familiar place. I'd worried that the children would become bored, walking the same path every day, or would stop seeing the land, so I developed several rituals for our walk. We pause at the rosemary to monitor changes in its fragrance, its buds and foliage, and to watch for the arrival of spit bugs, whose foamy nests delight the children. We pause at the wild grass to compare its growth to the children's growth, an inexact but joyfully chaotic measurement.

Learn the Names

When we talk about the natural world, we often speak in generalities, using categorical names to describe what we see: "a bird," "a butterfly," "a tree." We are unpracticed observers, clumsy in our seeing, quick to lump a wide range of individuals into broad, indistinct groups. These generalities are a barrier to intimacy: a bird is a bird is any bird, not this redwing blackbird, here on the dogwood branch, singing its unique song.

Most of us don't have much of a repertoire of plant, insect, animal, tree, or bird names; I sure don't. For many years, I wasn't particularly interested in learning the names of the flora and fauna, and imagined that learning the names would be a chore, a tedious exercise in memorization. My experience in Utah taught me that learning the names is an exercise in love. There, I was in an entirely unfamiliar place, and had only the clumsiest of generic names for what I encountered: a bush, a rock, a lizard. As I began to fall in love with the red rock desert, I wanted to know everything about it, including the names it holds. I bought a field guide and began to learn the names—the identities—of the plants, the creatures, the types of rock. Each name was a step closer into relationship. The names helped me locate myself in the desert.

I carry a field guide to the Pacific Northwest with me now, when I'm out with the children in my group. We take it with us when we walk to the school playground around the corner, and when we go farther afield. We turn to it when we encounter a bug we don't recognize or find an unfamiliar creature revealed by a low tide. And I've created lotto and matching games from the field guide, photocopying images of familiar trees, birds, marine creatures. We use the images for matching games and bingo games: Together, we're learning the names of this place that is our shared home ground.

Embrace Sensuality

In a culture that values intellect more than intuition or emotion, typical environmental education too often emphasizes facts and information in lieu of experience. There are plenty of plastic animals, nature games, videos, and books for children that invite children to intellectualize—and commodify—the natural world. Teacher resource catalogues offer activity books and games that teach about endangered species, rain forest destruction, pollution, and recycling. These books and games keep the natural world at a distance; the rain forest is, for most of us, an abstracted, distant idea, not our intimate place.

To foster a love for place, we must engage our bodies and our hearts—as well as our minds—in a specific place. Intellectual and critical knowledge needs a foundation of sensual awareness, and, for very young children, sensual awareness is the starting place for other learning. How does the air feel on your skin? What birds do you hear on the playground?

A friend of mine taught in a Head Start program in a housing development which had been the scene of several shootings and which had more graffiti than green. She wrestled with how to stir children's numbed senses awake in that harsh landscape where playing outdoors was dangerous. She decided to bring the sensual natural world into her classroom. She added cedar twigs to the sand table, and chestnuts, and stems of lavender. She included pine cones and sea shells in the collection of playdough toys. She supplemented her drama area with baskets of rocks and shells, and included tree limbs, driftwood, stumps, and big rocks in her block area. She played CDs of birds native to the Northwest. And in early fall each year, she welcomed the children to her program with feasts of ripe blackberries, making jam and cobbler with the children, telling them about her adventures picking the blackberries in a wild bramble in the alley behind her apartment building.

Explore New Perspectives

Living in a place over time can breed a sense of familiarity, and familiarity can easily slip into a belief that we've got the land figured out. We stop expecting to be surprised, to be jolted into new ways of seeing; we become detached from the vitality of a place.

Our challenge is to see with new eyes, to look at the familiar as though we're seeing it for the first time. When we look closely and allow ourselves to be surprised by unexpected details and new insights, we develop an authenticity and humility in our experience of place, and wake up to its mysteries and delights.

Several years ago, one of the 4-year-old children in my group posed a simple question: Why do the leaves change color? Her question startled me awake: I saw the transformation of color through her eyes, a phenomenon consciously witnessed only once or twice in her young life, and one full of mystery and magic. Her question deserved my full attention, not a recital of the muddled information that I remembered from my science classes in school, and not a quick glance at an encyclopedia. Madeline's question launched our group on an in-depth study of the lives of leaves that carried us through the seasons.

My co-teacher, Sandra, and I took the children on a walk through the neighborhood to study the trees. Moving from one tree to the next, we began to see a pattern, and shared our observation with the children: the leaves on the outermost branches began to change color before the leaves in the center of the tree. The children built on our observation, adding what they'd noticed: that the leaves first changed color on their outermost edges, while the center of the leaves remained green. I suggested that we gather leaves to bring back to our room, where we could study them up close and record what we observed, sketching the details that we saw and adding nuances of color with watercolor paint. As we sketched the lines of the leaves, children pointed out the resemblance between the skeletal lines of leaves—the "bones" of a leaf, the children called them—and the tendons and lines on our hands:

"The lines of the leaf feel like human bones." "The lines are like the lines on our hands." Excited by the children's observation, I suggested that we sketch our hands, just as we'd sketched the leaves, knowing that our sketching would help us see ourselves in new ways, as cousins to leaves.

As we sketched, I asked the children to reflect on why the leaves change color in the autumn. "What is it about autumn that makes leaves change from green to red, orange, brown?" In our conversation, the children generated several theories about the relationship between autumn and the changes in leaves: "In the fall, it's cold. Leaves huddle together on the ground to get warm. The trees are cold because they don't have any leaves to keep them warm." "The color is a coat to keep the leaves warm, because it's cold in the fall."

From this analysis, one child made a leap that deepened our conversation: "Leaves get sad when they start to die." From this decidedly unscientific conjecture, the children forged a potent connection to the leaves: "Like we give comfort to others when they're sad, the plant needs comfort." "I think a hug would help a leaf, and being with the leaf." "Maybe you could stay with it. You just give it comfort before it dies." "When it drops on the ground, that's when it needs you."

At Hilltop, we use an emergent pedagogy, developing curricula from the children's questions and pursuits. In our study of the lives of leaves, I experienced the value of this pedagogy, as the children and Sandra and I lingered with questions, theories and counter-theories, and with our not-knowing. Instead of falling back on environmental science lessons about chlorophyll and light, our emergent curriculum framework allowed us to explore Madeline's question in the spirit in which it was posed: a question about the meaning of change and the identity of leaves. Through our exploration, we became intimates of leaves, anchored in our place.

Learn the Stories

To foster an intimate relationship with place, we need to know the stories and histories that are linked to that place, just as we do in our intimate relationships with people. In our work with young children, our focus in gathering these stories is as much about the children's imaginings as it is about scientific facts. We can invite their conjectures to complement the facts, opening the door to heartfelt connections.

Visiting a Head Start program one afternoon, I watched Natalie catch ants on the asphalt slab that served as the program's playground. She hovered over a crack in the pavement, carefully picking up each ant that crawled from the crack and dropping it into a bucket. Curious about her intention, I asked what she was planning for the ants: "They're bugs and we hafta kill them." I imagined contexts in her life in which this could be true: had her family dealt with invasive insects at home? Had she experienced the pain of bee stings and itch of mosquito bites? I wanted respectfully to acknowledge these sorts of experiences, yet I didn't want them to become her only references for understanding and relating to the natural world. I said, "Sometimes, when bugs come into our houses, we have to kill them to keep ourselves healthy. And some bugs can bite us in painful ways. But sometimes, we don't have to worry so much about the bugs we find. I'm curious about these ants; where do you suppose they come from?"

Natalie was quick to imagine the ants' story: "The ants are in the hole talking. If they hear loud noises, they won't come out. We have to be very quiet! If they see us, they stay in because they're scared. When one ant wasn't looking, I got him! I'm faster than them—that's how I catch them."

"What's in the hole that the ants come from?" I asked.

"Maybe their family," Natalie mused. I offered her a clipboard and a pen, and invited her to draw her ideas about what was in the hole. She leaped at the invitation, and began to sketch, talking aloud as she worked: "They're a family. They talk to each other and bring food to their baby. In the house, there's food and a table and a bed and a seat."

Natalie stopped drawing to look into her bucket: "There's 15 ants in the bucket! That's more than one family. That's a lot of families.

They share one house in the hole. The ants come not fast because they're talking, saying their plan to come out to see what's outside. They want to find their family that's in the bucket. The ants in the bucket want to get out of the bucket and go to their family."

Natalie abruptly dumped the bucket upside-down next to the crack in the pavement, and tapped it on its bottom. "Go home, ants! Go to your home. Go to your family."

The invitation to imagine the ants' story helped Natalie look at her bucket from the inside as well as from above, and shifted her relationships with the ants. She moved from a defensive posture to that of being a protector. Particularly for children living in places where the natural world is degraded or dangerous, imagining the stories of a place can inspire new possibilities, can cast the children into an active role as people who care about and take action on behalf of a place.

Tell the Stories

We're often encouraged to see the earth as landscape, which is scenery—something to look at, but not to participate in. But when we collapse the distance between the land and ourselves and allow ourselves to become part of the story of a place, we give ourselves over to intimacy. This can be our work with young children—weaving them into the story of the place where they live.

One way I've begun trying to link the children to the land is by using observable markers anchored in place to measure our lives. "You'll start kindergarten in the fall, when the blackberries are ripe." "Christmas comes in the darkest part of winter, when the sun sets while we're still at school, and the sun doesn't rise until we're back at school the next morning."

And I've been playing a game with the children that I learned from Richard Louv's book, *Last Child in the Woods*, "The Sound of a Creature Not Stirring." We listen for the sounds we don't hear (a leaf changing color, an earthworm moving through the soil, blackberries ripening)—a way to focus our attention on the earth around us and to participate in what's happening in it.[4]

A Foundation for Action

Kathleen Dean Moore muses, "Loving isn't just a state of being, it's a way of acting in the world. Love isn't a sort of bliss, it's a kind of work. … Obligation grows from love. It is the natural shape of caring." And then she finishes her list of what it means to love a place: "10. To love a person or a place is to take responsibility for its well-being."[5]

From love grows action. In my work with young children, I share stories of local environmental activists who have used their love of place to fuel their action. For example, I tell the story of a group of children and their families who launched a campaign to save the cedar tree at the school playground where we often play.

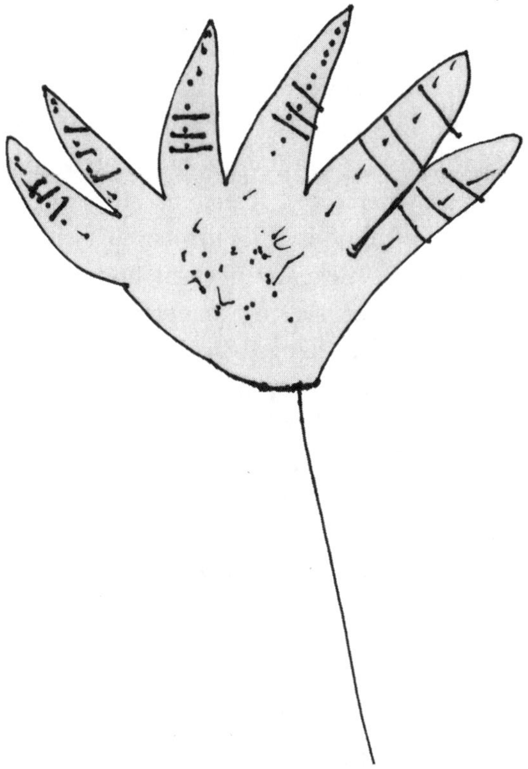

Children have loved the cedar tree at Coe School for a long time; children played at this tree even before you were born. One year, a mom was at a community meeting and learned that the city park department was planning to cut down the tree because it was damaging the asphalt on the playground with its big roots. She told the children in her daughter's kindergarten class, and those children and their families decided that they had to work to protect the cedar tree and to help the park department find another way to fix the problem of broken asphalt. The children and their families wrote letters to the city workers, telling them about how much they loved the cedar tree, and sharing their ideas for taking good care of the tree and the pavement on the playground. They had a meeting with the city workers, who hadn't known that the tree was important to the children. After the meeting, the city workers decided not to cut down the tree; they made a plan with the children and their families and the other kids at Coe School about how they could work together to fix the asphalt and take care of the tree.

I watch for opportunities for the children to add their own chapters to the story of activism on behalf of beloved places. I want them to see themselves as part of a community of people who are anchored by fierce and determined love to place and who take responsibility for its well-being.

I continue to explore my new home ground in the Northwest, seeking to open to it with a willingness to be changed by it. With the children, I flip through my field guide to find the name of an unfamiliar bush; I linger to watch a heron stalk fish; I make pilgrimages to the rivers where salmon spawn. Even as I give myself over to this place as *my* place, letting it shape who I am and how I live in the world, I resist the damp grey and crowded mountains; I still feel a tension between the land and sky of my childhood that my body knows intimately and loves deeply, and this cool and cloudy place. What seems to carry me through that tension—or to allow me to live with it—is my desire to live intimately in place, and to invite children to live here with me.

The poet Mary Oliver instructs us on how to open the natural world to children: "Teach the children. Show them daisies and the pale hepatica. Teach them the taste of sassafras and wintergreen. The lives of the blue sailors, mallow, sunbursts, the moccasin flowers. And the frisky ones—inkberry, lamb's-quarters, blueberries. And the aromatic ones—rosemary, oregano. Give them peppermint to put in their pockets as they go to school. Give them the fields and the woods and the possibility of the world salvaged from the lords of profit. Stand them in the stream, head them upstream, rejoice as they learn to love this green space they live in, its sticks and leaves and then the silent, beautiful blossoms. Attention is the beginning of devotion."[6]

And devotion is the beginning of action. ■

Ann Pelo is an early childhood teacher and teacher mentor in Seattle, Wash.

References

1. Rick Bass. *The Book of Yaak.* Boston. Houghton Mifflin Company. 1996.
2. Kathleen Dean Moore. *The Pine Island Paradox: Making Connections* in a Disconnected World. Minneapolis, Minn. Milkweed Editions. 2004
3. Edward D. McDonald, ed. *Phoenix: The Posthumous Papers of D.H. Lawrence.* New York. Viking. 1978.
4. Richard Louv. *Last Child in the Woods: Saving Our Children from Nature-Deficit Disorder.* Chapel Hill, N.C. Algonquin Books. 2005.
5. Kathleen Dean Moore. *The Pine Island Paradox: Making Connections in a Disconnected World.* Minneapolis, Minn. Milkweed Editions. 2004
6. Mary Oliver. *Blue Iris: Poems and Essays.* Boston. Beacon Press. 2004.

JORDIN ISIP

Bringing the Earth Home

Professional Development on Ecology

BY ANN PELO

I've been eager to engage the teachers at the childcare program where I work in reflection about environmental stewardship, consumption, and ecological justice. And I've wanted that reflection to have personal, as well as professional, resonance—to be more than an intellectual undertaking, but one that draws on and speaks to our lives beyond work.

In a recent staff meeting, I used Annie Leonard's short film, *The Story of Stuff*, to invite us into that reflection. The film traces the production of—well, stuff, from resource extraction to manufacturing to marketing to disposal. It's funny and sobering, and raises social and environmental issues about consumption and sustainability.

We began our staff meeting by watching *The Story of Stuff*. Folks' first responses were personal—thoughts about our own relationships with stuff, our consumption habits, our awareness of what we could be doing differently. We built on those initial responses by considering how our relationships with stuff show up in our work with children: What are we teaching children, either overtly or by our silences and inaction, about consumption and environmental stewardship? Teachers' comments were provocative and insightful:

> "We have the privilege of not being immediately impacted by the bad aspects of production and disposal: all of us—the kids and us teachers—live in a beautiful environment and are pretty much protected from seeing landfills and factories. When we don't raise the bigger

issues with kids, they get to live in a comfortable little bubble of privilege. Just like we get to, until things like this film wake us up."

"I think I'm making a good effort because I buy organic food and re-use my grocery bags. But I'm still complicit in the system if I don't burst through that bubble of privilege for myself and as a teacher with kids."

"There's a cold logic and intentionality to the system of production and marketing that really stands out in the film. We have to be *that* intentional about challenging it."

"It's painful to see images of environmental destruction; I don't want to make kids feel the despair that I feel when I look at polar bears stranded on floating bits of ice miles from land. I don't know how to raise environmental issues from a place of hope."

I decided to address the issue of despair by inviting us to articulate the ecological values that we want consciously to engage in our childcare program. I asked teachers to reframe the ideas they'd voiced as statements that began with the phrase, "We value______." People offered suggestions, and we talked together about them until we'd shaped them into statements that we embraced collectively. Here's a sampling:

We value raising issues of environmental stewardship and conservation with children—though we don't always know how. We want kids to be mindful of the earth and of stewardship, but not at the cost of their sense of playfulness and joy.

We value conservation of resources and we want to live in a way that acknowledges their scarcity. We want to think more about "need" and less about "want."

We value "reducing" more than "recycling." And we want to take care of what we have and use it well, for the long haul.

We value joyful, engaging experiences that aren't about "stuff" and want to put those kinds of experiences at the heart of our program.

We used these values, then, to brainstorm practices and actions that we might take up as a staff.

With and for the kids:

- Buy locally-grown produce.
- Talk with kids at lunch about where their food originated and all the people who worked to get it to their lunch.
- Institute a zero-waste lunch program.
- Get a yard waste container for Hilltop and begin composting.
- Have an event at which a week's collected garbage is weighed and sorted for what could have been recycled or re-used.
- Do regular critical thinking activities with the kids about media literacy and marketing.
- Invite kids to make toys for the room, instead of buying them: for example, dolls and stuffed animals, play houses and figurines.

For staff and families:

- Explore carpooling options for families and staff.
- Provide staff with bus passes.
- Buy staff and family appreciation gifts at local stores rather than at chains.

From that initial brainstorming, we chose several specific actions to take, and teachers stepped forward to spearhead those actions. Several teachers committed to launching a study group aimed at creating a zero-waste lunch program. A program administrator committed to setting up a place on our website where families and staff can post things that they're ready to give away. The union steward committed to bringing the need for bus passes for staff to the next round of union bargaining. And our cook committed to talking with local farms about buying our produce directly from them.

The Story of Stuff is easily available (it's free, online at www.storyofstuff.org); it's only about 20 minutes long, so it fits into an hour-long staff meeting with plenty of time left for discussion. It's been a powerful tool for the teachers with whom I work, giving us a shared reference for our ongoing critical thinking about consumption and about the practices we want to embrace, both personally and in our teaching.

Ann Pelo is an early childhood teacher and teacher mentor in Seattle, Wash.

MARILYN NOLT

Don't Know Much About Natural History

Education as a Barrier to Nature

BY RICHARD LOUV

> To a person uninstructed in natural history, his country or seaside stroll is a walk through a gallery filled with wonderful works of art, nine-tenths of which have their faces turned to the wall. —Thomas Huxley

David Sobel tells this story. A century ago, a boy ran along a beach with his gun, handmade from a piece of lead pipe. From time to time, he would stop, aim, and shoot at a gull. Today, such activity would be cause for time spent in juvenile hall, but for young John Muir, it was just another way to connect with nature. (Muir, it should be noted, was a bad shot, and apparently never killed a seagull.) Muir went on to become one of the initiators of modern environmentalism.

"Whenever I read Muir's description of shooting at seagulls to my students, they're shocked. They can't believe it," says Sobel, co-director of the Center for Place-based Education at Antioch New England Graduate School. He uses this example to illustrate just how much the interaction between children and nature has changed. Practitioners in the new fields of conservation psychology (focused on how people become environmentalists) and ecopsychology (the study of how ecology interacts with the human psyche) note that, as Americans become increasingly urbanized, their attitudes toward animals change in paradoxical ways.

To urbanized people, the source of food and the reality of nature are becoming more abstract. At the same time, urban folks are more likely to feel protective toward animals—or to fear them. The good news is that children today are less likely to kill animals for fun; the bad news is that children are so disconnected from nature that they either idealize it or associate it with fear—two sides of the same coin, since we tend to fear or romanticize what we don't know. Sobel, one of the most important thinkers in the realm of education and nature, views "ecophobia" as one of the sources of the problem.

Explaining Ecophobia

Ecophobia is fear of ecological deterioration, by Sobel's definition. In its older, more poetic meaning, the word ecophobia is the fear of home. Both definitions are accurate.

"Just as ethnobotanists are descending on tropical forests in search of new plants for medical uses, environmental educators, parents and teachers are descending on 2nd- and 3rd-graders to teach them about the rain forests," Sobel writes in his volume, *Beyond Ecophobia: Reclaiming the Heart in Nature Education.* "From Brattleboro, Vermont, to Berkeley, California, schoolchildren … watch videos about the plight of indigenous forest people displaced by logging and exploration for oil. They learn that between the end of morning recess and the beginning of lunch, more than 10,000 acres of rain forest will be cut down, making way for fast-food, 'hamburgerable' cattle."

In theory, these children "will learn that by recycling their *Weekly Readers* and milk cartons, they can help save the planet," and they'll grow up to be responsible stewards of the earth, "voting for environmental candidates, and buying energy-efficient cars." Or maybe not. The opposite may be occurring, says Sobel. "If we fill our classrooms with examples of environmental abuse, we may be engendering a subtle form of disassociation. In our zest for making them aware of and responsible for the world's problems, we cut our children off from their roots." Lacking direct experience with nature, children begin to associate it with fear and apocalypse, not joy and wonder. He offers this analogy of disassociation: In response to physical and sexual abuse, children learn to cut themselves off from pain. Emotionally, they turn off. "My fear is that our environmentally correct curriculum similarly ends up distancing children from, rather than connecting them with, the natural world. The natural world is being abused and they just don't want to have to deal with it."

To some environmentalists and educators, this is contrarian thinking—even blasphemy. To others, the ecophobia thesis rings true. Children learn about the rain forest, but usually not about their own region's forests, or, as Sobel puts it, "even just the meadow outside the classroom door." He points out that "it is hard enough for children to understand the life cycles of chipmunks and milkweed, organisms they can study close at hand. This is the foundation upon which an eventual understanding of ocelots and orchids can be built."

By one measure, a rain forest curriculum is developmentally appropriate in middle or high school, but not in the primary grades. Some educators won't go that far, but they do agree with Sobel's basic premise that environmental education is out of balance. This issue is the crux of the curriculum wars, particularly in the area of science. One teacher told me, "The science frameworks bandied about by state and local education boards have swung back and forth between the hands-on experiential approach and factoid learning from textbooks."

If educators are to help heal the broken bond between the young and the natural world, they and the rest of us must confront the unintended educational consequences of an overly abstract science education: ecophobia and the death of natural history studies. Equally important, the wave of test-based education reform that became dominant in the late 1990s leaves little room for hands-on experience in nature. Although some pioneering educators are sailing against the wind, participating in an international effort to stimulate the growth of nature education in and outside classrooms, many educational institutions and current educational trends are, in fact, part of the problem.

Surely children need a quality attachment to land not only for their own health, but in order to feel compelled to protect nature as adults—not only as common-sense conservationism, but as citizens and as voters.

For 25 years, psychologist Martha Farrell Erickson and her colleagues have used what they call "attachment theory," an ecological model of child development, as the framework for their ongoing longitudinal study of parent-child interaction. They apply those ideas to preventive intervention with parents in high-risk circumstances. The family's health, related to the health of the surrounding community, has become a growing concern to Erickson.

"The way we usually talk about parent-child attachment is that we rarely see the absence of attachment, even when the parents are unreliable, unresponsive, or erratically available. For example, a child with a parent who is chronically unresponsive (let's say a depressed parent, for example) will protect himself from the pain of rejection by detaching, acting disinterested in the parent—developing what we call an anxious– avoidant attachment."

I suggested to her that some of the same response or symptoms associated with attachment deficit occur with a poor sense of attachment to land. In my own experiment, the rate of development in my part of the country is so fast that attachment to place is difficult; to many of us who came here decades ago (in my case from Kansas), Southern California captures the body, but not the heart. In the world of child development, attachment theory posits that the creation of a deep bond between child and parent is a complex psychological, biological, and spiritual process, and that without this attachment a child is lost, vulnerable to all manner of later pathologies. I believe that a similar process can bind adults to a place and give them a sense of belonging and meaning. Without a deep attachment to place, an adult can also feel lost.

MARILYN NOLT

"It's an intriguing idea to approach a child's relationship with nature from the perspective of attachment theory," Erickson said. She continued:

> Children's experience with the natural world seems to be overlooked to a large extent in research on child development, but it would be interesting to examine children's early experiences with nature and follow how those experiences influence the child's long-term comfort with and respect for the natural world—comfort and respect being concepts that are central to the study of parent-child attachment. Given the power of nature to calm and soothe us in our hurried lives, it would be interesting to study how a family's connection to nature influences the general quality of family relationships. Speaking from personal experience, my own family's relationships have been nourished over the years through shared experiences in nature—from sharing our toddler's wonder upon turning over a rock and discovering a magnificent bug the size of a mouse, to paddling our old canoe down a nearby creek during the children's school years, to hiking the mountains.

Attachment to land is not only good for the child, but good for the land as well. As naturalist Robert Finch asserts: "There is a point … in our relationship with a place, when, in spite of ourselves, we realize we do not care so much anymore, when we begin to be convinced, against our very wills, that our neighborhood, our town, or the land as a whole is already lost." At this point, he argues, the local landscape is no longer perceived as "a living, breathing, beautiful counterpart to human existence, but something that has suffered irreversible brain death. It may still be kept technically alive—with sewage treatment plants, 'compensatory' wetlands, shellfish reseeding programs, lime treatments for acidified ponds, herbicides for ... ponds, beach nourishment programs, fenced-off bird sanctuaries, and designated 'green areas'—but it no longer moves, or if it does, it is not with a will of its own."

If a geographic place rapidly changes in a way that demeans its natural integrity, then children's early attachment to land is at risk. If children do not attach to the land, they will not reap the psychological and spiritual benefits they can glean from nature, nor will they feel a long-term commitment to the environment, to the place. This lack of attachment will exacerbate the very conditions that created the sense of disengagement in the first place—fueling a tragic spiral, in which our children and the natural world are increasingly detached.

I am not suggesting the situation is hopeless. Far from it. Conservation and environmental groups and, in some cases, the traditional Scouting organizations, are beginning to awaken to the threat to nature posed by nature-deficit disorder. A few of these organizations are helping to lead the way toward a nature-child reunion. They recognize that while knowledge about nature is vital, passion is the long-distance fuel for the struggle to save what is left of our natural heritage and—through an emerging green urbanism—to reconstitute lost land and water. Passion does not arrive on videotape or on a CD; passion is personal. Passion is lifted from the earth itself by the muddy hands of the young; it travels along grass-stained sleeves to the heart. If we are going to save environmentalism and the environment, we must also save an endangered indicator species: the child in nature.

Adapted from *Last Child in the Woods* by Richard Louv. ©2005 by Richard Louv. Reprinted by permission of Algonquin Books of Chapel Hill.

Richard Louv is an author and journalist focused on nature, family and community. He serves as chairman of the Children & Nature Network, an organization helping to build the international movement to connect children with nature. He also serves as honorary co-chair of The National Forum on Children and Nature. Louv is working on his eighth book.

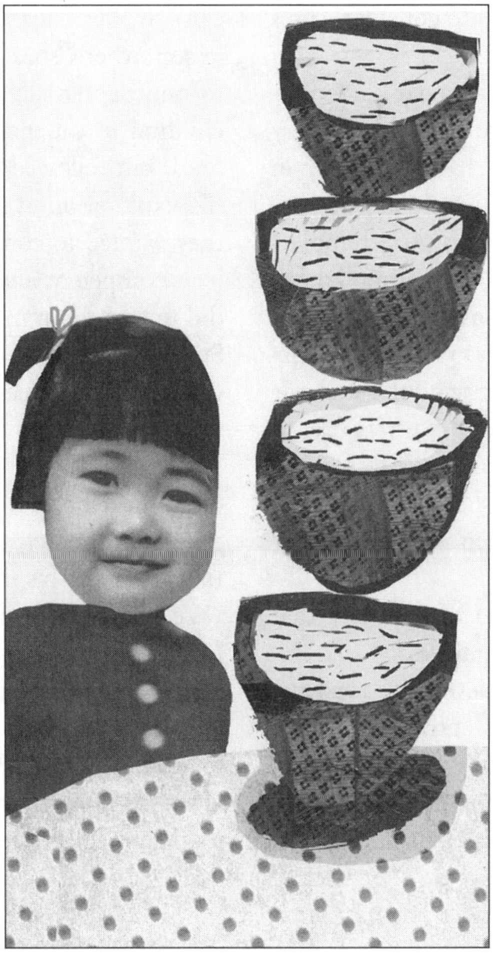
KATHERINE STREETER

Food Is Not for Play

BY *JEAN HANNON*

Not everyone's mealtimes look like mine. There will not necessarily be enough food tomorrow.

Food is not for play.

These are the lessons I learned from Ana*, and this is how she taught me:

Five-year-old Ana entered our classroom and went immediately to the large container of plastic snow play toys. She retrieved the dish-like items (recycled yogurt and applesauce containers) and meticulously placed them all in a neat row. Then Ana moved down the line of dishes carrying a much larger container and a makeshift ladle. She painstakingly scooped something invisible (to me) into each smaller container.

I understood that Ana was playing her version of "house"; she was dramatizing mealtime at the orphanage in northern China where she had spent most of her young life. Ana had moved to her new home and new family only three weeks before joining our classroom.

Harrison, a classmate, quickly learned that the simplest and most effective way to terrorize Ana was to make lunging gestures toward her open lunch box. Harrison never actually took any of Ana's carefully packaged and abundant lunchbox contents. But he intimidated Ana with the idea that he could take her food. Ana would cry, Ana's new friends would scold Harrison, and he would smirk. As I soothed Ana, I would talk to Harrison and encourage him to consider Ana's perspective.

Not all of the learning centers in our kindergarten classroom were available to the children every day. Some I kept for "special." It was a Friday in February and the children stood around one particular center in acute anticipation. As I removed the cover from the sensory table, Ana shrank back in horror. I had presented the class with a play area filled with rice. In it was enough to feed how many for how long? And I was encouraging the students to stick their hands into that food, to measure, to manipulate, to play! The look on Ana's face at the moment I lifted that cover and she first understood what I was suggesting has not left me in the intervening 10 years.

That experience helped me to conclude that using food for art or play is misguided.

Young children mostly believe their teachers. They believe that their teachers know a great deal and are generally truthful. Young children repeat their teachers' platitudes and embrace their classroom gestures. When young children play school they model their dramatic behavior after that of their teachers, and their imitative play is often embarrassingly accurate.

I have come to realize just how confusing my use of food for play and art was, not only for Ana, but for all my young students. While we collected cans of food "for the hungry," I also facilitated a lesson where students glued beans to cardboard to outline the letters of their names. I nagged the children to eat their lunches and not throw away food, but followed it by encouraging them in tactile exploration at the rice table. Perhaps because they wanted to continue feeling safe and cared for by a competent and thoughtful adult, the children did not question my particular brand of hypocrisy. Still, how could they not have been confused by the discrepancy between what I said about the value of food and the other lessons I provided?

Several things were inherent in my lessons: a disconnect between consumers, food, food workers, and ultimately the earth itself, a finite resource. Inherent also was the message of "them" and "us." "We" have enough and we can therefore waste. "They" do not have enough and must rely on the more fortunate and/or capable us.

I believe guilt is a useless emotion unless it leads to change. Ana's lessons forced me to reevaluate and change my teaching practice: In our classroom food is no longer part of our art or play. ■

* Names have been changed.

Jean Hannon retired from the primary classroom in 2008 and plans for the next chapter of her life to be just as fulfilling as teaching.

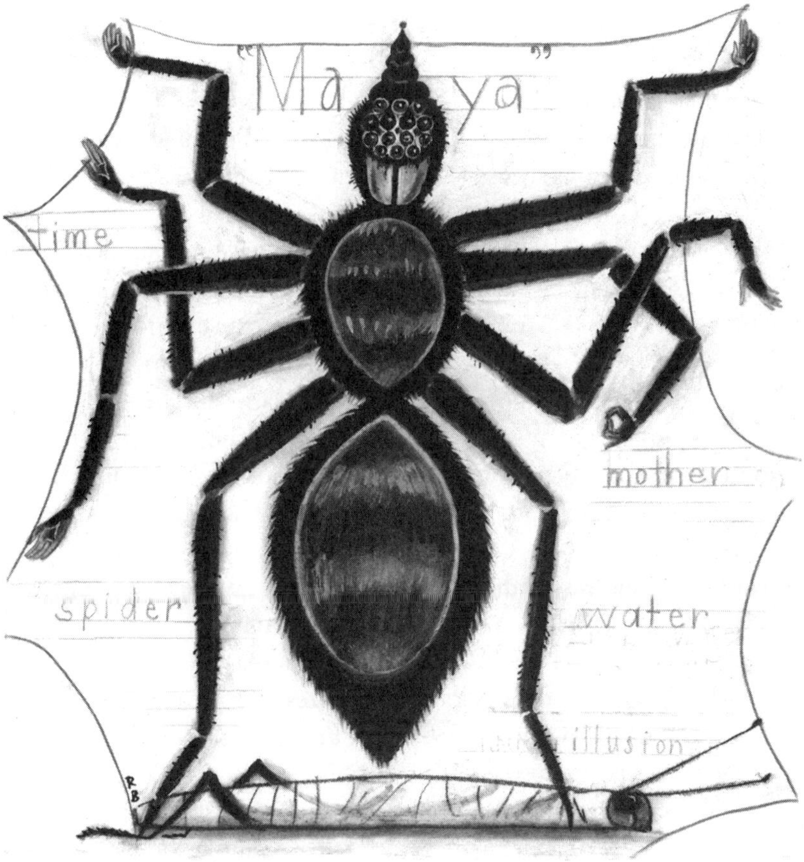

ROXANNA BIKADOROFF

Lessons from a Garden Spider

How Charlotte Transformed My Classroom

BY KATE LYMAN

"You're the best teacher in the whole world," said Maisee,* as she hugged me. Actually, it wasn't I who was "the best teacher," it was our new guest, a strikingly beautiful black and yellow garden spider.

Juan had found the spider in the bushes outside our classroom door, and I had set her on a wooden frame on a bookcase in my 3rd-grade classroom. Overnight, she had made a dazzling symmetrical orb web. My students watched in amazement as the spider pounced on a grasshopper and quickly wrapped it in silk. The "awesome!"s soon overtook the "ewww!"s as the students watched the spider feast on the grasshopper's blood.

In the few weeks that Charlotte (as my students named her) graced my classroom, the students learned many lessons from her. They learned about the web of life, the interdependence of predator and prey. Many changed their relationship to spiders from one of fear to one of respect.

They learned about the sad, yet ever-renewing cycle of life. They also learned many facts about spiders, their body structures, and their different habitats and mechanisms of survival. And in a world that will lose about a quarter of its wildlife in the next decade, I believe that observing and caring for one single spider helped us bridge the gap between the human and natural worlds.

Charlotte was an excellent team teacher. How could she have known that I had planned to do a lesson on food webs on the day that she first demonstrated her insect trapping skills to us? (*See sidebar.*)

As I watched my students hard at work on creating food web drawings, I thanked Charlotte for having provided a real-life demonstration of the concept. Teaching through words—even with the aid of illustrations in books—just didn't work with this class where 10 out of 14 of my students were learning English as a second language. (Six had Spanish as a first language, two had Hmong, one Khmer, and one Albanian.)

My classroom reflects the increasing diversity and pockets of poverty in areas of Madison, Wisconsin, a city commonly thought of as a white,well-off university town. About 65 percent of my school's families live on incomes below the poverty level, and 74 percent are from minority groups (mainly African American, Latino, and Hmong), with 33 percent designated as English Language Learners (ELLs). Some of the ELLs receive daily in-classroom support during the hour reading block and also for a few more hours a week during math and science instruction. However, the ESL teacher has to divide her time among three classrooms, all with a high percentage of ELLs, so the support cannot begin to meet every student's individual needs.

Not surprisingly, as the school year began, only five of my students were reading at grade level, and they all scored low on district tests. As I went over my class's test scores with my principal, I was reminded that more tests were looming: the 3rd-grade writing sample and the Wisconsin Third Grade Reading Test. I thought of all the standards that I was expected to meet.

I felt overwhelmed by the challenge of meeting the standards and bringing my students' test scores up while at the same time making school meaningful for them and inspiring them to learn.

The challenge of teaching diverse learners is multiplied by the testing regimens and the standards that give teachers little freedom to adapt the content and methods of their teaching to meet their students' needs. For example, our district now requires us to teach science through "FOSS" (Full Option Science System, developed by the University of California at Berkeley and published by Delta Education). It's a packaged program, complete with teacher training videos, step-by-step lessons, and packaged materials. We are supposed to teach science exclusively through FOSS and strictly adhere to the format of its lessons.

FOSS does have some advantages: Teachers find it helpful for teaching an area of science in which they may not have expertise. It also provides a structure and materials for beginning teachers. But many

Hands-On Learning: The Food Web

First I read aloud the book *Butternut Hollow Pond*, by Brian Heinz, which is about food webs. I asked for volunteers to act out the animals' actions as they captured and ate their prey. Next I handed each student a card with a drawing of a living thing on it. (Another teacher and I drew some pictures or copied them from other materials.) My cards included a blue heron, a leopard frog, grass, fungi, and a garden spider and a grasshopper. I chose a student to hold a ball of yarn and, while holding onto the end of the yarn, threw the yarn to his or her "predator."

The game went on, as the yarn was tossed from frog to heron to grass (representing death) to fungi to grasshopper to spider to frog, and so on, until all the students were holding pieces of yarn. The yarn crisscrossed the circle and formed a web of life.

When our web was completed, I asked students to predict what would happen if pesticide wiped out all the grasshoppers and other insects that the spiders ate.

"The spiders would die!" several students responded.

"And then the frogs wouldn't have enough food," added another. I asked all the students holding the grasshopper cards to drop their piece of yarn and they watched the web fall apart. Then the students went to work on drawing and labeling a spider's food web.

For instructions on how to build a frame for a spider web, see rethinkingschools.org/static/publication/rece/WebWork.pdf of us dislike the packaged, scripted manner in which FOSS is presented. I think it doesn't provide enough opportunities for the students to engage in genuine inquiry. I have found the FOSS units relating to natural science particularly objectionable.

For instance, the 3rd-grade FOSS "Structures of Life" kit attempts to teach some of the same concepts that Charlotte and I were introducing, but they remove living creatures from their natural habitats and use them as subjects of experimentation. One lesson I taught in this FOSS module explored the concept of habitat through crayfish that came shipped in bo xes (many dead on arrival). We were supposed to store them in plastic dishpans, with plastic bowls for their "shelters," and feed them aquatic plants and cat food.

The plastic bowls proved to be a very unsuitable habitat, as the crayfish proceeded to eat each other. This wasn't part of the planned FOSS curriculum, but the students and I discovered through further research a fact that was only briefly mentioned in my guide. When crayfish molt, they need to hide under rocks until their shells harden. Otherwise, they fall victim to predators, which, in our inadequate habitat, turned out to be other crayfish. This in itself would have been a great opportunity for further exploration. Looking back, I wish I had pursued the matter further. I could have encouraged the students to write to the creators of FOSS. At the time, I was happy only to separate the crayfish that had molted and to spare my students from coming to school to discover more half-eaten bodies.

Further on in the module (which, after the crayfish disaster, I decided to skip) students are directed to "harness" snails with thread and duct tape and attach the thread to paper clips and metric weights. The expressed aim of the lesson—"to investigate the pulling strength of land snails"—seemed to be in direct conflict with the first goal presented in the introduction to the kit, to "develop an attitude of respect for life."

I read through this lesson several times with horror. I could not figure out its purpose. When students are finished with the snail experiments, teachers are advised (if they cannot keep the snails or find another teacher who needs to use them) to "euthanize" the snails by putting them in a freezer. ("Terminate" is the euphemism used in other FOSS kits containing living creatures.) The FOSS guide warns teachers that students might ask where the snails went. Its recommendation? "Tell them that you returned them to the place where they came from. Let them extract from that what they will."

Charlotte, on the other hand, was a respected guest in our classroom. My class knew that she was borrowed from the bushes outside our classroom and that our plan was to return her. Never once did I see a student poke at her or disrupt her web creations. When students from other classrooms or my students' brothers and sisters came to visit Charlotte, my students taught them how to treat Charlotte with respect. My class became concerned about our spider's welfare at our school's Open House, when many families would be visiting with younger children.

Emily volunteered to write a warning note, which she taped to the bookcase:

> Charlotte here! This is a garden spider. The garden spider's name is Charlotte. Don't move the bookcase or the spider might fall. Charlotte is very kind. Do not touch her web. She made it to catch flies for our classroom. Don't take nothing from the bookcase. Don't touch the spider or she thinks you will hurt her. Please stay back. And her favorite food is grasshoppers.

In the next several weeks, as we continued to observe Charlotte, we learned about many different kinds of spiders through books and videos. Juan, a low reader and extremely reluctant writer, went through a small transformation after finding Charlotte. Even the teacher across the hall remarked at how he came to school every day with a smile on his face. Every day during independent reading time, I'd find Juan reading spider books. And now he was writing four or five sentences at a time about spiders.

We learned about a garden spider's life cycle. Charlotte again came through by laying her eggs and weaving an egg sac. There was some controversy over what to do with the egg sac.

"Let's keep it in our room," suggested Chou. "Then in the spring, we'll have a whole bunch of baby spiders in our room!"

"No!" protested several students. Much as they appreciated Charlotte's company, several objected to having hundreds of spiders running around our classroom. Lilly suggested we place the egg sac back on the bushes where Juan found Charlotte so her babies would be born there. But other students worried that kids from the school might disturb the egg sac. Eventually, we agreed to bring the egg sac to the Aldo Leopold Center, a nature preserve that we had visited on a class field trip.

Charlotte's Exit

The students knew from our studies that after creating her egg sac, the garden spider dies. At the start of every day they ran over to the wooden frame to see how Charlotte was faring. She surprised us by weaving a few more webs and continuing to eat grasshoppers. But then she moved to the corner of the frame and stayed there for several days.

What Rosita wrote at that point proved that my students' connection with Charlotte transcended language barriers. Rosita is able to read and write in Spanish but knows only a few words in English. Because most of the instruction is in English, Rosita rarely appeared to be paying attention. But she was paying attention to Charlotte.

This is what Rosita contributed to our class newsletter:

> Tenemos una araña en la clase que se llama Charlotte. Es una araña de jardín. Ella atrapó saltamontes y los envolvió con su teleraña. Charlotte ya tuvo sus huevos. Charlotte hizo una bolsita para que los metiera sus huevos. Charlotte ya no está en la tela que hizo. Charlotte está en la esquina. Charlotte ya no tiene el color amarillo. Ahora el color que tiene es gris. Charlotte no se mueve de su telaraña. Charlotte se va a morir cuando nacen los huevos.

> We have a spider in the class whose name is Charlotte. She is a garden spider. She caught grasshoppers and wrapped them with her web. Charlotte already laid her eggs. Charlotte made a little bag to put her eggs in. Charlotte is no longer in the web that she made. She is in the corner. Charlotte is no longer yellow. She is gray. She doesn't move from her web. Charlotte is going to die when her babies are born.

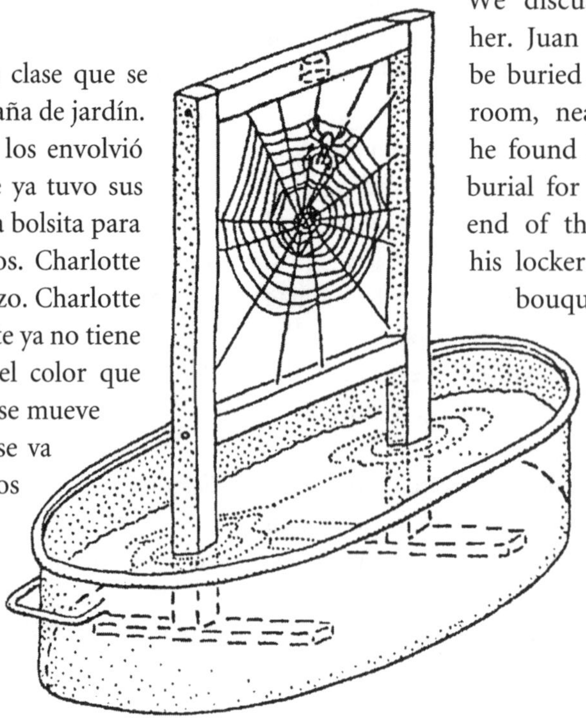

Rosita's observations were borne out the next morning.

"Oh no, Charlotte is dying!" moaned Maisee.

"Look at her color. She is turning gray," noted Chou.

"She's getting smaller," said Juan. "Why is she getting smaller?" Several students gently touched Charlotte.

"She is officially dead," concluded Lilly. Several moans and many sighs followed.

"Our only spider!" said Maisee.

"She was a good trapper," added Emily. "We will need to bury her."

Emily put herself in charge of the funeral arrangements, labeling a small casket (an earring box), "Are best friend." Emily and Maisee drew pictures of Charlotte to be placed by her grave. Lilly wrote her gravestone inscription: "Here Lays Charlotte. Room 27's Spider!" We discussed where to bury her. Juan said that she should be buried outside of our classroom, near the bushes where he found her. We planned the burial for the next day. At the end of the day, Chou ran to his locker and pulled a wilted bouquet of purple flowers from his backpack. Selfishly mistaking his intentions, I took the bouquet and thanked him. "Are they from your garden?" I asked. "Yes," he answered. Then he added shyly, "They're for Charlotte's grave."

The next day, we had Charlotte's funeral. Twice, by student request, we passed the box around the circle as students gravely inspected the dead spider. That afternoon, the class watched as I dug a hole and placed the box under the dirt. Lilly taped her grave marker to a tongue depressor and placed it in the dirt. Emily and Maisee added pictures that they had drawn of Charlotte. "So we'll always remember her," said Maisee. Denitra thanked Charlotte for being part of our class. "Thank you for teaching us how you spin webs and how you catch grasshoppers. You were a nice spider. We will miss you." We went around the circle. One student at a time thanked Charlotte.

Denitra asked to speak again, "And I hope your babies will be born here and make their own webs."

I have no doubt that Charlotte helped teach my class our district's science standards relating to "characteristics of organisms" and "life cycles of organisms."

She also engaged my students in learning and inspired them to expand their reading and writing abilities. Even after her burial, students continued to write about Charlotte.

Charlotte has even helped me teach multiplication, since story problems about multiple legs have endless possibilities.

Beyond Charlotte

Moving on from studying spiders to insects, we compared the body structures, behaviors, and life cycles of a variety of insects. Although I used some lesson plans and student sheets from FOSS, we observed the insects in the schoolyard and only borrowed living things that we could return.

We did not limit our studies of insects to observations and worksheets. Instead we learned and shared our learning through literature and videos, visual arts, music, and drama.

As the weather got colder, I continued to have guest animals in my classroom. But they were homeless companion animals from the Humane Society instead of wild creatures. Most of my students lived in apartments and few could have pets, so the opportunity to get acquainted with and care for a pet was a unique and exciting experience for them. (I was the only one with allergy problems.)

We further explored life cycles as we examined human beings from birth to death, and we shared and wrote about our own personal and cultural histories. We continued our examination of nature's cycles by studying the moon and its phases.

Later in the year, we returned to topics relating to life and environmental science. Charlotte taught my class to care deeply about the fate of one spider. I saw how those feelings transferred to their research about and advocacy for endangered species.

Charlotte also taught me many lessons. She taught me not to underestimate my students. They did improve their reading and writing. They did make progress in learning multiplication and mastering science concepts.

With motivation, trust, and classroom experiences that touch them as deeply as Charlotte did, my students will learn. As our spider's namesake in E.B. White's book points out, spiders are "naturally patient." They know that if they construct a well-designed web and wait long enough, their efforts will pay off. Teachers have a lot to learn from spiders. ■

* Names have been changed.

Kate Lyman has taught kindergarten through 3rd grade in public schools in Madison, Wis., for 33 years. She has done graduate work in multicultural education and in teaching English as a second language at the University of Wisconsin.

Part V

Emphasize children's social-emotional learning.

"Children can awaken in us an understanding of what it means to be inventive, engaged, delighted, and determined to rearrange the world. If we listen to and watch them closely, they will teach us to be more observant, inquisitive, and responsive in our work and in our lives."

Deb Curtis and Margie Carter
The Art of Awareness

JAQUAN FLEMING, MENDOTA GRADE SCHOOL, MADISON, WIS.

Holding Nyla

Lessons from an Inclusion Classroom

BY *KATIE KISSINGER*

Nyla came into our Head Start classroom wheeled by her special assistant and surrounded by three early intervention (EI) specialists. I could barely see her for the equipment, adults, and silence that encapsulated her.

Nyla had "severely involved" cerebral palsy. In addition to muscle dysfunction, she had orthopedic impairment, vision impairment, and was medically fragile. Her "feeding regimen" and "handling regimen" both involved technical training.

I was completely overwhelmed. My Head Start class had just merged with the early intervention program. It was 1992, and we were embarking on our first experience with inclusion classrooms, and although Nyla's special assistant and her three EI specialists had all been through the necessary training, I was one of her classroom teachers and I was intimidated.

Realities of Inclusion

The model we developed for our newly formed Head Start service was to merge the traditional "handicapped preschool," which had been serving all of the children ages 3 to 5 with disabilities, with typically developing low-income Head Start children, also ages 3 to 5.

The special education teachers and the early childhood teachers merged into a classroom team of four to plan for and address the needs of all the children.

I mostly loved the *idea* of inclusion. I had been struggling to teach about diversity and social justice in a northeastern corner of Oregon where there was almost no racial, linguistic, or economic status diversity. I thought including kids with disabilities in our classroom would help the preschoolers make meaningful connections with people who are different from them. I had no clue what we were getting into.

Facing Fears

After the second week of school, I have a tradition of spending the weekend thinking of each child in my class. I review what I learned about them, what I want to learn more about, and the ways I am beginning to feel connected to them. When I thought of Nyla, I drew a blank: a blank instead of a child with an emerging story, instead of a smile or a funny anecdote. I was surprised at myself, mad at myself, disappointed in myself. How could I have a child in my classroom for two weeks and not have one story or even an irritation to reflect on? What was this really about?

Then I had a memory. The summer I turned 5, my family went on our annual family vacation to visit relatives in Colorado. We went to the nursing home to see my Great-Granddaddy Greenwell. We had on our church clothes. It was hot, and my brothers and I were grouchy about having to dress up.

Almost 50 years later, I can still remember the odor when we walked through the doors of the nursing home. We hovered in the hallway and eventually saw a nurse wheeling Great-Grandpa toward us. He was a tall man, more than six feet, but in the wheelchair, he looked old, very wrinkled, and very scary to me. And he smelled even worse than the hallway. As the only girl child in our family, I suddenly became the designated representative. "Go hug Great-Granddaddy Greenwell," someone said. I took one trembling step forward and then whirled around and ran toward the door.

Recalling that memory, it struck me: That was the only close encounter I had ever had with a person using a wheelchair in my entire life up to that point. I was avoiding Nyla because I was afraid. It may sound odd, but once I realized this, I knew what to do. I had faced fears before.

On Monday morning, I went into the classroom and told the early intervention team that I wanted to take both the handling and feeding trainings for Nyla's caregiving. I completed both of those, but I had serious doubts when they introduced the feeding topic by telling us how many children had died in feeding incidents the prior year. When I was approved for safe caregiving, I asked the specialists if I could get Nyla out of her wheelchair and hold her for circle time. They were hesitant because this was not standard practice but decided we could try it.

As soon as I had Nyla in my arms, my relationship with her began. From that day on, for circle time, Nyla was either in my arms or in her "corner chair," which put her on the same level as the other seated children.

As soon as I changed my behavior and began a relationship with Nyla, the other children began to see her as a classmate. I have never had a clearer lesson about the power of the teacher as a role model.

Our class talked often about all of Nyla's equipment. The kids were really interested in her wheelchair and all of the equipment she used. We all talked together each time she used a different piece of equipment or if we were going to try to make her safe and comfortable on any of the traditional "toys" like the wagon and the wheelbarrow. And because holding her involved keeping her muscles supported, we looked at the ways her wheelchair and other pieces supported her muscles, including her footrest.

We began to address the ways her equipment got in the way of her connection to the other children. I started asking questions like, "Can't she be at the table with everyone else?" "Can't she stay in the room for this exercise and invite other kids to join her?" "Can't she ride in the wagon or wheelbarrow instead of the wheelchair when we play outside?"

Sometimes those questions led to my education about her fragile muscle system. Other times they led to the EI/special ed team's education about the value of Nyla's relationship to the other children or to play. These conversations and experiences transformed us all.

Questioning Injustice

After learning how to integrate Nyla and other special-needs children into the classroom community, we found that our inclusive classroom provided opportunities for students to question and address things that are unfair in the world.

For example, we ordered a set of rubber people dolls for children to play with in the dollhouse. We were all excited when we found the Lakeshore Learning Materials Company sold dolls that represented people with disabilities. When the toys arrived, we brought the boxes to circle time and opened them up together. Joshua unwrapped a man in a wheelchair. He exclaimed, "Here he is, the guy with the wheelchair just like Nyla's." Josh passed the doll around the circle and when Mikey got it, he said, "Wait a minute. There's a problem. This guy's feet don't reach the footrest on his wheelchair."

Sure enough, there was about a half-inch gap between the guy's feet and the footrests.

Another student said, "That would make his legs really tired, if they couldn't rest."

"What could we do about this problem? How could we make this work?" I asked.

"Let's look at Nyla's chair and see how it works first," said Mikey.

Then another child shouted, "What if we make a wood block to put in the hole between his feet and the foot rest?"

Several kids went scurrying over to the woodworking table and grabbed small scraps of wood. We were eventually able to craft a little wooden filler for the gap. The children were delighted with their invention and very pleased that the "guy" now could sit comfortably in his wheelchair.

I wanted to take things one step further, so the next day I asked the children, "Do you think we should tell the company about the problem we found with the guy's wheelchair?" They all agreed that we should. I set up our flip chart so I could write down their ideas. "What should we tell them?" I asked.

"Tell them it's stupid to make a chair that doesn't work," said Josh.

"Dear Mr. Lakeshore, that's a bad wheelchair you made," added another child.

"How about making better wheelchairs for kids to play with?" someone asked.

"We're not paying for this wheelchair because it's broke," Marisa declared.

Nyla was there in the circle, and although she did not have any formal expressive language at that point, she showed her excitement by squealing.

Eventually we wrote a letter to Lakeshore, saying we thought they made a mistake. We sent them a picture of our redesigned wheelchair and asked them if they knew how uncomfortable their wheelchair would be. We also said that we would not be buying more Lakeshore toys until they fixed this problem. We all went together to the post office to mail the letter, Nyla leading the way in her wheelchair with Mikey, the proud young engineer, helping to push her.

By the way, we never got a response from Lakeshore, but they have now fixed the gap problem with the wheelchairs.

Another day, our class started out on a field trip to the local feed store. It was a trip we had made the year before and loved. When we arrived, I had the horrifying realization that Nyla would not be able to visit the second floor, which had all the great farm tools. (This was part of our machines study.) I gathered up the children and said, "I just realized that I made a really big mistake. I forgot that this store does not have wheelchair access to the second floor."

I was going to ask the children what they thought we should do when one of the children interrupted me and said, "No, Katie. The store guy made a big mistake. He didn't think we would be friends with Nyla, but we are. And we're mad, because if she can't go, we're not going." Needless to say, we wrote another letter.

Nyla's Best Friend

In the process of developing the inclusion model, there was a great deal of questioning and, in some cases, trepidation on the part of parents. Nyla's mother, in particular, had expressed concerns about Nyla leaving the "handicapped preschool." She was used to working with the EI team and reluctant to have her daughter in a Head Start classroom. She wondered how Nyla's needs and safety could be ensured with so many other children in the classroom. And she wondered how Nyla's classmates would respond to her.

We were not always able to answer these questions to Nyla's mom's satisfaction. After about five months of indecision, she decided to pull Nyla out of the program. When we could not talk her out of her decision, I asked that we at least have a few days of closure and time for the children to say their goodbyes. It was a very hard few days.

On the last afternoon, Nyla's mother came to pick her up as we were finishing our "goodbye circle," where the child who is leaving sits in the middle of the circle and each person takes a turn saying what they like about the person and what they will miss when they're gone. It is always both a heartwarming and heartwrenching ceremony. This one was particularly wrenching.

Andy, a student who had overcome initial fear of Nyla's differences, got up from his seated space, knelt by Nyla and said, "Nyla, you are my best friend. I love you and I don't want you to go." I heard the classroom door close and when I looked up through my tears, I saw that Nyla's mom was gone. One of the other teachers came over to me and whispered, "She has changed her mind."

Later, Nyla's mom told me that in her wildest dreams, she had never believed that Nyla would have a best friend. And she was moved to see a whole classroom of children welcoming her daughter into their community.

I made important discoveries in those first years of working in an inclusion classroom. By facing my own fears and connecting with Nyla, I became a better role model for my students, who quickly grew to love and accept her. I realized that solidarity is something we can nurture from the youngest ages. ■

Katie Kissinger is an early childhood education consultant, adjunct faculty member, social justice activist, and author.

Fairness First

Learning from Martin Luther King Jr. and Ruby Bridges

BY *STEPHANIE WALTERS*

It was story time and my 1st-graders and I were reading the book *Virgie Goes to School with Us Boys.* Set in the South shortly after the Civil War, it is about a young girl whose parents do not want to send her to school. One of my students raised her hand and asked, "Ms. Walters, how can they do that? We know that isn't fair."

I explained that Virgie's parents did not think she was ready to make the long trek to school and that a century ago, many people believed girls would not benefit from learning in the same way as boys. And I felt cautiously optimistic that this student was transferring her understanding from a unit we had done on "fairness" to our everyday shared reading.

When I decided to teach a social studies unit on "fairness" as a jumping-off point for talking about justice, I was conflicted.

On the one hand, I believe it is important for young children to understand they have a role in creating a more just society—and that children have been present in movements to stamp out injustice, with the Civil Rights Movement and the anti-apartheid movement in South Africa being just two examples.

On the other hand, I lacked confidence that the unit could be a success. Although I had good rapport with my 16 students, all of them African Americans like myself, I was new to teaching 1st grade. I was not convinced I could convey the concepts that would get across my two key goals. My first goal was to help my students understand that children can work for change despite their ages. My second goal was to underscore that fairness and justice are not just global concepts, but that students can take action in their own corner of the world to right wrongs.

I was also nervous because my social studies curriculum and teacher's guide had nothing whatsoever on this topic; I knew I would have to develop all the materials myself. It would have been so much easier to have done a unit on "goods and services," since all the materials I needed were in the teacher's guide.

After reflection, I decided to go ahead with the unit on fairness and justice. I kept reminding myself that it's OK to stray from the pre-packaged curriculum.

Classroom Community

Since the beginning of the school year, I had tried to build a sense of community in our classroom. For example, we held daily meetings where we shared what was going on in our lives. The students paired up and told each other what they did the night before and what they planned to do after school. We then wrote a summary of these "news" reports, with each person reporting on their partner's news. (I modeled several times for my students what it would look and sound like to be eager, respectful listeners.) We had also done lessons about friendship and had begun a reading buddy program with a 4th-grade classroom.

In addition, we often talked openly in class about why some people are treated differently than others. I didn't pretend to know why, but I think it is important to be honest about the fact, since my students will face prejudice and racism during their lives.

I knew my students were aware of the ideas "fair" and "unfair" and decided to start the two-week unit with those concepts rather than the words "justice" and "injustice."

In our first lesson, we discussed what it meant to be fair. I wrote their answers on a piece of chart paper labeled, "Fairness."

"Letting everyone get a turn," was Tammy's example.

"Sharing your toys with your friends," was Bryan's idea.

Andre's contribution was that we have to make sure everyone has room in the circle.

I took down more of their examples, but I was a little concerned. My students were not giving the answers I wanted, which were answers dealing with the concept of "justice" in a broader social context. I took a step back and realized my expectations were unrealistic, and that my students' answers were important because they were from their own experiences and set the stage for deeper understandings as they mature.

We repeated the exercise with a paper headed, "Unfairness."

"Not letting someone play with your favorite game," Quincy said.

"Pushing in front of somebody in line," was Nathaniel's suggestion.

"Not letting other children play with you or come to your birthday party with you because of the way they look," said Inez.

While I appreciated all the responses, Inez's answer excited me. It began to get at the idea that whether people are treated "fairly" or not is not necessarily random or arbitrary, but may be related to something about the person's identity. And because I did not have to explain what she meant to the other students, I was hopeful that my students might intuitively have a deeper understanding of the concept of "fairness" than I had originally credited them for.

At the end of this first lesson I asked my students, "Are people always fair? What should we do when we see people treated unfairly?"

They were stumped by the questions but I was encouraged enough overall to move on.

Young Martin Luther King Jr.

I then tried to make the bridge from "fair" and "unfair" to "justice" and "injustice"—which, even for older students, is somewhat of a stretch. Although the transition was not always smooth, I wanted to move beyond "unfair" in the individual sense of being pushed around on the playground, to issues such as discrimination and prejudice on a social level.

I proceeded to do two lessons on Martin Luther King Jr. Immediately, I had doubts. Was King the right choice? Would it be better to focus on a leader who does not get such attention? Still, I forged ahead. For one thing, I had several high-quality, age-appropriate books about King. Second, because they were only 1st-graders, I didn't think my students had been exposed that much to King.

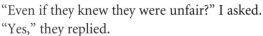

I also wanted to look at King's life from the perspective of his early years, when he was not much older than my students, and explore how those experiences might have helped make him a warrior for justice and peace.

I asked students what they knew about Dr. King. In essence, they knew he was a black man who worked for peace and that he had died. They knew nothing of King's childhood days in Atlanta, Ga., and were excited as I read to them from *The Young Martin Luther King Jr.: "I Have a Dream."* One story, for example, told of young Martin riding the city bus in Atlanta when a white woman boarded the bus and demanded his seat. When he stood up for his rights and refused, she slapped him. My students were appalled.

"How could she do that?" one of them wanted to know.

I asked, "That wasn't fair, was it?" All emphatically said no.

I asked them to draw a picture showing what would have been fair, and they were eager to share their drawings.

"This is Martin Luther King sitting down and this is that lady standing up, because he should not have to get up just because she is white," Stephan said in explaining his picture.

Some students were able to write down by themselves what their picture said to them. For students who had not yet reached this level, I wrote what they said on a note card.

I asked my students what they would have done if they had been in young Martin's shoes. It was a difficult question for them. I also explained to them it was not until King became a grown-up that he began to work to change things for African Americans in the United States.

Then I posed a question that was key to my goal for the unit: "Do you think that young children can help to change things in our world that are not fair?"

Only two of my students answered yes. This surprised me, since we had just discussed the story of young Martin. When I pressed them on why they felt that way, one student said that kids were just too young to do anything. They did not know enough to change things that were unfair.

"Even if they knew they were unfair?" I asked.

"Yes," they replied.

Ruby Bridges

Then we read *The Story of Ruby Bridges* and *Through My Eyes* (the autobiography of Ruby Bridges).

In 1960, Ruby Bridges became the first African American to attend William Frantz Elementary School in New Orleans, following court-ordered desegregation. In reading the books, my students heard about a 6-year-old girl (the same age as many of them) who stared down angry white mobs in order to help desegregate the New Orleans public schools. They saw illustrations and photographs of this tiny little girl walking to school surrounded by U.S. marshals. They were amazed.

After reading and discussing the books, we talked about the meaning of Ruby Bridges. What did we learn from her efforts? What did her story say about the role of children in helping to create change? As a class, we brainstormed words that described Ruby.

Right away, James came up with the word "brave."

"She showed us that kids can do something to change unfair things," he said.

Nathaniel drew a picture of Ruby when she was praying over the group of white people who stood outside her elementary school every day. "This is Ruby Bridges," he wrote. "She prayed for the people who didn't like her."

Tammy drew a "before and after" picture. In the "before" side, she had a picture of Ruby going to a school labeled "black." On the other side, she had Ruby outside a different school she labeled "black and white."

"Ruby Bridges helped to change laws so black and white (children) could go to school together," Tammy wrote.

When I saw Tammy's picture, I felt a sense of accomplishment. Somehow the unit had helped at least some of my students make that bridge from "unfair" on an individual level to "injustice" on a social level. I also felt clear progress toward one of my goals: that my students understand that young children can make a difference.

However, this is where I worked myself into a corner of sorts. Upon further reflection, I realized that the way I had approached the unit made it difficult to accomplish another key goal: to convey to my students that they could take actions in our own classroom and school community to change our environment for the better.

By emphasizing "brave" and "historical" figures such as Ruby Bridges and Martin Luther King Jr., I inadvertently gave my students the impression that only larger-than-life heroes can work for change. Yet I had wanted to convince my students that any action they take to improve our community—no matter how small—is significant. In the future, I know I must create lessons that allow students to decide on what is necessary to make changes in their own lives, and what steps they can take to facilitate those changes.

After I finished this unit, I realized how much more I would have liked to do. I wanted to bring the unit to more contemporary times and study issues of unfairness that the children face in their lives today. I also wanted to study other people's struggles for justice throughout the world.

Despite its shortcomings, I was pleased I did the unit on "fairness."

For the students, I believe the discussions provided background for even more meaningful lessons on "fairness" and "unfairness," "justice" and "injustice," as they get older. For myself, I now have some curriculum materials on "fairness" and some experience in how to approach the topic.

I also overcame my fear that I was doing something wrong. I learned that it can be worthwhile to deviate from the standard curriculum, especially when it involves an important concept that my students face every day.

That year, my students learned of young people who played a role in changing unfairness. After that, I started working on encouraging my students to consider how they could play a role in changing today's unfairness. It's rare that a unit goes perfectly, but that's OK. Progress in teaching, as in social justice, often comes slowly. ■

Stephanie Walters is an editor of *Rethinking Schools* magazine. She is on leave from her position as a teacher in Milwaukee, Wis., public schools and is a staff person for the Milwaukee Teachers' Education Association, an NEA affiliate.

Staying Past Wednesday

Helping Kids Deal with Death and Loss

BY KATE LYMAN

The first time that death took a seat in my classroom was about 15 years ago. Jessica*, a kindergartner in my class, and her brother had died over the weekend in a fire at a babysitter's house. I prepared to return to school on Monday, to face the empty seat at her table, answer the inevitable questions, and deal with my students' fears and grief.

When I got to school, the staff was told to go to the library for a brief meeting. The principal announced the tragedy and warned teachers not to broach the subject. "Trained personnel" (the school psychologist and social worker) would talk with the children. Teachers could answer questions but were to get on with school business as soon as possible.

"I'm giving this until Wednesday," whispered the teacher of my student's sibling. "After Wednesday, we won't talk about it anymore."

Death—like sex, AIDS, genocide, racism, and poverty—is silenced in the elementary classroom. That silence sends a strong message to children: This may be your reality but it is not the truth that we honor in this institution. You must set aside your classmate's death or your ancestors' history or your 13-year-old sister's pregnancy. You are here to discuss and write and learn about matters of more importance.

The Monday after Jessica's death, my students gathered on the rug. Many had heard about the fire. They burst out with facts (many erroneous), questions, and feelings. There was an undertone of fear for their own safety.

I took the students' lead and, ignoring the principal, I moderated a sharing session. After about 30 minutes, the tone switched from curiosity and fear to sadness. What about Jessica? Where was she now? How could we remember her and tell her that we miss her? I asked the students for ideas. They wanted to decorate her table space, to write about her, to draw pictures of her, and to send something to her family. I told them I would clear off a bulletin board for remembering Jessica and sent them to their tables to draw and write.

The bulletin board stayed up until the end of the school year. Questions, stories, and projects about Jessica did not end on Wednesday.

Death and Loss

Since then, I have often included a unit of several weeks on death and loss in my curriculum. Some years, especially when I taught kindergarten, the unit was precipitated by the death of a classroom guinea pig or by a robin found dead on the playground. Books such as *The Tenth Good Thing About Barney*, by Judith Viorst, sparked student discussions on a range of topics: the loss of a favorite pet (Barney was a cat), the death of a grandparent, and the many different views on afterlife.

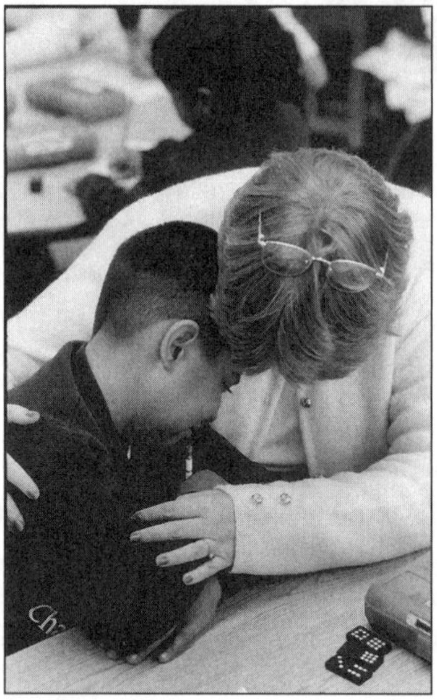

JEAN-CLAUDE LEJEUNE

More recently, when teaching 1st through 3rd grade, I have incorporated the unit as a regular part of my curriculum, sometimes as part of a discussion on AIDS awareness. The unit's immediacy invariably becomes clear. One year, for example, while I was preparing for the unit, a student who had been in my classroom the year before died in a car accident. A few years later, the mother of a girl in my class came in to tell me that her cousin was dying of AIDS and probably would not survive the night. Several days later, as part of our unit, this student solemnly shared her eulogy of her mother's cousin.

More recently, in my 2nd/3rd-grade classroom, I planned for the class to create a "death and loss quilt" as a follow-up to a field trip to view panels from the NAMES (AIDS Memorial) Quilt. For students who had several stories to tell, we talked about whom they would choose for their quilt panel; we discussed hard questions like who had meant the most to them and whom they missed the most. For several students, the loss of a parent through separation was akin to death because the parent had dropped out of their lives.

On the day we began our work on the quilt, Lisa came in late, which was not atypical. She is often quiet and withdrawn, but she appeared unusually upset and on the verge of tears. She sat down at her seat and laid her head on her arms. With some coaxing, she agreed to meet with me in the hall.

"What's the matter?" I asked.

"Nothing."

"You seem to be feeling very sad." No response. "Did something happen at home?"

"Yeah, but it's nobody's business," Lisa said, her body racked with sobs. I sat with her a while and asked how I could help. She blurted out, "Well, my aunt killed herself last night, but my mom says it's nobody's business."

I suggested that Lisa speak with a counselor but she didn't want to. She wanted to go back to the classroom. Feeling as if I were in a movie, I told her what the class was writing about. She sat down and wrote about her dog who had run away. Being unsure myself if it were too soon, I tentatively suggested she write about her aunt.

"No. Too hard," was her tearful answer.

Then I noticed that Mariah was also in tears. Usually a prolific writer, she had written only her name and the date. I went over to talk to her.

"I want to write about my mom, but it makes me too sad," she confided.

I told her that Lisa was having a similar problem and suggested they share their feelings. They went to the bench in the hall. When they came back, they were both ready to write. Lisa quickly wrote her story:

> My aunt, Linda, lived in Stevensville for a long time, since she was a kid. When my grandma moved out, she had to move out. She got an apartment. And it was very small. It was one room. Everybody said she was a slob because she left cigarette wrappers around. Everybody said she was crazy. She died and I miss her.

When Mariah finished her story, she shared it with the class:

> Brenda was my mom. I will never see her again. I loved her and I still do. I always will. Whenever I came over she gave me sea shells because I hadn't seen her for too long. When they got divorced I was 4. We went out for ice cream from Dairy Queen. We don't know where she lives. That's why I'll never see her again. I have to stay with my dad. I want to stay with her, but I can't.
>
> She loves Cheetos. I know she loves me. My mom couldn't take care of me. But my dad could. My mom and dad probably had a fight over me. But I don't know. I was only 4. I wished it never happened.
> I wished on a star. It was the first one; I know it. I wished on Lauren's sea shell that was painted.
>
> I know she loves me. I know it. I just know it. She is a friend and a special mom. She is special because she's my mom, and I love her. And she's part of my family.
> I love you mom!!

Struggling Through

I was having a hard time handling the intensity of the girls' feelings. I struggled through the day and the rest of the year. Students worked on their quilt squares in art class. They wrote and decorated acrostics (poems or short stories formed around the letters of a person's name) about their loved ones. I read the book *Words of Stone* by Kevin Jenkes, which paralleled Lisa's and Mariah's issues. In this book, two children who have experienced the loss of a parent (one through death and the other through abandonment) discover what they have in common and become friends.

Lisa and Mariah also became friends and continued to write about their losses. While Lisa's writing seemed to serve as a private emotional outlet, Mariah asked again and again to read her stories to the class. She welcomed questions and input from classmates. She seemed relieved to discover that her loss was not unique.

"Oh, that's just like me," contributed Jamie. "But my mom's in jail. I hardly ever can see her."

The support that Mariah gained from the class enabled her to begin to heal from her loss. Lisa, however, went on an emotional spiral downward, was treated for depression, and was briefly institutionalized. As the school, her family, and her therapists struggled to deal with her mental illness, writing was one of the few activities that sustained her. She wrote stories about her aunt at every opportunity, even on paper towels used to serve snacks.

For both girls, writing had become necessary and cathartic. As I watched them write about their pain and grief, I wondered what would have happened if I hadn't made room for their stories. Would they and the other children have learned that grieving, compassion, and working through loss have no place in school, perhaps no place in life?

I have always believed that the most powerful lessons are those relevant to the students' lives. Death, tucked away in the "life cycle" part of our science standards, has never been a major part of our official curriculum. But ever since Jessica's death 15 years ago, it has forced its way into my classroom. It has taken a seat and proclaimed its presence. It refuses to move out on Wednesday. ■

* Names have been changed.

Kate Lyman has taught kindergarten through 3rd grade in public schools in Madison, Wis., for 33 years. She has done graduate work in multicultural education and in teaching English as a second language at the University of Wisconsin.

Part VI

Learn from and stand with families.

"Collaboration is not a passive phenomenon; it requires risk-taking with some passion about it. … Collaboration involves more than a coming together. It requires more from the participants than simply sharing their perspectives. At best, it requires that the participants reach a new level of understanding—a perspective that was not apparent before. This is the real power of collaboration."

Elizabeth Jones and John Nimmo
Collaboration, Conflict, and Change: Thoughts on Education as Provocation

ETHEL JEANNE ALIE'NOR RENIA

Welcoming Kalenna

Making Our Students Feel at Home

BY LAURA LINDA NEGRI-POOL

When I was a child, our home was filled with the sounds of Spanish, mariachi music, and boisterous conversations. At home, my Nana cooked enchiladas, menudo, and tamales. During family celebrations we broke piñatas, danced, and hung papel picados. I was surrounded by six siblings, multiple cousins, tíos, and tías. My home was filled with light, color, art, texture, and love.

My school, in contrast, was drab, white, and unappealing.

I recall only one time when my Mexican American identity was validated during elementary school. When I was in 3rd grade, my mother organized a Cinco de Mayo event at our school. My father, siblings, and I cut out the papel picados, made the piñatas, formed the papier mâché sculptures, and created paper flowers. Seeing my culture represented at school made me feel at home there for the first time.

I want my students to have more than one memory like that. I've worked in early childhood education for more than 30 years, and I feel passionate about embracing families from nondominant cultures into the early childhood communities I work in.

As the result of a personal process of identity and cultural reclamation, I came to understand how my personal experiences influence this passion.

My experiences inspired me to find ways to make sure that other marginalized children and families see themselves and their lives reflected in our classroom community.

Welcoming Kalenna

One fall day, I held an open house to welcome the new children and families enrolled in our preschool program. When Kalenna entered our classroom, I immediately felt an affinity with her. Kalenna's dark, thick hair and chocolate brown skin set her apart from most of the other 14 children in the class. Our community college lab school served predominantly European American children whose parents were taking classes. Her mother, Diane, spoke with an accent that made me wonder if English was not her first language.

"Do you speak a language in addition to English?" I asked Diane.

She smiled and answered, "Marshallese." Our journey had begun.

I sensed Diane's feeling of relief and surprise when I asked about her language history. I knew from my own experiences what it was like to not be seen, to be treated with a question mark. I wondered how many times others had asked her, as they had me, "what she was" rather than respectfully and authentically inquiring about her. My question was an open and honest acknowledgment of her differences.

Over the next few months, I tried to infuse our classroom environment with the sounds, textures, and objects that surrounded Kalenna in her home.

First I had to learn about the Marshall Islands. I had no idea where or what the Marshall Islands were, let alone anything about the Marshallese language and culture. I started with a map, where I learned that the Marshall Islands are a collection of 1,225 islands and islets in Micronesia. From the internet, I learned about the ongoing struggle of the Marshallese people to maintain their language and culture given their history of domination by Germany, Japan, and the United States. Following World War II, the United States conducted nuclear tests on the islands—including Bikini Atoll. These tests exposed many inhabitants to high radiation levels.

After gaining some knowledge of her origins, I was able to begin to speak more confidently with Kalenna's family. I began regular conversations with Diane, each of us sharing information about our family and culture.

I discovered a website with Marshallese music and language. I printed a list of simple words and phrases and brought it to the classroom. I showed Diane what I had found and asked her to translate a song into Marshallese. Each morning the children, student teachers, and I sang a greeting song utilizing the home languages of the children and adults present in our classroom, including

Tips for Teachers

My own experiences of marginalization, invisibility, and outsider status propelled me to find ways to implement curricula and environments that embrace, validate, and honor the life experiences and cultures of children like me—those who are not white and not surrounded solely by the English language. Here are some simple ways teachers can help young students from marginalized communities to feel, hear, and see themselves reflected in the classroom:

- Spend time talking with and building relationships with parents and other family members.
- Learn to greet children in their home languages.
- Pronounce children's names correctly and with as much of an authentic sound as you can.
- Use fabrics and materials familiar to the children in the classroom for tablecloths, wall hangings, containers, and clothing.
- Play CDs and tapes of music from the children's culture during play periods, rest time, and meal time.
- Invite parents to cook family recipes with the class.
- Take and post pictures of the children and their families and their homes in the classroom.

Spanish, Chinese, and Afrikaans. Diane taught us how to sing our good morning song in Marshallese.

I asked Diane if she could help me locate items from the Marshall Islands that the students might use in the classroom. She brought in a hat, a basket, clothing, a hairpiece, and a necklace. We incorporated them into our dramatic play area. The children frequently wore the hairpiece and hat. The large basket with shells held an assortment of classroom materials throughout the year. The children loved wearing the seashell necklaces. They knew that the items belonged to Kalenna and treated them with care and respect.

I invited Diane to record the book *No, David,* by David Solomon, on audiotape in Marshallese. The book was a favorite in our classroom due in part to the artwork, the simple text, and message of unconditional love. In the story, a little boy repeatedly gets in trouble for typical misbehaviors, including making a mess, overfilling the bathtub, and playing with a baseball in the house. The story concludes with the mother expressing her enduring love for him despite his antics. The children already could "read" each page in English. I partnered Diane with a mom who spoke Spanish. Together they recorded the book in their home languages. The mothers joined us at circle time to read the book aloud and to allow us to hear their voices on tape. From then on, Kalenna listened frequently to her mother's voice reading *Jaab, David.*

Bridging Cultures

One of my best memories of Kalenna is of the day she brought some of "her music" to class. I had invited her mother to share music that they listened to at home, in part because I was having difficulty locating Marshallese music.

Kalenna and I went to the CD player and began to listen. At first we listened to it as background music while the students played. Later Kalenna went to the large rug area. I began to move to the music and told her how much I liked it. Then she began to dance. As she danced, a magnificent smile appeared on her face. She clearly had a specific routine that she'd learned for that particular song. I began to mimic her movements. When the song ended, I rewound the tape and started it again. She began to teach me the moves. We laughed and moved, reveling in our intimate shared enjoyment. The other children watched, pausing in their own play to see our scene unfold. Later, some came and joined us. Kalenna's delight was evident as our dance continued. I had finally touched her where she lived.

JEAN-CLAUDE LEJEUNE

A few years ago a former teacher of mine told me that he always pictured my face while reading of a young Mexican woman in the novel *The Pearl.* I was shocked. I never knew that he saw me as Mexican, that he associated me with the language, the culture, and the stories. I was touched, yet felt a loss. The loss was about not having my identity validated some 25 years earlier.

How I yearned to have a teacher who could see me, hear me, and dance with me. ■

Laura Linda Negri-Pool has worked in the field of early childhood education for more than 30 years. Her work experiences have included Head Start, Early Head Start, private child care, and teaching community college. She is Education Coordinator for Nike Child Development Programs in Beaverton, Ore.

Children's books about holidays often reinforce stereotypes and myths. According to The Pilgrim's Party, A Really True Story, *by Sadyebeth and Anson Lowitz, "[w]hen it was all over, the Indians gave three cheers for the Pilgrims. Never before had they eaten such wonderful food."*

Holiday Lessons Learned in an Early Childhood Classroom

BY *JULIE BISSON*

I've always loved holidays, and the rituals and special foods that go with them. Growing up, I relished the meticulous tree decorating during the Christmas season and I counted the days until Christmas Eve when Santa would slide down our chimney. I can still smell the crisp New England air and feel the warm sun on my face as my siblings and I traipsed through the pumpkin patch every fall searching for the perfect jack-o-lantern candidate. When I moved away from home, I carried my love of holidays and special cultural traditions with me, and to this day, I gather friends and loved ones in my home several times a year to join me in holiday rituals.

I carried my love of holidays into my life as an early childhood teacher. My story as a teacher follows a trajectory from holiday-themed curricula to holiday activities that focused on superficial and stereotypical elements of cultures and from there, to downplaying mainstream cultural holidays and highlighting less conventional ones. But my story doesn't stop there. With support from other anti-bias educators and a family who challenged me to rethink my approach to holidays, I became clearer about how to weave holidays into the fabric of the classroom in a way that connects to children and families and supports anti-bias learning.

My Early Thinking: Holidays *Are* the Curriculum

As a beginning teacher of preschoolers, I loved preparing holiday activities for the children in my classroom. Each month, I made a new holiday-themed flannel board, changed the colors in the easel paint cups to match the season, rotated books so that I had the appropriate holiday-themed books on the bookshelf, and played music relevant to the season. Holiday activities often took control of the curriculum.

As I look back on those years I realize that this holiday-based curriculum wasn't very meaningful to the children. I'd bet that there were children in my classroom who didn't celebrate Halloween, Christmas, or Easter. I don't know for sure, though, because I don't remember having any conversations with families about what they celebrated at home or what they thought about the holiday activities that we did at school. Since the holidays were not connected to the children's family lives, the activities I offered were, at best, a fun sensory experience. But they weren't meaningful experiences that made connections between the children's lives at home and at school or that assisted children in learning more about the ways they are similar to and different from one another.

Because I focused so much of our time on holidays, we lost out on opportunities for other activities and discussions that could have emerged from children's interests and from current happenings. Instead of pursuing the children's curiosity about how we get our skin color, for instance, which could have led us to stimulating literacy, community, and social learning, I kept us narrowly focused on the holiday of the month. I now know that the children weren't the center of my curriculum but, rather, my holiday curriculum was at the center of my teaching.

Feeling the Tension: I'm Leaving Out Some Holidays!

A few years into my work with young children I began learning about anti-bias practices and decided to expand my focus on holidays to include a holiday that I thought would introduce children to a new culture. When the Mexican holiday Cinco de Mayo rolled around, I invited my friend Joanna, a Spanish major in college who had lived in Spain for a year, to come talk with the children about Cinco de Mayo. I thought this would be a great way to introduce the children to a new holiday and teach them to value diversity. The fact that my white friend who had spent a year in Spain—not Mexico—wasn't exactly the best teacher about Cinco de Mayo didn't cross my mind. She had lived among people who spoke Spanish and at the time, I thought that was good enough.

Joanna arrived at the center that day with Spanish music cued up on her tape recorder. When the children met her at the front door she greeted them with a few Spanish words: "Hola! Buenos días!" Joshua, 4 years old, turned on his heels and ran into the office, calling me, "Julie, your housekeeper is here!" At the time, I chalked up Joshua's comment as "one of those cute things kids say."

Looking back on this now, I am appalled. I'd neglected to read up on the holiday before I jumped in. I didn't know much at all about Cinco de Mayo and didn't do my homework ahead of time. If I had, I would have learned that Cinco de Mayo is mostly a U.S. holiday, only regionally celebrated in Mexico. I also hadn't taken the time to find out about the children's experiences with people who are Mexican. Joshua's comment wasn't a harmless "cute" comment, but an indication that he associated Spanish speakers with housekeepers, a flag that ought to have alerted me to back up and reassess my plan.

Over the next few years, as I learned more about anti-bias education, I changed my holiday strategies again. I began to see how inundated children and adults are with images and messages about dominant culture holidays, especially in the fall and winter. For the children who celebrate those holidays —Halloween, Thanksgiving, Christmas, New Year's, Valentines Day, and Easter—this is a positive reflection of their family lives. But I wanted the children in my class to understand that the dominant-culture holidays are only part of the picture. And I wanted children who celebrated holidays outside of the mainstream to see their families' values and beliefs represented. I began to downplay dominant culture holidays and to highlight less mainstream holidays, like Kwanzaa, Solstice, El Día de Los Muertos, Sukkoth, Noruz, Diwali, and others.

My early efforts to include a range of unfamiliar holidays were clumsy. I continued to plan holidays in a haphazard way, choosing holidays because I was curious or intrigued, rather than because they supported goals I had for the children's education, like learning about important events in the lives of children in the class or strengthening critical thinking skills. The holiday activities I offered to children were not connected to the children or their families, and they often were not accurate reflections of how real people today celebrate a holiday. And, as with my experience with Joanna at Cinco de Mayo, I often reinforced stereotypes or misinformation.

How I Resolved My Unease

I finally understood how holidays can create connections with families and enhance an anti-bias approach when a multiracial family offered to share their holidays with my class. Erika's mom is Chinese and her dad African American. They joined us one afternoon to talk about how they celebrate both Kwanzaa and Chinese New Year. This was the first time that a family had come into my classroom to share their special celebrations. The experience was magical, for me and for the children. The children were captivated by the stories of lighting the kinara and participating in the dragon parade, and Erika beamed as her parents told their family's holiday stories. Not only did I get firsthand information about holidays that I didn't celebrate personally, but I also felt closer to Erika's family. Finally, I felt that I understood what we mean when we say we should build home-school connections. It became clear to me that one of the best ways to introduce an unfamiliar holiday is to have a family who celebrates it tell their story.

That was a turning point for me. As I worked closely with other teachers on this topic and continued welcoming families into the classroom to share their holiday stories, it became clear that the questions about what and how to celebrate were answered by learning more about the children and families in the classroom and what they celebrate—or don't. It has less to do with what I am interested in or what I celebrate in my own family and more about what best meets the developmental and educational needs of the children. This was a huge revelation for me and it had a tremendous impact on how I would approach holidays in the future.

Principles for Anti-Bias Holiday Practices

I've developed a set of principles that grow from my conviction that attention to holidays is an important way both to honor the community and to embrace anti-bias education goals. Those goals include: 1) foster in children a positive self- and social-identity; 2) give children tools for comfortable, empathic interactions with people who are different from them; 3) strengthen children's ability to think critically about bias; and 4) grow a willingness to take action to address unfairness. The aim of anti-bias education in early childhood education isn't cultural studies. Rather, the emphasis is on fostering identity, encouraging relationship across differences, strengthening critical thinking, and developing activism. Holidays, when used as one part of an overall approach to diversity, can further anti-bias goals and deepen children's awareness of how people are both similar to and different from one another, a core disposition in anti-bias education.

In an early childhood classroom, holidays ought to be more about learning than about celebrating. When a family shares their holiday practices, they might read a book, offer some food, or tell a family story rather than launch a full-fledged party. When I introduce a holiday, I use a picture book or tell a persona doll story. And, even with this focus on learning rather than celebrating, holidays ought to be only a small part of the curriculum.

Principle 1. Get clear about goals for holiday activities.

Holidays are one way to further anti-bias learning: a primary goal of anti-bias education is to explore the fundamental principle that we are alike *and* different. When sharing family rituals with each other, children learn that while people may celebrate the same holiday, they often celebrate in different ways. For instance, many children celebrate Christmas, but some may hang stockings for Santa to fill, while others go to church to honor the birth of Jesus—and some folks do both.

Expanding children's awareness of others is another anti-bias goal that holidays address. When I have a classroom where most children celebrate Easter, I stretch the children's understandings by first acknowledging their experiences: "Next week, many of you will be celebrating Easter. You might search for hidden eggs, or you might go to church, or have a special brunch with your family." Then, I introduce a larger context: "There are other holidays that people celebrate that happen in spring. One is Passover, a holiday that honors the time in history when Jewish people were freed from slavery in a country called Egypt. I've brought a book to read about a boy named Sam, who is the same age as you, and how he celebrates Passover in his house."

NORMAN BRIDWELL/CLIFFORD'S HALLOWEEN / SCHOLASTIC

Some children's literature about holidays reinforces racial stereotypes.

Principle 2. Work closely with families to find out what and how they celebrate.

My experiences with having families bring their holiday stories into the classroom cemented my conviction that teachers need to work closely with families to find out what and how they celebrate. When families enroll their children, I use a combination of questionnaires, meetings, home visits, and other exchanges to ask questions like: "How important are holidays in your family?" "What holidays or other special days do you celebrate or observe?" and "What are some of the ways that you celebrate these special days?" I also describe the many ways that families might share their special days in the program. I use this as a time to find out if a family doesn't celebrate any holidays or if a family has concerns about their child participating in or learning about any particular holidays. If I learn that a family doesn't celebrate holidays, I work with them to make a plan for how to talk about holidays in a way that respects their family's beliefs.

And when I talk with families about holidays, I try to be mindful that for some people, holidays hold unhappy memories and that they may not want to share holiday stories with me or the class.

When identifying holidays to include, I'm careful to recognize at least some of the special days that each of the children celebrates, even dominant culture holidays. I try to remember that even though dominant culture holidays are highly visible in our society, children who celebrate those holidays deserve to have their stories told and to hear their teacher acknowledge what is important in their families.

Principle 3. Consider whether or not to introduce holidays that are not celebrated by children and families in the program.

Some years there are a myriad of different holidays celebrated by children and families in the classroom. When that is the case, children will get the idea that there are many days and ways to celebrate, and I may not introduce any other holidays for us to learn about. However, if families celebrate a small set of special days (particularly if those are the usual mainstream holidays), I may introduce some other holidays. This locates children's experiences in a larger context and communicates that, "Just as your family celebrations are special and important to you, other families' holidays are special and important—whether you are familiar with them or not."

When choosing an unfamiliar holiday to share with children, I consider holidays with the potential for making connections to children's own experiences so they can see the ways in which they are similar to the individuals who observe the holiday. I consider holidays celebrated in our local community. This increases the possibility that the children may know people who celebrate that holiday or that they'll see decorations or places of worship related to the holiday. I also explore holidays to which families may have a more distant connection: for example, when I had a child in my group who had been adopted from Guatemala, I introduced All Saints Day—when giant colorful kites are flown in cemeteries to establish links with the dead—knowing that we could make the holiday real through our connection to Maria. Without that connection, a focus on this holiday would very likely leave children feeling that Guatemalans are an exotic "other" rather than people, just like them, who celebrate what's important to them with their families.

I've learned to do my research ahead of time to become familiar enough with a new holiday to ensure that it is being introduced in a historically accurate way that considers multiple perspectives as well as ways that families might celebrate it. I find a lot of useful information about the history of a holiday and how it is celebrated in children's books. Cultural centers, libraries, and the internet are other sources I use.

To introduce an unfamiliar holiday to the children, I read a children's book or tell a persona doll story about a child or family that celebrates the holiday, emphasizing that this is how one family celebrates this holiday, rather than talking about it general terms; I want to avoid the stereotypes that grow from broad cultural descriptions. By anchoring unfamiliar holidays in stories about real children and families, children can connect these new holidays to their lives.

Principle 4. Decide how to handle religious stories and aspects of holidays.

Over time I've learned to give special attention to the religious aspects of holidays. Since most holidays have a religious story, I have to decide whether and how to acknowledge this story. If I decide to avoid religious aspects, I know that I need to make decisions about what I will focus on. One danger I've learned to watch for: when the religious story is de-emphasized, it can be tempting to focus on the commercial aspects of a holiday, instead. For example, I've noticed that some teachers choose to avoid the story of Jesus Christ's birth when discussing Christmas and instead focus activities on Santa, reindeer, and presents under the tree. But some children and families celebrate Christmas as Jesus' birth and don't believe in the Santa Claus story; they do not see themselves honored or reflected in this perspective and take issue with Christmas being represented in a commercial way. Another approach that I've seen teachers take is to avoid religious stories and, instead, highlight family togetherness and the values of giving and receiving during the Christmas season.

When I do include the religious story I tell it as one way that people believe and celebrate, instead of as the true or preferred perspective. For example, when talking about Christmas, I say, "Some people celebrate Christmas as the birthday of a person named Jesus Christ. They may go to church and sing and pray together to celebrate Jesus' birthday."

Principle 5. Plan how to handle stereotypical images and messages in holidays.

I carefully examine all children's books, educational materials, and holiday decorations before I use them, in an effort to avoid stereotypical images. I strive to present accurate information about holidays through activities and discussions and I make sure I know all sides of a story behind a holiday before sharing it.

During the same year that I invited Joanna into my classroom to talk about Cinco de Mayo, I dressed kids up as pilgrims and Indians for our community Thanksgiving feast. What I didn't understand then is how offensive and inappropriate it is to dress children up to be someone from another culture. I see now that I reinforced misinformation and stereotypes, as well as the myth of harmony and collaboration between Native Americans and the Pilgrims.

These days my approach to Thanksgiving is to talk about how families come together to celebrate on this day, emphasizing the values of relationship, community, being thankful, and sharing special food. I also use Thanksgiving as an opportunity to call children's attention to the unfair and untrue images of Native Americans, laying the groundwork for critical thinking about Native American stereotypes throughout the year.

When stereotypical images and messages do surface, I talk about them with children and families. Many books about Thanksgiving, for example, offer insulting images of animals dressed up as Native Americans celebrating Thanksgiving with Pilgrims. When coming across these images, I might say to children, "This picture looks unfair to me. I wonder how a person who is Native American might feel if she saw this picture." This could start a valuable discussion about thinking critically about unfairness that children could choose to act on, an important anti-bias goal.

Holiday celebrations can be simple and tender, a way to come together as a community to tell stories, do an activity together, and share food. Many teachers struggle with holidays, unsure what path to take. Like me, they're eager to celebrate with children, and, like me, they want to "get it right"—to be respectful, and joyful, and inclusive. When we turn to the families in our programs as a way to begin sorting out how to celebrate, we often find willing collaborators who can help us chart a new course. Support from other anti-bias educators also helps. Holidays can bring anti-bias goals and community stories to life in delightful, celebrative ways. ■

Julie Bisson has been teaching and learning in the field of early childhood education for more than 25 years. She is a consultant, trainer, college instructor, and author of *Celebrate: An Anti-Bias Guide to Enjoying Holidays in Early Childhood Programs* (Redleaf Press, 2002).

DAVID BACON

Strawberry Fields Forever?

An Early Childhood Teacher Draws on her Past to Teach Children of Migrant Farmworkers

BY CIRILA RAMÍREZ

When I was a child, my mother couldn't help us with our homework. She had gone to work as a maid in a Mexican *hacienda* at age 11 and hadn't learned to read or write in Spanish. She was embarrassed when asked to sign her name. She worked in the farm labor fields of the Salinas Valley until she was 80 years old.

I thought a lot about my mother's life when I worked on a school-readiness project with the children of Mexican farmworkers in a migrant labor camp outside of Watsonville, Calif. I wanted the children I worked with to be proud of where they came from, and I wanted to help them develop literacy in Spanish before they were launched into kindergarten.

In some ways, the camp was a familiar setting. I grew up in migrant labor camps in California and Texas. My childhood camps share one big similarity with the camp I worked in: they are isolated and hidden from the world around them, and become small, contained little worlds for the inhabitants.

I had been to the camp outside of Watsonville before, although I barely recognized it. It had been torn down and rebuilt a few years back, and bore little resemblance to the cold, isolated, run-down dump I first visited in the early 1980s.

Back then, the camp was surrounded by strawberry fields, which served as the children's playground. Two gigantic, gnarled weeping willows guarded the entrance like menacing gatekeepers.

The trees hid the squalid living conditions from view. The majority of the homes had no screens or windows. I remember visiting a family consisting of a mother, father, three small children, and a young adult male. The home was a large room that served as living room, bedroom, and kitchen. There was a closet-sized bathroom in the corner. The room was dark and cold, and the family used the stove as a heating source.

Twenty years later, many things had changed. The old weeping willows had been cut down and replaced with brand-new, prefabricated two-story apartments. There was a laundry room, a large playground for the children, and a community room for meetings. There were computers for parents who wanted to learn how to use them. On the surface, it looked wonderful.

But was it wonderful? Did these new improvements signal better working conditions for the children's parents? Did they bring about a better life for the children? And, were these kids destined to have trouble in school?

DAVID BACON

Getting Students Ready

An organization called First 5 Santa Cruz County funded the school-readiness project for which I worked. The school district was concerned about the number of migrant children who failed kindergarten each year and wanted us to focus on reading and writing in English. I was more concerned with what was developmentally appropriate for the children. To me, that meant finding out what the children knew about the world around them and incorporating their interests into the curriculum. For example, if they were interested in tortillas, I created a lesson on the subject. We would start by reading a book on tortillas and then make our own flour and corn tortillas. The activity would include math and science concepts to meet school district requirements. If their parents worked picking strawberries, I created activities to validate their parents' work.

Because I spent so much time in the camp, I had a unique opportunity to interact with the students and their families. After a while, I noticed that many of the children exhibited only limited vocabulary in Spanish, their primary language.

I decided that I needed to incorporate lots of literacy activities to help the children develop an extensive vocabulary in Spanish. I believed that if the children had a strong and rich vocabulary in their first language it would make it easier for them to learn English. I brought a variety of books for the children to read. We read a book in the morning and one before they got ready to go home. Books served as a refuge for Jaime*, who often came in upset because his father yelled at his mother. I also set up small-group activities to encourage the children to interact in positive ways with one another. One activity the children enjoyed was looking at and discussing pictures of themselves and their parents. I would sit nearby and listen to their conversations. Alejandra would talk about making *carnitas* (marinated pork meat), and Jaime would describe his Spiderman tennis shoes. As the students got more comfortable with me and with each other, rich and descriptive conversations took place.

Living in the Present

Migrant families' main priorities hadn't changed much in the 20 years between my visits to the camp at Watsonville. They were concerned with keeping a roof over their heads and food on the table—just like my mother was when I was growing up. "The rest will take care of itself," she would tell me. "The present is what is important, not what will happen tomorrow or a week from now."

An outsider to this world might have a hard time understanding the idea that "right now" is more important than the future. Some would say it's backward thinking. But these families—as well as my own—share many parallels with families of mainstream America. They want a home, and they want their children to get an education. It is frustrating for them when they can't help their children with their homework or communicate in a meaningful way with the administrator at their child's school. For many, it's painful to admit they are not literate in their own language. Their children's homework is foreign to them. And often they cannot afford to think beyond the present because survival requires all their attention.

At the camp I saw dedicated teachers as well as other volunteers come in one day a week to assist the children with their homework. They brought to mind the impact Mr. Smith, my history teacher in high school, had on me. He believed in me—a special education student who ended up in his class by mistake. Within a few days I found myself beaming with joy that someone believed in my potential. He also instilled in me a love of history.

Looking back, I realize that growing up in migrant camps and my mother's life helped shape the kind of teacher I have become. My mother is now 90 years old and suffers from Alzheimer's disease. She longed to become a citizen, but not knowing how to read or write English made the dream impossible. She often worked seven days a week from before sunrise until sunset. She had little time for socializing and less for listening to the conversations of a 3-year-old.

I entered the field of child development to escape working in the fields myself. I know it is important for students to learn English—especially if they are to succeed in school. But I believe we can accomplish that by validating what they already know in their first language. By providing a variety of activities that integrate their lives in the camp with concepts of math, science, and literacy, we can provide an environment that will get them ready for kindergarten. We can give them the tools to become independent learners and thinkers. And more important, we can teach them not to be ashamed of living in a migrant camp.

Now my hope is that the mainstream education establishment can step up, recognize these students' educational progress, validate their heritage, and believe in their potential. ■

* Names have been changed.

Cirila Ramírez is a board member of Fuerza en Diversidad, Inc. (Strength in Diversity). She serves as a consultant for several Latino family childcare associations in the development of new leaders and board members.

MARILYN NOLT

Talking the Talk

Integrating Indigenous Languages into a Head Start Classroom

BY *CATHIE DEWEESE-PARKINSON*

When I became a Migrant Head Start Director in Cornelius, Oregon, in 1995, I joined a staff dedicated to involving parents and supporting children's language and culture. At first we thought that meant having teachers in every classroom who spoke Spanish. But soon we realized that we needed to expand the languages at school to include indigenous languages spoken by the families originally from southern Mexico or Guatemala. In many of those families, the father spoke Spanish as a second language, while the mothers and younger children spoke only Mixteco, Triqui, Zapotec, Canjobal, or another indigenous language.

We began to bring the families' languages into our teaching. We turned to our Parent Child Center, where moms would come daily to learn about child development; we hired some of those moms—indigenous community members—as teachers or as assistants, depending on their teaching qualifications. Thanks to intensive in-house professional development and a deeply committed staff trainer, several of the assistants, bilingual in Spanish and indigenous languages, became teachers.

We also relied on migrant parents for recommendations of teachers. When one teacher returned to Oaxaca to fulfill his traditional responsibility as mayor, the Triqui parents brought another one.

After several years, we requested a grant to intensify this work. One Triqui teacher and one Mixteco teacher developed materials and training intended to improve staff understanding about the children's language learning experience and to teach key classroom words to use with the children. All teachers were paid to participate in these trainings. The indigenous teachers developed and published four children's books illustrated with photos of the children and text in Triqui, Mixteco, Spanish, and English. Triqui and Mixteco speakers accompanied teachers on home visits to assure adequate communication with indigenous parents.

While the validation of the children's languages and culture was important, there was also programwide respect that made a real difference to these indigenous families. We listened to and incorporated the families' needs, even adding Saturday service at the request of the parent committee, to accommodate the strawberry harvest schedule. Everyone understood that parents were a critical part of the program.

Challenges We Faced

Even at the height of our language capacity, we never had enough speakers. Good pickers could earn more in the strawberry fields than as assistants in our classrooms.

While some families thought their languages were important, others were affected by discrimination in the U.S. and Mexico; they saw their home languages as a source of suffering and no longer useful. We addressed these differences by using a fluid approach to language. Generally teachers tried to respond to children in the language in which the children spoke. The indigenous speakers spent individual time with children conversing and reinforcing the language, as well as including words or phrases in the general classroom life.

As Head Start came under pressure to hire teachers with college degrees, we struggled with how to keep indigenous teachers on the teaching staff. Head Start's narrow definition of "qualified" has returned indigenous teachers to the role and pay level of assistants—or pushed them out of the classroom altogether.

When I reflect back on my experience, I am proud of how we created a program that respected the children's languages and culture. I'm not sure if our work with indigenous home languages in the classrooms was intensive enough to directly impact most children's academic progress. We know that some struggled in school and others did very well. It's likely that only the most determined or isolated families will maintain these languages in the U.S. The pressure is too great and the numbers of speakers too small. Yet even for those families in transition, the inclusion of their languages is critical to the respect and recognition of their culture and their dignity as human beings. ■

Cathie DeWeese-Parkinson has worked with children and families for more than 30 years, including 14 years with Migrant Head Start in Oregon as an Education Specialist and as a County Director. She reviews programs for Head Start and is working on a parenting program in Tijuana, Mexico, where she lives.

ABE HERZOG-ARBEITMAN, 2ND GRADE, NORTHAMPTON, MASS

Heather's Moms Got Married

BY MARY COWHEY

My 2nd graders gathered on the rug, discussing the impending 50th anniversary of the historic *Brown v. Board of Education* decision. I asked how their lives would have been different without *Brown.*

"I wouldn't have all these friends … 'cause I wouldn't know them," said Sadie.*

Michelle raised her hand and said, "I wouldn't exist." Michelle is a biracial girl, with an African American mother and white, Jewish father. Her mother Barbara had stayed for morning meeting that day and she elaborated:

"Because of *Brown,* I was able to get a good education and went to a college that was integrated. That's where I met Michelle's dad. We fell in love and decided to get married."

Samuel, who is Panamanian and Pakistani, said, "My mom is brown and my stepdad is white, and they got married." He turned to ask Barbara, "In those days could a brown person and a white person get married?" Barbara said they got married in Massachusetts in 1985, and it wasn't a problem.

Angela, an African American girl, had quietly been following the discussion and finally raised her hand. "Because of that [the *Brown* decision], things are more fair, like I can go to this school and have all different friends. Still, not everything is fair, and that makes me sad."

Sadie asked Angela what still wasn't fair. "Well, your parents could get married, because you have a mom and a dad, but I have two moms and they can't get married. That's not fair."

What Can One Elementary Teacher in Anytown, U.S.A., Do?

- Do not presume that students live in traditional families with both married heterosexual birth parents. Name a wide variety of configurations that are possible in the diversity of human families. Part of that naming process includes using books and resources that portray family diversity, including the video *That's a Family*. Invite students to respond to the question, "Who is in your family?" Allow students to share and display their family stories and pictures.
- Explore and challenge gender stereotypes with your students. Use children's books such as *Amazing Grace, William's Doll, Oliver Button Is a Sissy, China's Bravest Girl: The Legend of Hua Mu Lan, Riding Freedom,* and *Beautiful Warrior* as springboards for discussions. Activities can include students brainstorming lists of stereotypical behavior for boys and girls, then making captioned drawings of boys and girls engaging in nonstereotypical behaviors. These can be made into a class book or hallway display, "Boys Can/Girls Can." Once students learn to question gender stereotypes, they can recognize and reflect on stereotypical characters and behaviors in other books and media. They can extend their understandings of stereotypes to recognize and challenge other forms of bias.
- Teach a lesson on teasing and name-calling. Children's literature, such as *Oliver Button Is a Sissy* or *The Hundred Dresses*, can be an excellent point of departure for discussion and activities. These can help establish a baseline of classroom expectations that we are all respected members of this classroom community and that no put-downs will be tolerated.
- Answer students' questions about gay and lesbian issues in a straightforward, educational manner. Do not ignore or quash their curiosity. Remember that the two main points of reference are respecting differences and equality for all people. Elementary children are not asking about sexuality. When they ask what "gay" means, it's sufficient to say, "Gay is when a woman loves a woman or a man loves a man in a romantic way."
- Replace the phrase "moms and dads" with "parents and guardians" in your classroom and in your school, from informal conversation and classroom teaching to official school documents such as registration forms and emergency cards. Not only is this phrase more inclusive for students with gay or lesbian parents, but also for those being raised by foster parents, grandparents, aunts, and others. It accepts and affirms all of the families in your school.
- Consider showing a video like *Oliver Button Is a Star* as part of a professional development workshop for faculty and staff. *Oliver Button Is a Star* is a documentary that weaves a reading and musical production of *Oliver Button Is a Sissy* with interviews with adults like arctic explorer Ann Bancroft, author/illustrator Tomie dePaola, and dancer Bill T. Jones, who recall their childhood experiences. It includes scenes (some from my classroom) where 1st and 2nd graders do activities about name-calling and challenging gender stereotypes. *That's a Family* and *It's Elementary* are good choices too.
- In the event that you encounter an intolerant colleague, administrator, or parent, keep the following points in mind:
  - The diversity of families in our school is more beautiful and complex than any one of us could presume to know. Whether we have any self-identified ("out") gay- or lesbian-parented families in our school community or not, it is safer to assume that they are here than not.
  - An estimated one in 10 students may grow up to be gay or lesbian adults.
  - All of our students deserve a safe and supportive school experience.
  - Gays and lesbians are entitled to the same rights as others. We are talking about equal rights, not special rights.
  - We are not talking about "sexuality" when we discuss gay and lesbian issues any more than we are discussing sexuality when we read Cinderella or any other story with all heterosexual characters.

—Mary Cowhey

Sadie considered this for an instant before asking, "Who made that stupid rule?"

With the honesty and incisive thinking I cherish in 2nd graders, Angela and Sadie had cut to the chase. When it comes to discussing gay marriage in 2nd grade, these are the questions that matter most: Is it fair to exclude some families from the right to marry? Who made that rule (and how is it changing)?

I should pause here to say that I don't teach in Anytown, U.S.A. I teach in Northampton, a small city of 29,000 in western Massachusetts, which has been known as a haven for women and for lesbians. Northampton's status as a refuge from homophobia has been profiled in dozens of newspapers and media outlets around the country and around the world.

While the numbers vary from year to year, I have always had at least one child in my class with lesbian parents. This year, one third of my students have lesbian parents. While I probably have more lesbian-parented families than most teachers, the reality is that teachers may not know by looking if they have a child with gay or lesbian parents, aunts, uncles, grandparents, or family friends.

I teach at Jackson St. School (JSS), a public elementary school with about 400 students. Our school is a celebration of economic, racial, linguistic, and family diversity. Families speak a variety of home languages including Albanian, Spanish, Khmer, Vietnamese, Chinese, French, and Hindu. About 39 percent of the students are children of color, with the largest share of those being Puerto Rican. Forty percent of the students receive free or reduced lunch.

The school welcomes family involvement, with a weekly family newsletter and regular potluck dinners. It has a Family Center, which hosts a weekly Parents' Hour with coffee and conversation, as well as a family portrait project, in which a professional photographer takes free family portraits at Open House. These photos are displayed in the front hallway, heralding for all visitors the breadth of the school's diversity. Over the years, many parents have told me that even before speaking to anyone in the school, just looking at those family photos in the front lobby made them feel welcome, like they could fit in.

An Eye-Opener

I began teaching at Jackson St. School when I was fresh out of my teacher-preparation program. I decided to start the school year with home visits to my new students and their families. At one of the first homes I visited, a parent greeted me wearing a button that said, "We're here. We're gay. And we're on the PTA." Beth and Karen Bellavance-Grace began talking about being foster parents for the state department of social services and being adoptive parents. As we began talking about family diversity issues, I asked if they would be willing to advise me on good books and teaching ideas. My education in teaching family diversity and learning from my families began on the first day of my teaching career, before I even set foot in my classroom.

When I speak to teachers and future teachers about gay and lesbian issues in elementary schools, they often ask how I can "get away with that." This is particularly ironic in Massachusetts, which was one of the first states to recognize the rights and needs of gay and lesbian youth in schools. In 1993, during the administration of Republican Gov. William Weld, the Massachusetts Governor's Commission on Gay and Lesbian Youth recommended that:

- High schools establish policies protecting gay and lesbian youth from harassment, violence, and discrimination
- Teachers and counselors receive professional development to respond to the needs of these students

Bringing the Lives of Lesbian and Gay People into Our Programs

"Most people still get queasy talking about gay and lesbian issues at middle or—heaven forbid—elementary levels," writes Mary Cowhey. "Teacher self-censorship, often based on the fear of raising potentially controversial topics, remains the status quo in many schools."

That's sure been my experience; when I talk with other early childhood educators about how we can make sure that lesbian and gay people are visible in our childcare and primary classrooms, people usually blanch, sharing their squeamishness about parents' responses and about imagined questions that the children might pose about sexuality. There is an attitude of "Don't ask, don't tell": "If we don't have lesbian or gay families in our program, there's no need to raise the issue," the thinking goes. "And even if we do, that's their family's business, not anything we need to address with the rest of the children."

Mary Cowhey's story challenges us to reconsider. She says, "These are the questions that matter most: Is it fair to exclude some families from the right to marry? Who made that rule (and how is it changing)?"

As early childhood educators, we have a responsibility to honor a rich diversity of families and to make visible the full complement of people in our world. And we have a responsibility to raise issues of fairness and equity, inclusion and bias. When we make lesbian- and gay- headed families visible in our programs, our emphasis is on relationships—who people love and how people form families; sex and sexuality are not our focus.

We may not have lesbian or gay families enrolled in our programs, but we can make them visible in a range of ways, from persona dolls to lotto games to puzzles to books that include lesbian and gay characters. In my work as a childcare teacher with 3-, 4-, and 5-year-old children, I often change the gender of characters in chapter books to make sure that children hear stories about adventurous female characters, male characters who tend to hearth and home, and about lesbian and gay people. The following is a letter that I wrote to families to let them know about how I used the classic children's story Trumpet of the Swan to create a lesbian protagonist.

Dear *families,*

Your children and I have made a daily ritual of reading from a chapter book at nap time. The kids settle on their mats, curled up with their stuffed animals and cozy under their blankets, and I settle on the floor in the middle of the room and read a chapter from our current book.

This week, we began our next book, The Trumpet of the Swan, by E.B. White. This classic book tells the tender, slightly bittersweet story of a Trumpeter swan who is born without a voice, unable to cry "Koho!" like other swans. The book traces the swan's journey from infancy to adulthood, through the adventures of learning to read, write, and play the trumpet to communicate. The swan spends time as a camp bugler in Montana and a jazz trumpeter in a New York nightclub and with the swan boats in Boston. As the swan grows into adulthood, it falls in love with another swan and they become mates.

I read this book for several reasons. This book introduces the children to one experience of disability, as Louise describes her feelings when she realizes that she is different from the other swans and as she seeks ways to communicate with them. My brother is deaf and this was one of his favorite books as a kid; he's told me that he took comfort in reading about Louise's struggles and triumphs with communication.

Another reason that I read this book is because it offers gentle openings for conversations about lesbian and gay relationships. I've changed the gender of the swan hero from Louis to Louise. Children deserve to hear a story about a powerful, passionate, adventurous female, and to learn about the love that can flourish between two women. The book lends itself to a re-telling which nudges some anti-bias issues to the surface. Chapter books with powerful female protagonists are few and far between; it's even more rare to find books that present lesbian and gay relationships in a straightforward, matter-of-fact way.

My goal in reading this book is to make the lives of lesbian and gay people and people who have a disability visible for the children—visible and estimable. It's important to me to reflect the diversity of our community, diversity that includes many different sorts of families and people with disabilities. I hope for children to expect to encounter a range of people, and to feel relaxed and at ease with them.

We've only just begun the book. Today, we read about Louise's mother and father waiting on their

(continued on page 181)

- Schools establish support groups (gay-straight alliances)
- Schools "develop curricul[a] that incorporate gay and lesbian themes and subject matters into all disciplines, in an age-appropriate manner"

Despite that progressive policy, established under a Republican governor, teacher self-censorship, often based on the fear of raising potentially controversial topics, remains the status quo in many schools. Another problem, as progressive as the Weld commission's report was, is that it focused solutions primarily at the secondary level, with gay-straight alliances and so forth. Most people still get queasy talking about gay and lesbian issues at middle or—heaven forbid—elementary levels.

Teaching About Same-Sex Couples

In my classroom, issues of family diversity often arise spontaneously. Once a group of my 1st-grade readers decided to act out *The Carrot Seed*, a simple story about a boy who plants a carrot seed and cares for it diligently, despite the discouragement of his brother, mother, and father. After the skit, all the other students wanted a chance to act it out too. I said we could do it once more before lunch. I began pulling sticks with student names at random from a cup, to assign the four roles. After I pulled the first three sticks, a boy had already claimed the part of the brother. One girl had taken the role of the mother and another girl had taken the role of the kid who plants the seed. The last stick I pulled was Natalie's, and the remaining role was for the father. A boy quickly said I should pull another stick. Natalie sprang to her feet without hesitation. "That's OK!" she said, "I'll be the other mom!"

In 2004, same-sex marriage became legal in

Massachusetts. Heidi and Gina Nortonsmith, parents of one of my students, had been plaintiffs in the *Goodridge v. Mass. Department of Public Health* landmark lawsuit that resulted in the legalization of same-sex marriage in our state. They were given the first place in line at Northampton's crowded City Hall on the morning of May 17 to get their marriage license.

(continued from page 180)

nest for their eggs to hatch, about their encounter with Sam, a boy who will play an important role in the book, and about the eggs hatching and the cygnets taking their first swim. Kids held their breath as a fox nearly captured the mama swan, and clapped their hands with delight when the eggs hatched. They seemed wrapped in the loveliness of the pond in the woods where the swans have their nest. And they were tender about Louise, whose voice doesn't work. Will commented, "I think the baby swan is sad that she can't say 'Cheep.'"

I expect us to talk about disabilities as Louise struggles to find a way to communicate. And, as Louise falls in love with and courts Serena, we'll talk about women marrying women and men marrying men.

I'm interested to hear about any of this that comes home with your children, as well as any thoughts you have. Your children are reflective, thoughtful people, eager to discuss ideas and feelings. When we read My Father's Dragon, they debated the fairness of capturing the baby dragon; they talked together about whether zoos are fair to animals. Your children dig into big issues with passionate and careful thinking. The Trumpet of the Swan meets them right where they are.

Ann Pelo is an early childhood teacher and teacher mentor in Seattle, Wash.

After the court's decision, my students got "marriage fever." During "sharing time" Maggy reported on how she was the flower girl and her sister was the "ring barrier" at their friends' wedding. Avery Nortonsmith proudly showed the silver ID bracelet that he, his brother, and his moms all got on their wedding day, inscribed with the historic date. Sarah talked excitedly about preparations for her moms' wedding, how she and her sister and six of their girlfriends would be flower girls. I went to the wedding with my daughter and saw about half the families from my class. It was one of the most joyous and supportive celebrations I have ever witnessed.

My 5-year-old daughter caught the fever too, and conducted wedding after wedding in her imaginary play. Each night she'd say, "Come on Mom and Dad, you're getting married tonight." "We got married eight years ago," my husband would remind her. Undeterred, my daughter would say, "No, that was your commitment ceremony, but this is gonna be your wedding."

Even snack time conversations raise the issue of gay marriage. Beth Bellavance-Grace, who now works as an aide at our school, told me about a kindergarten conversation she heard. A girl announced to her table, "I know who I'm gonna marry when I grow up. I'm gonna marry Ella."

"You can't marry a girl," a boy at her table replied.

"That was just in the olden days," she replied. "But now I can."

Discussing Diversity

When we discuss family diversity, I define family as "the circle of people who love you." After I showed *That's a Family* one year, Marisol responded, "Yuck, that is so weird to have two dads!"

James turned to her and spoke with an air of sophistication. "What's the big deal about two dads?" he asked. "I got two dads. I got one in my house and one in the jail. Lots of kids gots two dads."

Marisol considered this a moment, then said, "Oh, I didn't think of that. I have two moms. I have my mom at home and a stepmom at my dad's house."

"See?" James said with a shrug of his shoulders. "I told you it's not so weird."

I had one student who was co-parented by three women. One morning we were having a math exhibition and the students had invited their parents. Thomas' three moms came in one at a time, each from their different jobs. James knew that his parents wouldn't be attending, but he kept looking to the door whenever another parent entered. He finally went over to Thomas and asked, "It be OK if I could borrow one of your moms?"

Margaret Spellings, appointed U.S. Secretary of Education by President George W. Bush, once criticized PBS for producing *Postcards from Buster*, a children's show that included a family with lesbian parents. I wish Spellings could have spent some time in my classroom. And I wish many Americans would approach the issue of same-sex marriage with the same openness as my 2nd graders.

The refusal to extend equal rights to families with gay and lesbian parents hurts children like my students, giving them the message their families are not equal, are somehow inferior. And, as my 2nd graders will tell you: That's not fair. ■

* Most students' names have been changed, except for those presented with last names, who asked to have their real names published in the interest of modeling family pride.

Mary Cowhey has been teaching 1st and/or 2nd grade at Jackson St. School in Northampton, Mass., since 1997. She is the author of *Black Ants and Buddhists: Thinking Critically and Teaching Differently in the Primary Grades* (Stenhouse Publishers, 2006).

COURTESY JOSE MARTI CHILD DEVELOPMENT CENTER

Activism Brings Us Power

An Interview with Hilda Magaña, Program Director, José Martí Child Development Center

BY JACQUELINE LALLEY

For families who enroll in Seattle's José Martí Child Development Center, preschool is infinitely more than a place where children go while their parents are at work. The program, which is dual-language, was founded as part of El Centro de la Raza in 1972, when neighborhood residents took over an abandoned school and turned it into a center for social services and early childhood education, a force for activism, and a symbol of ethnic pride and multiculturalism. It served 122 children in 2008. Below, the program director talks about the center's relationship with families and how their involvement transforms their lives.

How do you promote child development while engaging in social justice? Being a child development center and being part of El Centro de la Raza enables us to blend activism into the early childhood curriculum. During enrollment, we explain to parents our philosophy (*see sidebar, Principles of El Centro de la Raza*) and mission as we talk about the needs of our children. We talk about how the curriculum is developmentally research-based and also blends in language, culture, community involvement, and awareness of social justice. We explain how children and families attend rallies, participate in family literacy nights, and come to other events where the topics are chosen based on their needs. By enrolling their children in the center, parents become involved in social and political activities—both local and national, and even international.

For example, this year there was a big rally on immigration reform on May 1. Our children made signs for the rally and attended it with their parents, staff, and other community members. The sign-making was a classroom activity, and the children were learning their alphabet, making art, and learning to be involved in their community all at the same time. Going to the rally as a group added concrete experience with community activism, for them and their parents.

What impact does activism have on children as they develop?

We have many beautiful examples of kids learning from their parents' leadership. I have seen people

Principles of El Centro de la Raza

To share, disburse, and distribute our services, resources, knowledge and skills to our participants, community, visitors and broader human family with all due dignity for their individual needs and condition. To do so creatively with warmth, cultural sensitivity, fairness, enthusiasm, compassion, honesty and optimism in all areas of work.

To struggle to eliminate institutionalized racial, sexual, age and economic forms of discrimination, which hamper the human potential in our society.

To support the majority of people in this country; i.e., all workers—including, but not limited to farm workers, factory workers, service workers and office workers in their struggle for collective bargaining rights, safety, benefits and just wages and salaries.

To promote the recapture of the culture, language and respect for the Chicano! Mexicano! Latino! community as a priority in all of our work, without falling into ethnocentrism; to strengthen and help the struggle to recapture the cultures of our sister communities.

To promote strong and positive working relationships with other minority communities in all areas of work, service, political and social activities.

To provide a collective, healthy, safe and friendly workplace for members of our community and all participants in our sphere of influence.

To struggle against all forms of racism, sexism, individualism, ageism, and violence in our work and our community center.

To struggle for the creation of programs and services which a society must provide for the development of our community and its people.

To struggle for a clean, safe, and nuclear waste-free environment for our people and future generations. To work for a rational use of natural resources in the interests of the preservation of mother earth and the peaceful development of humankind.

To support the rights of self-determination of Native Americans, African Americans, Asian Americans, and Latinos, as well as our brothers and sisters in developing countries around the world. To promote the development of foreign policy by our government which puts into practice principles of sovereignty, justice, democracy, self-determination, international respect, and above all, peace with dignity.

To strengthen the family as an elementary formation of society which contributes to the development of society as a whole. To help each other and our community fulfill roles as parents, spouses, sisters, brothers and children, based on the absolute equality of men and women. To respect and recognize the rights of children as full and privileged members of our society. To strengthen the extended family relations. To develop programs which fulfill our obligation as family members of the larger society to bring up the future generations with clear vision that leads us to recover our fighting spirit. To struggle to ensure that family life is nourished and respected. To protect the rights of women and children to live their lives free from any form of abuse: physical, psychological, or sexual.

To struggle for a dignified human existence for all people in our society, which includes access to quality healthcare and housing, equal employment and education opportunities, a voice in democratic processes regarding political and social affairs, a responsible economic system which eliminates the vast differences in income; all of which are causes of poverty and deprivation in our society.

who were born during the founding years of the program, were enrolled in and graduated from the program, took part in rallies and activism with their parents—and have come back and become community activists as adults. Here they learned to express themselves verbally and in action. It's not enough to speak—you need to take action. Being part of an organization like this brings us more power. It's more than just volunteering here and there. As Paulo Freire says, social justice means being a part of something so that you can have more impact at deeper levels.

What are some examples of family involvement at your center?

We deal with issues of education, environmental justice, immigration, language, and culture, and many other issues—including stopping the war. Our children are part of a choir, Children Singing for Peace, and they sing at many rallies to stop the war, rallies where their parents are also participating. This year when there was a conference with the Dalai Lama, 73 of our families participated. Parents sent a letter asking the Dalai Lama to give his attention to immigration issues.

Parent involvement enabled us to win the FAMILIES COUNT Family Strengthening Award, presented by the Annie E. Casey Foundation and the National Council of La Raza. Three-fourths of our parents wrote letters to explain to these organizations how participating in our program has impacted them. Because of the award, our center is receiving mini-grants for our Family Literacy Nights.

Our activities go beyond our early childhood program. People from all backgrounds who participate in social services gather together at El Centro de la Raza to become stronger in the community. Campaña Quetzal is a coalition of parents from our center and other organizations, providing parent leadership on a number of issues, including getting equal distribution of financial resources to schools and promoting dual-language programs at schools. The first year they had a summit with more than 500 people, mostly parents from Seattle schools, and our parents led a workshop.

As an early childhood program, people come to us for help. When we learned that a student group at the University of Washington wanted to do a screening and find [immigrants] at the university who were undocumented, we asked to meet with the president. The president refused. We had a rally with MEChA leaders, and succeeded in putting a stop to this policy. We have staff and parents who are graduates, students, and staff at the university, and they thought the policy was a bad idea. It would have served to humiliate people. [Our families] see the injustice and the need for leadership. Parents need to provide that leadership because that helps not only themselves but others.

Ecological Oath / Juramento Ecológico

I promise	Prometo
To use my eyes	Usar mis ojos
To see	Para ver
The beauty of nature	La belleza de la naturaleza
Use my hands	Usar mis manos
To help	Para ayudar
Protect	A proteger
Earth	Suelo
Water	Agua
Forests and animals	Bosques y animales
And with my good example	Y con mi buen ejemplo
Teach others	Enseñar a otros
To take care of	A cuidar
And use correctly	Y usar adecuadamente
Our natural resources	Nuestros recursos naturales

Our number-one principle is environmental justice. Our children take a beautiful ecological oath (see sidebar above), which they recite in public. Recently, parents and staff hosted an event about stopping global warming through community action, such as recycling, and invited the mayor of Seattle and other leaders to speak.

Whatever issues we are working on, our children and parents are part of it. The teachers are

very good at presenting the issues at the developmental age of the children. In our own organizing work on many issues to better the community, children have concrete examples and experience with working to create better society.

What kind of leadership is needed to have this kind of family involvement in an early childhood program?

Our executive director has been an exemplary leader in our community, showing how to take effective action in a nonviolent way and right the wrongs in our community. Through our activities, events, and leadership, we've been able to have a very clear vision, and that shapes the curriculum we teach our children. We have learned from the examples of Martin Luther King Jr., Rosa Parks, and César Chávez. The current leaders of our community are giving our center information, and we're effective because we take action on it. ■

Jacqueline Lalley is a writer and communications consultant for nonprofits. She is on the web at invitingpositivechange.org.

Part VII

Advocate for children, families, and early childhood workers.

"We will carry what we know—what it can mean to have your country under you like a hammock, what it is to take part in the world instead of using your people as fodder in a war to control the world's meaning and expression. We will disrupt through witness, remembrance, and the courtship of the imagination. We will escort children past the darkest warrens of the forest. We will construct kites that stay aloft in the rain. We will champion what is beautiful."

Barry Lopez
Resistance

LAURA DESANTIS

Who Cares for Our Children?

The Childcare Crisis in the Other America

BY VALERIE POLAKOW

Lack of child care is frequently the tipping point that catapults a low-income family into poverty, destitution, and homelessness. For single mother families, in particular, child care is an urgent and vital need. In my recent book, *Who Cares for Our Children?,*[1] I argue that child care should be viewed as a human right for all children and their working parents. In the book, I present the voices of ethnically diverse low-income mothers from across the country—New York, Michigan, Iowa, and California—and tell their compelling stories of struggle and resilience as they juggle work and family responsibilities while desperately searching for safe, affordable, quality child care. Their stories form the heart of the book that points to a critical analysis of gendered public policies that perpetuate family poverty through low-wage work, mandatory welfare-to-work requirements, restricted access to postsecondary education, and lack of investment in the early lives of infants and young children. The appalling conditions of child poverty and lack of universal child care provisions in the United States stand in sharp contrast to the social citizenship rights enjoyed by women and children in most European countries.

The excerpts that follow are drawn from the book's introduction, "Who Cares?," and the concluding sections of chapter eight, "The Right to Child Care."

***

> I tell people I know how you feel because I've been there. ... What do you do? I mean, you cannot leave your children at home, and you can't take a day off and you don't have child care. ... I mean, we just had two children that were burnt, that died in a fire ... last year, we had one lady, she had to leave her son at home to go to work. ... It's very sad. It's very, very sad. ... We say these children are our future, but we just throw them away!
> *(Clara, a special education teacher commenting on the acute shortage of affordable child care in New York City)*

Caring for Children: A Private or Public Responsibility?

In 2004, 77.5 percent of women with children 6-17, 62.2 percent with children under 6 years old, and 57.3 percent with children under 3 years old, were in the labor force.[2] However, there is still a dearth of family support policies available to working parents. As Janet Gornick and Marcia Meyers point out, "This exceptionally private conception of family life leaves American families to craft individual solutions to what is essentially a social dilemma: If everyone is at the workplace, who will care for the children?"[3] The United States stands alone among all major industrialized countries in failing to provide paid parental leave, child care, and health care to all its children. As mothers are the primary caregivers for children, child care is indeed a woman's issue where economic independence, autonomy, and social equality are directly linked to access, availability, and affordability of good quality child care. Far-reaching changes in the structure of families and women's employment have, in the past decades, increased the need for child care and there has long been a "care deficit" for working mothers, both married and single.[4]

The Care Deficit

Under the 1996 Personal Responsibility and Work Opportunity Reconciliation Act (PRWORA) welfare legislation, the need for child care expanded exponentially as poor single mothers were coerced, under threat of sanctions and benefit cut-offs, into the low-wage labor market leaving infants as young as 12 weeks old behind.[5] Paradoxically poor women's care for their own infants or young children does not count as a legitimate work requirement; and their rights to make decisions about their own children's nonparental care is severely undermined by the inflexibility of the welfare-to-work mandates. The underlying assumptions behind this legislation are that poor mothers are work-aversive, dysfunctional parents, and unfit to care for their own children. Such legislation impugns their dignity and "repudiates them as mothers."[6] While welfare "reform" has dramatically increased the demand for care, particularly for infants and toddlers, the public supply is grossly underfunded, leading states into a race to the bottom for the cheapest of publicly subsidized child care. At present there are long waiting lists in over 20 states and only one in seven income-eligible children actually receives any childcare subsidy.[7]

While universal K-12 public education exists for all children in the United States, there is still no entitlement for young children to an early childhood education. During the past decade, state-funded prekindergarten initiatives have been implemented in 38 states, but lack of funding has resulted in restricted access, and poor quality in many programs.[8] Head Start still serves only 50 percent of income-eligible 4-year-olds nationwide, and most programs do not provide wrap-around care for working parents. From public preschool intervention programs, licensed private and community-based centers and family daycare homes, religious-affiliated centers, employer-sponsored child care, for-profit chains, to license-exempt care and the vast unknown informal care sector—child care is a patchwork of uneven quality and market-driven provisions demonstrating the glaring inequities in childcare services for young children. As child care costs between $4,000-$10,000 a year, low-income families must often compete with families on welfare for scarce childcare subsidies. In 20 states a family earning $25,000 a year is not even eligible for childcare subsidies. Subsidies also do not pay the full cost of care, and in the majority of states, the reimbursement rates are based on outdated market surveys.[9] When state reimbursement rates are low, many childcare providers are reluctant to accept children whose parents cannot pay the difference in copayments, which may run as high as $200-$300 a month, further exacerbating the segregated system of care. Hence the care deficit ricochets with alarming costs for the well-being and healthy development of children.

Gornick and Meyers argue that there is an urgent need for new public policies that would redistribute the costs of caregiving.[10] While affluent working mothers compete to enroll their toddlers in the "baby Ivies" paying up to $15,000 a year,[11] how does a food-service worker mother earning $6 an hour at her local Taco Bell purchase quality care? If she lives in New York City where there are 38,000 children on waiting lists for subsidized care,[12] she has few options open to her other than the cheap informal care sector.

Making choices in the best interests of one's child is arguably a vital parental responsibility. But low-income women have few choices. And the poorer they are, the less autonomy they have as providers and caregivers. Why should poor women in the United States not have the right to make choices about the care of their own children? While conservatives yet again urge middle-class mothers to choose the traditional terrain of a stay-at-home motherhood, in order to raise their own children and "preserve the family," poor mothers are still located in the space of a marginal motherhood, and family values for *them* are constructed as something entirely different. Neither the extensive psychological literature on early development nor the array of studies pointing to the importance of high-quality childcare experiences appear to have influenced the design of welfare "reform" and its underfunded, made-on-the-fly, inferior childcare provisions. Mothers working just beyond the edges of poverty find that they, too, must settle for *less*; less than what they choose, and less than what they want for their children as the increasingly privatized childcare market creates dangerous disjunctions between quality care and affordable care.

***

Child Care as a Human Right

Most industrialized democracies have recognized the importance of creating a "positive state" for women and children through the provision of strong family support policies[13] that incorporate child care as a key social citizenship right. However, attempts to create a legal right to child care in the United States through litigation have been largely unsuccessful, and state constitutional provisions that grant children the right to public education have not been extended to early education and the right to child care. Martha Davis and Roslyn Powell argue that because of its failure to offer basic social protections and family supports to its citizens, the

United States is an outlier in the international arena and that it is a misguided strategy to rely *only* on domestic law to attempt to establish childcare provisions.[14] The absence of child care should not be viewed as another competing demand of a special interest group, but rather, child care should be framed as a fundamental human right, emanating from international human rights standards, and an affirmative obligation of government.

The affirmative obligation of government to create family support policies and childcare provisions is recognized in three international human rights conventions, which the United States has failed to ratify: the Convention on the Rights of the Child (CRC), the Convention on the Elimination of All Forms of Discrimination Against Women (CEDAW), and the International Covenant on Economic, Social, and Cultural Rights (ICESCR). The CRC, adopted by unanimous consent at the United Nations in 1989, was implemented in 1990 and has been ratified by 191 countries. In the CRC, children, for the first time, are recognized as "rights bearers," as citizens, and as social actors.[15] The CRC also addresses children's rights to receive care and protection and the promotion of their best interests for "full and

harmonious development." Article 18 emphasizes that State Parties must provide "appropriate assistance to parents ... in the performance of their child-rearing responsibilities" and take "all appropriate measures to ensure that children of working parents have the right to benefit from childcare services."[16] Countries that have ratified the CRC are required to submit periodic reports that are subject to international review and scrutiny. Although the reports and recommendations are not binding, they do serve a critical purpose in creating an international discourse of childcare rights that has had the power to shape domestic policy changes in numerous countries that have ratified the Convention.[17]

CEDAW, hailed as an "international bill of rights for women," was adopted by the UN General Assembly in 1979 and entered into force as a treaty in 1981. CEDAW has been ratified by 169 countries, excluding the United States. There is explicit recognition in CEDAW of the links between women's equality, the right to work, family life, and the necessity for government to ensure that these rights and opportunities are upheld by focusing on provisions for the care of children. Article 11 specifically addresses women's "right to work as an inalienable right," including "the right to maternity leave with pay or with comparable benefits." State parties are enjoined to make it possible to "combine family obligations with work responsibilities and participation in public life ... through promoting the establishment and development of a network of childcare facilities."[18] Similarly, ICESCR ratified by 145 countries, but not the United States, ensures the "equal right of men and women to the enjoyment of all economic, social and cultural rights" including rights to "fair wages," "a decent living for themselves and their families," paid maternity leave, and adequate social security benefits for working mothers.[19]

The United States clearly violates the social and economic rights that are embedded in these three human rights conventions, specifically those that address women's rights and children's rights. From a cross-national comparative perspective, the United States fails on almost all indices of child and family well-being. The U.S. poverty rate is characterized by Gornick and Meyers in their 12-nation comparative analysis as "exceptional" and of particular concern, given high rates of poverty even among two-parent working families. Among single-mother families who are employed, 45 percent live in poverty in the United States, a dramatic contrast to levels of 8 percent in Denmark, and 4 percent in Sweden.[20] The Luxembourg Income Study (LIS), which provides the database for international comparative studies, shows that the United States has the highest average income in the industrialized world (after Luxembourg), yet ranks worst in child poverty rates among 19 rich industrialized nations.[21]

Most of the major industrialized countries have introduced maternity and parental leave provisions so that the work of caring for newborns and the formation of critical early bonds may occur within the family. Major trends in the past two decades have been to extend parental leaves during infancy, so that there is an affordable alternative for families who are permitted to take paid job-protected leaves. Europe has been instrumental in leading this trend, particularly in Scandinavia. As Kamerman documents among OECD countries, only South Korea and Switzerland have no national statutory provisions for parental leave, and the United States is one of only three countries that offers no paid leave. In the advanced industrialized nations the norm is 44 weeks, which includes maternity, paternity, and parental leaves, and the average time for a paid leave is 36 weeks. "U.S. policy," says Kamerman, "exists in dramatic contrast to the policies that exist around the world and especially in our peer countries."[22]

The U.S. Family and Medical Leave Act (FMLA) of 1993 offers only 12 weeks of unpaid leave to employees for childbirth, adoption, or carin g for an ill family member and only to those previously employed for a period of 12 months by companies with 50 or more employees, thereby excluding 42 percent of the private workforce. Low-income parents, particularly single mothers, cannot afford to take unpaid leave, and California is currently the only state that actually provides paid family leave to mothers and fathers. State Temporary Disability Insurance (TDI) is available in five states (California, Hawaii, New York, New Jersey, Rhode Island), which provide partial short-term wage replacement for disabilities (such as pregnancy and childbirth), but these states include only 25 percent of the nation's population, and in 45 other states women have no rights to any paid leave.[23]

The absence of family support policies, such as paid parental leave, takes a heavy toll on the lives of infants and their struggling-to-make-it parents. The dearth of childcare provisions and the developmentally damaging care that so many young poor children are subjected to violate their human rights. Poor women in particular, as solo mothers, as earners, as caregivers of their children, are stripped of their rights to live as fully functioning human beings, when the conditions for living are distorted. Furthermore, welfare "reform" legislation violates poor mothers' human rights by wresting from them the fundamental right to care for their own infants, as they are forced into the low-wage workplace in order to avoid destitution. With no paid parental leave and with their infants left alone or subject to the perils of the unregulated license-exempt childcare sector, how is it possible for poor women to make decisions in the best interests of their babies?

Children as Rights Bearers

The Convention on the Rights of the Child confers rights on children so that children, too, are agents and "rights bearers," and should be treated as ends not means, for each has "a life to live, deserving of both respect and resources."[24] Not so, not yet, in the United States. Unique in its unparalleled wealth and global dominance, and too, in its obdurate violations of domestic human rights whose first and primary victims are always children—the United States increasingly has come to occupy its own singular and eroded human rights milieu.

Poverty in a land of plenty is a moral disgrace; so too is the consequential childcare crisis among America's millions of low-wage families. Many other countries take seriously the fundamental care gaps that must be filled in order for children and their mothers to remain healthy and stable, by developing carefully crafted social protections aligned with the key international human rights treaties. There is a stark contrast in assumptions and sensibilities about how poor children are viewed in Europe and the United States. Viewed instrumentally, children have no rights to care, to early education, to housing, to health care, and to adequate nutrition. As dubious public goods, their young lives are cheap. And it is cost-benefit analyses of young children's lives that dominate the coldhearted discourse about the childcare crisis, and enable the deplorable perennial question about whether investing in child care and early education is worth it. This privatized tunnel vision results in a shameful indifference, where "individuals become angry at even the notion of the public good,"[25] with often brutal consequences for young children and their families.

Unequal life circumstances and the lack of fundamental social and economic rights entrap poor women and entangle their lives in a web of resource deficits that diminishes their own development as human beings, and profoundly alters their own children's life chances.

Children's distress, their fears, their shaken sense of trust and security that ensue when child care harms, when it does not work, when it is not there when needed—must be heeded and attention must be paid. There are seeping wounds and developmental scars that are readily produced in socially toxic landscapes. Consigning young children to overcrowded, unsafe, indifferent spaces, where opportunities for discovery, imaginative play, active learning, and the formation of stable relationships are absent, or worse, twisted into harsh regimens of compliance—is a violation of their human rights to grow and develop.

And it is always poor children whose lives count for less. ■

Valerie Polakow is a professor of educational psychology and early childhood at Eastern Michigan University. She has written extensively about women and children in poverty, family and childcare policies, and human rights.

References

1 Valerie Polakow. *Who Cares for Our Children? The Child Care Crisis in the Other America.* New York. Teachers College Press. 2007.
2. U.S. Department of Labor, Bureau of Labor Statistics. *Women in the Labor Force: A Data Book, Report 985.* Washington, D.C. 2005.
3. Janet Gornick and Marcia Meyers. *Families That Work.* New York. Russel Sage. p.8. 2003.
4. Arlie Hochschild. "The Culture of Politics: Traditional, Post-modern, Cold Modern and Warm Modern Ideals of Care." In *Social Politics.* 2 (3). pp. 331–346. 1995.
5. While the federal law required mothers with infants over 12 months to meet mandatory work requirements, states were permitted to set their own requirements and implement even stricter work activation requirements: Massachusetts, Michigan, Wisconsin, Ohio, and New York implemented 12 week requirements.
6. Gwendolyn Mink. *Welfare's End.* Ithaca, New York. Cornell University Press. p. 103. 1998. See also Peggy Kahn and Valerie Polakow. "Mothering Denied: Commodification and Caregiving under New US Welfare Laws." In *SAGE Race Relations Abstracts.* 25 (1). pp. 7–25. 2000.
7. Children's Defense Fund. *Child Care Basics.* Washington, D.C. 2005.
8. Helen Blank, Karen Schulman, and Danielle Ewen. *Seeds of Success: State Prekindergarten Initiatives 1998–1999.* Washington, D.C. Children's Defense Fund. 1999). See also W. Steven Barnett, Jason Hustedt, Kenneth Robin and Karen Schulman. *The State of Preschool: 2005 Preschool Yearbook.* New Brunswick, N.J. National Institute for Early Education Research. 2005.
9. The reimbursement rates are pegged at the 75th percentile of local market rates, but most states have not updated their market surveys. Michigan's current subsidy rates for example are based on 1999 survey and 66 percent of subsidy expenditure is in the unlicensed informal care sector. See also Peggy Kahn, Peter Ruark, Rick McHugh, and Jackie Doig. "Impacting Poverty: Current Trends and Issues." A Presentation to the National Association of Social Workers, Lansing, Mich., May 18, 2006. See also Karen Schulman and Helen Blank. *Child Care Assistance Policies 2005: States Fail to Make Up Lost Ground,*
Families Continue to Lack Critical Supports. Washington, D.C. National Women's Law Center. 2005.
10. Gornick & Meyers, ibid.
11. Victoria Goldman. "The Baby Ivies: Preschool Pedagogy for up to $15,000." *New York Times.* January 12. p. 22. 2003.
12. Barbara Carlson and Rebecca Sharf. *Lost in the Maze: Reforming New York City's Fragmented Child Care Subsidy System.* New York. Welfare Law Center. 2004.
13. Barbara Hobson and Ruth Lister. "Citizenship." In Barbara Hobson, Jane Lewis, and Birte Siim, eds. *Contested Concept in Gender and Social Politics.* Cheltenham, U.K. Edward Elgar. pp. 23–54. 2002.

14. Martha Davis. "Child Care as a Human Right: A New Perspective on an Old Debate." Presented at *Women Working to Make a Difference, IWPR Seventh International Women's Policy Research Conference.* Washington, D.C. June 2003.
See also Martha Davis and Roslyn Powell. "The International Convention on the Rights of the Child: A Catalyst for Innovative Child Care Policies." In *Human Rights Quarterly.* 25 (3). pp. 689–719. 2003.
15. Susan Kilbourne. "Placing the Convention on the Rights of the Child in an American Context." In *Human Rights.* 28 (2). p. 27. 1999.
16. Convention on the Rights of the Child. *Preamble, Article 18 (2), (3).* United Nations Office of the High Commissioner for Human Rights. 1989.
17. Davis & Powell, ibid.
18. *Convention on the Elimination of all Forms of Discrimination against Women. Article 11, 1 (a), 2 (b), 2 (c).* United Nations Division for the Advancement of Women. 1979.
19. International Covenant on Economic, Social, and *Cultural Rights. Article 3, 7 (a) (i) (ii); Article 10 (2).* Office of the United Nations High Commissioner for Human Rights. 1966.
20. Gornick & Meyers, ibid.
21. Timothy Smeeding, et al. *United States Poverty in a Cross-National Context (No. 244).* Syracuse, New York. Syracuse University. 2000.
22. Sheila Kamerman. "Parental Leave Policy: As Essential Ingredient of Early Childhood Care Policies." *Social Policy Report.* 14 (2). p. 13. 2000.
23. Davis & Powell, ibid.
Kamerman, ibid.
Gornick & Meyers, ibid.
24. Martha Nussbaum. *Women and Human Development: The Capabilities Approach.* Cambridge, U.K. Cambridge University Press. p. 65. 2000.
25. Toni Morrison. "Racism and Fascism." *The Nation.* 260 (21). p. 760. 1995.

It's All of Our Business

What Fighting for Family-Friendly Policies Could Mean for Early Childhood Educators

BY ELLEN BRAVO

At the end of her lunch break at an Atlanta child-care center in August 2002, Stacey Calvin checked on her 2-year-old son, Jevon, who attended the same facility. She found him sitting on the floor shaking and grabbed a thermometer—his temperature was 104.1. Immediately, Calvin picked the boy up, carried him toward the door, and began dialing her supervisor's cell phone. Her boss insisted she finish her shift. "He said if I clocked out there was a chance I wouldn't ever clock in again," she recalls. Calvin stood her ground and kept her job. Her luck ran out two years later, when she was eight months pregnant. After she slipped on some stairs before work, the doctor told her to take a day off as a precaution. Although Calvin felt fine the next day and badly needed the income, her boss told her she could not return until after the baby was born. "Women don't know their limitations," he claimed.

How could this happen? Because in the United States today, the workplace has not kept up with profound changes in the workforce, including the significant increase in employment among women and growing demands for care of both young children and seniors. Obsolete standards in the workplace make families feel that child care and leave are personal problems, but in reality, they're political, the result of outdated workplace policies designed for a bygone era when most families had employed fathers and stay-at-home mothers.

Business leaders and their political boosters deny the need for family-friendly business standards—ones that allow all workers to be both responsible family members and conscientious employees. But such changes will improve working conditions for early childhood workers and their families and for the children they educate.

Why Are We in This Boat?

It's easy to forget that until 1978, it was perfectly legal in this country to fire someone for being pregnant. You may not think Congress knows much, but even they understood that pregnancy does have something to do with sex. After much organizing by grassroots groups, Congress passed the Pregnancy Discrimination Act (PDA).

Groups then organized to pass the Family and Medical Leave Act, which did include a job guarantee and covered men as well as women and a broader range of care needs, including personal illness. Although it was a critical first step, the FMLA is fairly meager. It's unpaid, rendering it moot to large numbers of workers. It applies only to firms of 50 or more employees and covers only those who work at least 25 hours a week and have been on the job at least a year. That leaves out more than half of private sector workers, including most early childhood teachers and caregivers.

The FMLA has another enormous limitation: it applies only to serious illness. Fortunately, most kids don't get leukemia, but they do all get stomach flus and colds and a host of other ailments not covered by this law. Not to worry, business lobbyists proclaim, workers can use their sick days for that. Problem is, half the workforce doesn't have any paid sick days to use. Many who do have the benefit aren't allowed to use it to care for a sick family member.

For early childhood educators that means both having to come to work sick themselves and having to deal with sick children whose parents aren't allowed to stay home with them or able to pick them up if they fall ill at day care.

What's at Stake?

The consequences of outmoded family policies are especially hard on children and families. Common sense tells us that kids fare better when their parents are available to care for them. Research underlines the significance of this connection. For instance, we now know the importance of parental bonding for early brain development and of paid leave for reducing infant mortality. Yet more than 60 percent of new mothers in the U.S. take less than 12 weeks of leave after the birth of a child and more than half receive no pay during that leave. At these crucial early developmental stages, a lack of parental leave can translate into barriers to healthy growth and development.

Medical researchers have found that sick children have shorter recovery periods when their parents participate in their care, as well as better vital signs and fewer symptoms. The presence of parents has been shown to reduce hospital stays by 31 percent and to speed up recovery from outpatient procedures as well. We know that low-wage families are more likely to have children with health and learning issues. Yet these workers are the least likely to have access to any schedule flexibility or paid time off.

Carissa Peppard works as an occupational therapist in the birth-to-3 setting, often with families who are just realizing their child may be on the autism spectrum.

"If parents can't take the time off for early diagnosis," she says, "they miss key interventions that can lead to independence. They need time find a specialist and to identify a childcare center that will provide appropriate care. The only doctor in the field may be three hours away."

Clearly these issues affect early childhood educators whether or not they have children of their own. When parents don't have adequate time for bonding and to care for sick kids, their children are more likely to have serious problems when entering prekindergarten and kindergarten, their prime development years.

What's Being Done?

To make significant progress toward policy change, we must come to understand the core issue isn't a matter of personal choices but a systemic problem (family values too often stop at the workplace door), that this problem requires government action, and that the appropriate role of government is to create standards that reflect prevailing public values.

I coordinate a network of state coalitions working to expand paid leave and other family- flexible options. These groups are made up of diverse allies—grassroots groups fighting for kids, economic justice, worker rights and aging populations, alongside progressive employers, teachers and school principals, interfaith councils and disability activists. The network, known as the Multi-State Working Families Consortium, is a new model of collaboration, where groups raise funds together and share them equally. They also share strategies, materials, and organizing tips.

Each of these groups and many others are winning changes at the state and local level, as well as working together for new federal policies. In 2004, a state coalition in California successfully won expansion of its Temporary Disability Insurance (TDI) program to cover leave for family care purposes. Groups in New Jersey, another state with TDI funds, won a similar victory in spring of 2008, and New York may soon follow suit. Washington State created a new social insurance fund to cover parental leave.

In 2006, San Francisco passed the first city-wide ordinance to guarantee a minimum number of paid sick days to all employees. The District of Columbia followed in 2008. Groups from Milwaukee to Montana are introducing similar measures in city councils and state legislatures.

I see early childhood educators as a great asset to this organizing. The first step is to find ways to speak out, both about providers' own needs as workers and about the consequences for children when parents aren't able to be present in times of need. This can be done through letters to the editor, op-eds, testimony at public hearings, and rallies. For the public and decision makers, early childhood teachers embody legitimacy and authority regarding what children need. Caregivers also have access to large numbers of parents. Sharing information, connecting parents with coalitions, arranging for coalition members to set up tables during registration, parent-teacher conferences, PTA meetings and the like, are all ways to serve as internal organizers for these campaigns.

More Work to Do

Many employers have done a great job making the workplace family-friendly, enabling workers to have control over their schedules and treating them as whole people who have lives outside of work. Research reminds us over and over that workers who feel respected return the favor by improved loyalty and performance.

And family-friendly policies are not an unmanageable cost for employers. Even when looking solely at the bottom line, the costs pale beside the price tag for employee turnover, estimated at 150 percent of compensation for salaried employees. The expense for family-friendly benefits for low-wage earners is relatively inexpensive when you consider the steep cost in replacing a worker—recruitment, training, and lost productivity add up to more than $5,500 for someone earning $8 an hour.

Spreading the word about best practices is important. But expecting all business owners to implement them is like thinking 2-year-olds can decide when they need a time out. We need to guarantee a reasonable floor for all workers, and that means public policy changes. These include guarantees of paid sick days, accessible and affordable family leave paid for by the shared risk of a social insurance fund, equity for part-time workers, and quality dependent care. It also means a reasonable work week with no mandatory overtime. Such policies will work only with a meaningful wage floor: money is a work-life issue.

Young children need quality education and love from caregivers every day. Sometimes, though, they need to be home with their parents or to have their parents participate in plans for their care. Early childhood educators can help make that possible by becoming involved in coalitions to win policies that put family values to work. ■

To hear and watch workers telling their own stories and to link with campaigns in your state, go to 1000VoicesArchive.org and select the special series Family Values at Work. For more information, visit www.valuefamiliesatwork.org.

Ellen Bravo, former director of 9to5, National Association of Working Women, teaches women's studies at the University of Wisconsin-Milwaukee and coordinates the Multi-State Working Families Consortium. Her latest book is *Taking on the Big Boys, or Why Feminism Is Good for Families, Business and the Nation* (Feminist Press, 2007).

ROB DUNLAVEY

Improving Conditions and Status for Early Childhood Educators

By Charles Bruner

Improving working conditions and professional status for early childhood educators is critical to developing high-quality early childhood and school-readiness programs. Making these improvements with special attention to career ladders and opportunities for educators in low-income, immigrant, and minority communities is critically important as states and communities develop new standards for child care and create new preschool programs to serve these families. Colorblind approaches simply will not produce the gains that are needed to close the gaps that children in poor, immigrant, and minority communities experience at the time of school entry.

Poor teacher compensation has long been a major challenge for the field of early care and education. In 2004, according to the Bureau of Labor Statistics, the median annual salary of a childcare worker was just under $18,000. The vast majority of childcare workers qualify as low-income or living in poverty.

Such low worker compensation is extremely harmful to program quality. Low worker wages are directly correlated to increased rates of turnover, often ranging in childcare centers to annual rates of 25 percent to 50 percent. A constantly changing staff makes it difficult for children to form solid social and emotional relationships with the adults who have primary responsibility for them.

Low wages also mean that workers seldom have the discretionary resources they might use to invest in their own career development. These low wages are tied to the absence of sufficient public subsidies to increase wages and professional development supports. Most working families simply are not in a position to pay enough out of their wages for child care both to provide for decent wages for childcare workers and to make their own work pay. In short, there is a mismatch between what parents can afford to pay for child care and what is needed to ensure decent wages that can support quality care.

Current state efforts to develop quality rating systems and tie enhanced reimbursement to those systems are one means for raising compensation, with an attention to quality. As these are developed, however, they must recognize the importance of developing a quality workforce through the multicultural lens. As an example of the current lack of attention to these issues, few quality rating systems being established in states assign any value to teacher bilingualism or to cultural congruity in determining what rating level programs achieve.

Raising compensation for childcare center and family childcare home providers also can have a positive economic impact on poor, immigrant, and minority communities by increasing the assets in those communities. Numerous childcare economic impact studies have shown that early care and education is big business, rivaling industries such as the insurance and financial services industries in job generation and the income they produce. Not only do they enable parents to work in other jobs, but they are a significant part of the local economy, particularly in poor, immigrant, and minority communities. Therefore, raising compensation as well as skills and career pathway opportunities can have a positive economic impact on whole communities.

Recommendations

A set of principles can be used to construct multiple pathways and a scaffold that will support the development of a highly qualified, bilingual, multicultural workforce. These principles should be used together to develop effective national, state, and local infrastructures and policies:

- Redefine the core competencies for providing high quality care and education to include effectively addressing the development and learning needs of ethnic, minority, and foreign-born children.
- Invest in multiple delivery systems and alternative pathways that help teachers, especially from under-represented backgrounds, further their education. A key component is ensuring articulation between non-credit granting training, two- and four-year degree programs.
- Build capacity within community colleges, four-year colleges and training institutions to provide effective coursework and training for quality early childhood education appropriate to an increasingly diverse population of young children.
- Provide adequate resources, support and time for people (and particularly low-income, nontraditional and immigrant students) to pursue and successfully complete the pathways toward a degree.
- Link the creation of new workforce standards with the financing of the early childhood system and appropriate compensation levels that support the retention of a high quality, well-trained early childhood education workforce.
- Monitor and track the impact of professional policies on the diversity of the early childhood education workforce. ■

This chapter is excerpted from Charles Bruner with Michelle Stover Wright, Syed Noor Tirmizi, and the School Readiness, Culture, and Language Working Group of the Annie E. Casey Foundation. *Village Building and School Readiness: Closing Opportunity Gaps in a Diverse Society.* Des Moines, Iowa. State Early Childhood Policy Technical Assistance Network. 2007. The working group also produced *Getting Ready for Quality: The Critical Importance of Developing and Supporting a Skilled, Ethnically and Linguistically Diverse Early Childhood Workforce.* Oakland. California Tomorrow. 2006.

Charles Bruner is executive director of the Child and Family Policy Center. He served 12 years as a state legislator in Iowa.

J.D. KING

Caught in a Quagmire

The Effort to Improve Wages and Working Conditions for Childcare Teachers

BY PATTY HNATIUK

The Center for the Child Care Workforce's Worthy Wage Campaign slogan from the 1990s still rings true today: "Parents can't afford to pay and teachers can't afford to stay—there has got to be a better way." However, the better way being pressed by lobbyists and politicians is to plunge the system into the quagmire of marketplace idealism and for-profit providers, whose sights are so focused on the bottom line that they can't see the important mission of educating children. Nor do their proposals have workers' interests at heart. We will only free ourselves from the effects of commercialized child care when we coalesce to move forward with constructive demands for equitable, coherent, well-funded systems.

The for-profit workforce is bumping up against the universal prekindergarten (UPK) movement in the U.S. Universal prekindergarten is an effort, organized and funded at the state level, to provide preschool programs to all 4-year-old children, regardless of income. The push towards UPK impacts issues like employment and working conditions, and the funding of childcare programs in communities. Side by side with the push towards UPK is an expanded privatization of child care, with corporate chains like Bright Horizons gobbling up childcare programs. These realities compel early childhood workers to find ways to organize and to join ranks with organized school teachers.

The problem of decades of low salaries among the 2.3 million in the workforce is oppressive to women and children. On May 1, 2008, which is "Worthy Wage Day" in the childcare field, the American Federation of Teachers (AFT) held a briefing on Capitol Hill during which early childhood educators discussed low wages and other problems plaguing the profession. Most striking in the AFT's presentation was a comparison of mean hourly wages of early childhood educators and other teachers.[1]

Elementary Teacher—$23.41

Kindergarten Teacher—$22.62

Preschool Teacher—$12.45

Childcare Worker—$9.05

The mean annual salary of childcare workers in the United States in 2006 was $18,820. According to the AFT, since 1973 the hourly wage of childcare workers with some college education has gone up *39 cents*. Professions with mean hourly wages comparable to childcare workers include parking lot attendants ($8.33), bell hops ($8.83) and animal trainers ($14.39).

Incremental wage increases for employed childcare teachers and providers attending college need to be guaranteed. As students successfully complete courses, reward systems placed within shared career lattices need to be established. At present, the wage scales vary widely between Head Start, corporate, community, school-age, and family childcare programs. Wage scale consistency, not based on market value or volume of stockholder investments, is required to bring about more equity for the workforce. When wages are linked to education, teachers and providers need tangible support for accessing higher education—support like tuition assistance and loan forgiveness programs; higher education is often out of the reach of teachers and providers, which leaves them in a closed loop of low wages that can't be improved by additional education which would move them up a wage ladder.

States typically distribute funds for UPK pilot programs through school systems and in school districts. According to the National Women's Law Center, some states have been successful subcontracting between school districts and the local childcare centers. However, when school districts hold the purse strings, suspicions can arise in communities about how fairly the money will be allocated. In Boston, for instance, the Mayor's UPK initiative, while well-intended, has caused real problems in existing community-based childcare programs. Parents of preschoolers have understandably opted to send their children to free early learning centers housed in the schools, thus exiting community childcare programs and forcing closures of preschool classrooms, layoffs, and a scramble among program directors to maintain balanced budgets. The centers are not being "invited in" to the schools or to union pay scales in many areas of the country. Administrative collaborations at the state and local levels can help to assure that children's early education and care not be disrupted when one agency controls the funding. It should be possible to allocate funds within districts and communities (even rural regions) to support early education for children in a variety of settings.

Teachers and providers should be able to join teacher unions and form the early education flanks in public education. Childcare teachers are eager for the recognition and compensation afforded their counterparts in the schools. When school districts subcontract with childcare programs for prekindergarten, the amount of funding needs to be sufficient to provide good quality—including pay scales for early education teachers that are comparable to those of elementary school teachers. Also, the childcare community needs assurances that health, education, and safety standards will not be compromised and that funding agreements will be met over the long term.

By bringing public schools and childcare sectors together, all teachers will be more fully able to engage in meaningful dialogues about developmental early education principles and how to best prepare all children to progress within elementary schools. The "entering school ready to learn" mantra doesn't cut it. Teacher understanding and acknowledgment that from birth children are *learning already* can open the way for more long-term student achievement and success. When primary school teachers and early education teachers engage in shared professional development opportunities focused on diverse children and families, it can be a win-win for all concerned.

Untangling the Complexities

Early education and care employs a female workforce (the younger the students, the greater the number of women in the education workforce). Women's comparable worth in wages still remains well below that of men, and in childcare jobs the wages are even lower. There is still a notion that women should educate and care for young children out of love or duty, and that they ought not to be concerned with compensation. These patriarchal attitudes and realities disempower workers from organizing and asserting themselves.

There is long-term gain from investing in early education and care of young children. Because high staff turnover has a negative impact on children's development in early education, and the number one reason for turnover is low wages, it makes sense to invest socially, politically, and economically in solutions to the childcare compensation crisis. Notable efforts to bring justice to the staffing crisis emphasize empowerment of the workforce and grassroots movement-building to bring about change, including the Worthy Wage Campaign and the Leadership Empowerment Action Project led by the Washington, D.C.-based Center for the Child Care Workforce. These organizing models have expanded the ranks of diverse leadership, won state and local victories, and contributed to childcare worker empowerment. However, the field at large continues to lack unity and shared vision.

There are several reasons for the discord. States and sectors have different standards and regulations. In states with large numbers of for-profit, anti-union childcare chains, there are paid lobbyists actively working against stronger standards and regulations in order to keep group sizes large and staff-child ratios low, thus maximizing profits. The high rates of teacher turnover, because of poor wages, benefits, and working conditions, lead to destabilization of the workforce, engender low staff morale, and work against building stability and unity.

Furthermore, there are multiple funding streams, especially among public childcare providers. Head Start and Early Head Start have their own distinct federal funding. Community-based child care has languished for decades with underfunding and inequitable funding rates from public sources, and relies instead on fees from parents with ever-tightening family incomes.

And the field itself suffers from an identity crisis. How can care be education and education be care? How can a large and dispersed workforce come to consensus about the purpose of the field? There are no simple answers. However, there needs to be a sense of urgency to try to articulate a "better way" for children, the workforce, and parents.

A Vision for a Better Way

Massive public investment on the order of billions of dollars is required to close the wage gap between those working outside of public school systems and those working in them. New revenue sources need to be enacted. Of course, we need direct financial assistance to programs and increases in state and federal subsidies to income-eligible families. At present, only a small percentage of eligible families receive subsidized support for the cost of full-day child care and early education.

In addition, we need accountable administrative systems with locally based paid staff and infrastructure to provide data collection, technical assistance, training, and services in multiple languages. There also needs to be an infusion of funds to increase entry-level minimum wages, as well as a raise in teacher salaries across the board in subsidized early education and care systems.

A blending or integration of full-day early childhood programs can succeed in partnership with service delivery through public education systems. We can make more attempts at merging dollars and funding streams, without disrupting children's current programs. In fact, school and community satellite programs can link with health centers, resource and referral agencies, multilingual parent education and employment centers to create "seamless" collaborations. Representative local community councils can lead and guide decision-making and data collection regarding local assets and needs. All teachers and providers should fit into roles in progressive career development systems and receive equitable pay for commensurate education, along with shared professional development opportunities. Early childhood educators should qualify for unionized teaching positions, with benefits, in developmental, linguistic, and culturally appropriate classrooms and home settings.

What educational attainment will be required of all teachers? How will access to higher education (including loan forgiveness, scholarships, student supports, and advising) be expanded? What options exist for credit for prior learning, as well as offerings in languages other than English and support for immigrants and English language learners seeking additional education?

Federal financing is sorely needed for resources to support higher education in preparing teachers to meet state standards to teach in early childhood settings. However, caution must be applied. As standards become more rigorous (in support of better quality programs), there is a danger of stratifying the education levels among teachers and providers across race and class lines. Approximately 30 percent of the childcare workforce is made up of people of color (African American, Asian, Latino), according to a 2002 report from the Center for the Child Care Workforce. Teacher preparation to meet state standards should go hand in hand with improved access to higher education.

If comparable education for comparable pay continues to become the rule, community-based childcare and Head Start teachers will need to be advised on how to incorporate college courses they have already attained, earn credit for prior learning, and join in higher education from multiple points of entry.

Child Care, Commercial Fare

I once attended a research conference in Toronto where I heard Helen Penn, the noted early education scholar from London, make a dismissive remark that little could be learned from U.S. childcare systems because they are *primarily commercial.*

This gave me pause and I reflected on U.S. child care. The origins of organized child care (day nurseries) in the U.S. were employer-sponsored—in tenements adjoining factories. However, during World War II, under the Lanham Act, the U.S. created childcare centers serving 400,000 children when mothers were needed to work in defense industry jobs. It happened virtually overnight. And the system was shut down just as fast. Of the 3,000 centers opened under the act, 2,800 were closed as women were sent home from work to make way for returning soldiers.[2]

We live in different times. Today the largest childcare sponsors are corporate conglomerates, with the bulk of U.S. child care based (after the military) in the for-profit sector. And it shows no signs of slowing down.

In January 2008, Bright Horizons Family Solutions reached an agreement to be acquired by an affiliate of Bain Capital—a private equity firm founded in 1984 by former GOP presidential candidate Mitt Romney and others—for $1.3 billion. Bain has invested in such diverse companies as Staples, Burger King, Toys 'R' Us, and Hospital Corporation of America. This is its first foray into education. Bright Horizons manages more than 600 early-care and family centers in the U.S., Canada, the United Kingdom, and Ireland, serving more than 700 clients including nearly one fifth of the Fortune 500 companies.[3] It boggles the mind to consider the market value of our childcare programs today—not in terms of children's futures, but rather, stockholder shares.

While the Bright Horizons centers are well-equipped and corporately housed and situated, the majority of its nonunionized workforce is no better compensated than childcare teachers in other centers. Program directors grapple with staff turnover issues, just like their counterparts in the nonprofit sector. The leveraged buyout of Bright Horizons by Bain—Bain provides the down payment, Bright Horizons pays the off the debt—has raised serious concerns in the childcare industry about what will happen next. Private equity firms are not publicly traded companies and operate virtually free of public accountability. After Bain bought KB Toys in 2000, the toy company closed stores, laid off employees, and filed for bankruptcy in 2004. The Service Employees International Union's (SEIU's) Kids First campaign is promoting public awareness about Bain's acquisition of Bright Horizons. In it, a Bright Horizons parent, Deborah Brown, states: "Our children's education depends on maintaining good programs and treating staff well. Parents will not tolerate cuts in quality to pad the pockets of CEOs."

Movement Signs for Optimism

Compensation activists understand the issues and complexities facing the field. Public policy connections to systemic change and transformation in early education have been drawn for years. In fact, historically, major U.S. policy devel-op-ments have emanated from grassroots movements, not been bestowed from above.

One sign of achievement for advocates is the inclusion of compensation and rewards systems in legislative mandates and plans for workforce development with the advent of UPK. Of course, fiscal solutions must be devised in order to meet the legislative requirements.

Labor activists have made strides—particularly of note are successes by the SEIU in the family childcare arena. Its organizing drive, Kids First, combines comprehensive, inclusive policy papers[4] and legislative referenda that demonstrate how to build a campaign with and for providers. Kids First incorporates policy analyses and recommendations in pressing forward in community organizing, along with legislative agendas and strategies.

Evelyne Dalembert, a longtime family childcare provider in Somerville, Mass., and Steering Committee member of Kids First with Local 888, explains that in family childcare homes, "With 10 children, we must hire an assistant, yet we only receive $27.50 per day, per child, and that ends up paying us less than minimum wage. This is not acceptable.

"We have to stand up for ourselves and not expect that others will do it for us," she goes on. "We are the ones working with kids all day, many from 7:00 a.m. to 6:00 p.m. We know what's going on and we have to help each other and decide what we want for ourselves.

"Most providers want more education, associate's degrees or higher, but we need tuition assistance and strong advising and support systems to guide us through the processes of higher education. Some of us have been out of school for 20 years."

SEIU notes lessons from other states, including the TEACH Early Childhood Program, which provides scholarships for tuition, fees, and books, stipends for earning course credits and degrees, and CDA assessment fees. It was developed in North Carolina and has spread to 21 states. Wage supplement initiatives in states, such as the WAGE$ Projects, provide six-month bonuses to providers who achieve certain levels of education to supplement their low wages.

No Panacea, Just Hard Work

While there are signs that state and federal officials are taking early childhood education more seriously than in the past, advocates know not to rely solely on elected officials to fix the compensation crisis. They surely have roles to play, legislation to pass, and funding to approve. Their constituents need to keep them accountable. Yet no one argument or organizing strategy will bring about the systemic changes necessary to establish equity in the paid childcare workforce. Meaningful systemic change will require numerous ongoing actions in and outside of government and on multiple fronts, including introspection and leadership choices within the field itself.[5]

There needs to be a broad-based movement for change to keep plugging away as always, relying on ourselves, our unions, organizations, and allies to call for and take actions to achieve social and economic justice. This is how we pull the workforce in early education and care from the quagmire. Our success will rely on how effectively we forge strategic alliances and build inclusive movements across sectors, cultures, and regions. ■

Patty Hnatiuk has taught, designed courses and programs, and written in the early childhood field since 1971. She is co-author of *The Early Childhood Mentoring Curriculum: Handbook for Mentors* and *Trainer's Guide* (Center for the Child Care Workforce, 1997) and was a founder of the national Worthy Wage Campaign. She is an instructor in education at Wheelock College in Boston.

References

1. American Federation of Teachers, AFL–CIO. *Fact Sheet: Legislative Briefing,* May 2008. Washington, D.C. 2008.
2. American Association of Family and Consumer Sciences. "Public Policy Resolution." In *Child Care for the 21st Century.* Alexandria, Va. 2003.
3. Robert Daniel. *Bright Horizons Going Private for $1.3 billion.* www.marketwatch.com/ January 14, 2008.
4. Service Employees International Union. *A Shared Vision for Professional Development and Quality Enhancement in Massachusetts Family Child Care: A Discussion Document from Service Employees International Union (SEIU) Kids First, Local 888.* Boston, Mass. 2007.
5. S. Goffin and V. Washington. *Ready or Not: Leadership Choices in Early Care and Education.* New York. Teachers College Press. 2007.

Part VIII

Resources

"Teacher research is largely about developing the professional dispositions of lifelong learning, reflective and mindful teaching, and self-transformation. The real value of engaging in teacher research is that it may lead to rethinking and reconstructing what it means to be a teacher and, consequently, the way teachers relate to children."

Andrew J. Stremmel
Nurturing Professional and Personal Growth Through Inquiry

10 Quick Ways to Analyze Children's Books for Racism and Sexism

BY THE COUNCIL ON INTERRACIAL BOOKS FOR CHILDREN

Both in school and out children are exposed to racist and sexist attitudes. These attitudes—expressed over and over in books and other media—gradually distort their perceptions until stereotypes and myths about minorities and women are accepted as reality. It is difficult for a librarian or teacher to convince children to question society's attitudes. But if a child can be shown how to detect racism and sexism in a book, the child can proceed to transfer the perception to wider areas. The following 10 guidelines are offered as a starting point in evaluating children's books from this perspective.

1. Check the Illustrations.

Look for Stereotypes. A stereotype is an oversimplified generalization about a particular group, race, or sex, which usually carries derogatory implications. Some infamous (overt) stereotypes of blacks are the happy-go-lucky, watermelon-eating Sambo and the fat, eye-rolling "mammy"; of Chicanos, the sombrero-wearing peon or fiesta-loving, macho bandito; of Asian Americans, the inscrutable, slant-eyed "Oriental"; of Native Americans, the naked savage or "primitive brave" and his "squaw"; of Puerto Ricans, the switchblade-toting teenage gang member; of women, the completely domesticated mother, the demure, doll-loving little girl, or the wicked stepmother. While you may not always find stereotypes in the blatant forms described, look for variations which in any way demean or ridicule characters because of their race or sex.

Look for Tokenism. If there are racial minority characters in the illustrations, do they look just like whites except for being tinted or colored in? Do all minority faces look stereotypically alike, or are they depicted as genuine individuals with distinctive features?

Who's Doing What? Do the illustrations depict minorities in subservient and passive roles or in leadership and action roles? Are males the active "doers" and females the inactive observers?

2. Check the Story Line.

Liberation movements have led publishers to weed out many insulting passages, particularly from stories with black themes and from books depicting female characters; however, racist and sexist attitudes still find expression in less obvious ways. The following checklist suggests some of the subtle (covert) forms of bias to watch for.

Standards for Success. Does it take "white" behavior standards for a minority person to "get ahead"? Is "making it" in the dominant white society projected as the only ideal? To gain acceptance and approval, do persons of color have to exhibit extraordinary qualities—excel in sports, get A's, etc.? In friendships between white and non-white children, is it the child of color who does most of the understanding and forgiving?

Resolution of Problems. How are problems presented, conceived and resolved in the story? Are minority people considered to be "the problem"? Are the oppressions faced by minorities and women represented as related to social injustice? Are the reasons for poverty and oppression explained, or are they accepted as inevitable? Does the story line encourage passive acceptance or active resistance? Is a particular problem that is faced by a racial minority person or female resolved through the benevolent intervention of a white person or male?

Role of Women. Are the achievements of girls and women based on their own initiative and intelligence, or are they due to their good looks or to their relationship with boys? Are sex roles incidental or critical to characterization and plot? Could the same story be told if the sex roles were reversed?

3. Look at the Lifestyles.

Are minority persons and their setting depicted in such a way that they contrast unfavorably with the unstated norm of white middle-class suburbia? If the minority group in question is depicted as "different," are negative value judgments implied? Are minorities depicted exclusively in ghettos, barrios, or migrant camps? If the illustrations and text attempt to depict another culture, do they go beyond oversimplifications and offer genuine insight into another lifestyle? Look for inaccuracy and inappropriateness in the depiction of other cultures. Watch for instances of the "quaint-natives-in-costume" syndrome (most noticeable in areas like clothing and custom, but extending to behavior and personality traits as well).

4. Weigh the Relationships Between People.

Do the whites in the story possess the power, take the leadership, and make the important decisions? Do racial minorities and females of all races function in essentially supporting roles?

How are family relationships depicted? In black families, is the mother always dominant? In Hispanic families, are there always lots of children? If the family is separated, are societal conditions—unemployment, poverty, for example—cited among the reasons for the separation?

5. Note the Heroes.

For many years, books showed only "safe" minority heroes—those who avoided serious conflict with the white establishment of their time. Minority groups today are insisting on the right to define their own heroes (of both sexes) based on their own concepts and struggles for justice.

When minority heroes do appear, are they admired for the same qualities that have made white heroes famous or because what they have done has benefited white people? Ask this question: "Whose interest is a particular hero really serving?"

6. Consider the Effect on a Child's Self-Image.

Are norms established which limit any child's aspirations and self-concept? What effect can it have on images of the color white as the ultimate in beauty, cleanliness, virtue, etc., and the color black as evil, dirty, menacing, etc.? Does the book counteract or reinforce this positive association with the color white and negative association with black?

What happens to a girl's self-image when she reads that boys perform all of the brave and important deeds? What about a girl's self-esteem if she is not "fair" of skin and slim of body?

In a particular story, is there one or more persons with whom a minority child can readily identify to a positive and constructive end?

7. Consider the Author's or Illustrator's Background.

Analyze the biographical material on the jacket flap or the back of the book. If a story deals with a minority theme, what qualifies the author or illustrator to deal with the subject? If the author and illustrator are not members of the minority being written about, is there anything in their background that would specifically recommend them as the creators of this book?

8. Check Out the Author's Perspective.

No author can be wholly objective. All authors write out of a cultural, as well as a personal context. Children's books in the past have traditionally come from authors who were white and who were members of the middle class, with one result being that a single ethnocentric perspective has dominated children's literature in the United States. With any book in question, read carefully to determine whether the direction of the author's perspective substantially weakens or strengthens the value of his/her written work. Is the perspective patriarchal or feminist? Is it solely eurocentric, or do minority cultural perspectives also appear?

9. Watch for Loaded Words.

A word is loaded when it has insulting overtones. Examples of loaded adjectives (usually racist) are "savage," "primitive," "lazy," "superstitious," "treacherous," "wily," "crafty," "inscrutable," "docile," and "backward."

Look for sexist language and adjectives that exclude or ridicule women. Look for use of the male pronoun to refer to both males and females. While the generic use of the word "man" was accepted in the past, its use today is outmoded. The following examples show how sexist language can be avoided: ancestors instead of forefathers; chairperson instead of chairman; community instead of brotherhood; firefighters instead of firemen; manufactured instead of manmade; the human family instead of the family of man.

10. Look at the Copyright Date.

Books on minority themes—usually hastily conceived—suddenly began appearing in the mid-1960s. There followed a growing number of "minority experience" books to meet the new market demand, but most of these were still written by the white authors, edited by white editors, and published by white publishers. They therefore reflected a white point of view. Not until the early 1970s did the children's book world begin to even remotely reflect the realities of a multiracial society. The new direction resulted from the emergence of minority authors writing about their own experiences. Unfortunately, this trend has been reversing, as publishers have cut back on such books. Nonsexist books, with rare exceptions, were not published before 1973.

The copyright dates, therefore, can be a clue as to how likely the book is to be overtly racist or sexist, although a recent copyright date, of course, is no guarantee of a book's relevance or sensitivity. The copyright date only means the year the book was published. It usually takes about two years from the time a manuscript is submitted to the publisher to the time it is actually printed and put on the market. This time lag meant very little in the past, but in a time of rapid change and changing consciousness, when children's book publishing is attempting to be "relevant," it is becoming increasingly significant. ■

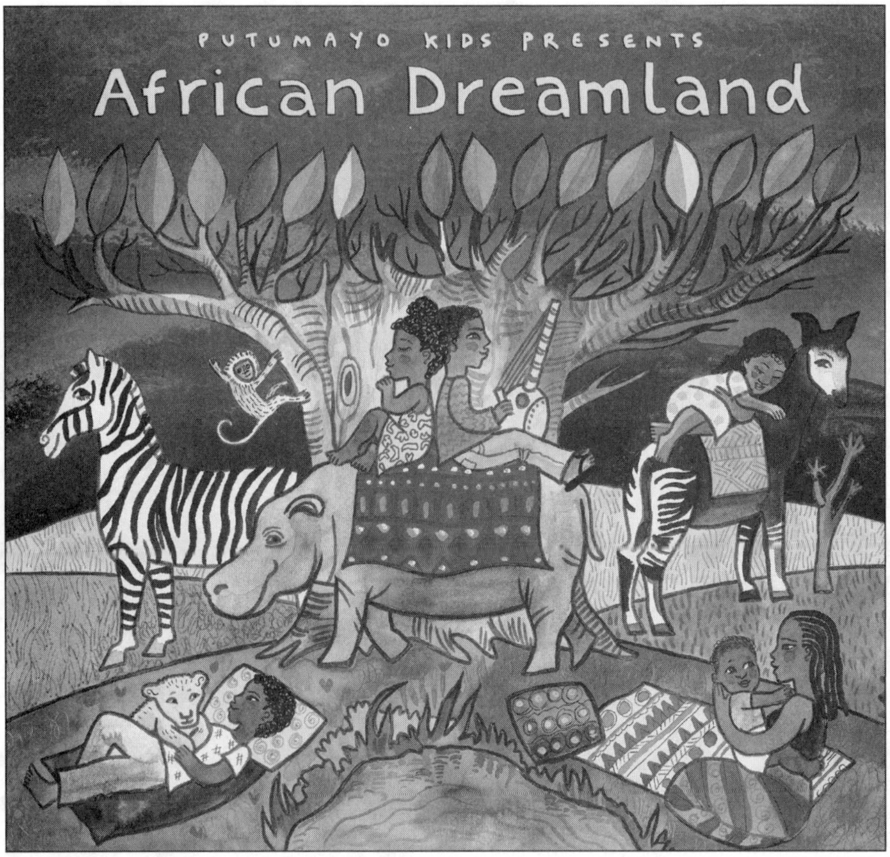

Putumayo Kids presents African Dreamland / Putumayo World Music / Artwork by Nicola Heindl

Music for Social Justice

BY RITA TENORIO

What a joy it is to share music with children! Whether it serves as background while children arrive, inspiration for starting the day together, a soothing offering during quiet times, or a source of reflection, music can build and sustain early childhood community.

Music is one way to expose young children to cultural diversity and to invite them to look at the world in different ways. Young children notice and are able to analyze similarities and differences. They have an emergent ability to respect others and to notice fair and unfair behavior. Early childhood educators should build on those dispositions in children by exposing them to familiar and unfamiliar people, events, and images. We should give young children opportunities to discuss concepts like fairness and stereotyping, and to explore the ways in which people see the world with multiple perspectives. Noticing and honoring "differences" is the basis for children's ability to engage in deeper critical analysis about fairness and injustice as they grow and mature. Music can help lay the foundation for children's awareness of and comfort with differences.

I have always believed that "children's" songs have an important role. But there is so much more. Listening to Raffi is good, but children should also hear Pete Seeger and Stevie Wonder, José Luis Orozco and Sweet Honey in the Rock. Music from many different genres and cultures is an easy and powerful strategy for introducing culture to students.

Music as a part of multicultural/anti-racist education should be integrated into the overall curriculum. Music shouldn't be used as the sole way of exposing children to "other" cultures. Rather than teaching a song as a connection to a specific country or culture, consider how to introduce a song's message as an example of a broader topic or concept being taught. Music can help students see that many different people have experiences, ideas, and feelings to share.

Here are some ideas that help add variety and depth to the music we can share with students.

A Foundation: Ella Jenkins—This American folk singer has given us 50 years of material to use with children. I particularly like her variations on popular songs (like "May-re-mack") that give a cultural perspective different from the one in the usual renditions of those songs. Her repertoire includes nursery rhymes, holiday songs, bilingual songs, African American folk songs, international songs, and rhythmic chants. Drawing from cultures all over the world, Jenkins sings in many languages, exposing her audiences to diverse cultures and promoting greater cultural awareness.

Historical Insights—Where did that song come from? "All the Pretty Horses" is one example of a song that enslaved African Americans used to communicate with each other without alerting their white owners. There are songs like "I've Been Working on the Railroad," "Pop Goes the Weasel" and "San Sereni" that have their roots in the labor movement. There are songs that connect to the Civil Rights Movement and the struggle for equal rights. These songs are wonderful jumping off places for stories about the past.

Folk Songs—Songs made popular in the 1960s and 1970s, like "If I Had a Hammer," "Somos el Barco," and "All Work Together" are easy to learn and can give a strong message of working for social justice if we call attention to the words and purpose of the song. I've enjoyed using these songs as part of the opening activities of the day. As we talk about the meaning of "justice," "freedom," or other ideas in the song, we can set the tone for the day and consider how we want to be treated throughout the day. These types of songs also are perfect for adding verses that continue the theme while adding personal perspectives. In fact, when we create verses with children, we help them see what a folk song is: music that people change and add to over time, based on important concerns or experiences.

Ella Jenkins

Songs of Struggle—Teachers can use songs from various organizations to inspire children. "De Colores" is the anthem of the United Farm Workers movement. The melody and words may be familiar to Spanish-speaking children, but the song also gives the opportunity to tell the story of César Chávez, Dolores Huerta and the thousands of others who worked to secure bargaining rights for farm workers. "Step by Step" is the anthem of the United Mine Workers. The images of "many stones to form an arch" and the "drops of water" working together to turn the mill are concrete metaphors that can be used to develop the classroom community.

New Songs, Current Musicians—Several music publishers have excellent collections of songs for children and their teachers that celebrate the world through music. One of my favorites is the collection from *Teaching Tolerance* called "I Will Be Your Friend." It includes a CD, music, and activities for the songs that focus on peace and justice. This collection includes music from all the categories above. It is a must-have for any early childhood classroom.

UMG Recordings' album, *Peace Makes the World Go Round*, is a collection of peace related songs by recognized artists. This CD has such songs as "Peace Train" by Yusuf Islam (formerly Cat Stevens), and "What a Wonderful World," sung by Louis Armstrong. "What's Going On" by Marvin Gaye is as relevant now as when it came out in 1971.

Other current favorites: At Long Last Records has an album called *Labor of Love: Songs of Work and Play*. I like the music for naptime that comes from Ellipsis Arts called *World Music for Little Ears*, or *Dreamland* in the Putumayo World Music collection. The group Black Sheep performs a song called "Time to Think." In our materialistic culture, children need to hear messages that help them to consider the important things that they have: family, food, and a place to sleep. This song reminds us not to take our world for granted.

Dan Zanes is an artist whose songs easily connect with young children. His combination of traditional and new music sends his audience a wide variety of sounds, inspiring messages of love and hope.

Finally, one of my favorite resources is the music published by Putumayo World Music. They have wonderful collections for children, but the broader catalogue offers just as many possibilities for music to use with students. There is a wealth of albums that focus on various genres and cultures. The "World Playground" series is especially relevant.

Woody Guthrie

This list barely scratches the surface. My hope is that it helps us begin to see that almost all music can be "children's music." As we work as educators to teach about social justice, we need numerous ways to send our messages about celebrating differences, inviting multiple perspectives, and taking collective action to address injustice. Music is a powerful and effective vehicle for our social justice teaching. ■

Rita Tenorio is the principal of La Escuela Fratney in Milwaukee, Wis.

Books and Multimedia Resources

We asked the contributors to Rethinking Early Childhood Education *to recommend some of the resources that they find useful in their work. Below are their recommendations.*

Julie Bisson recommends:

Anti-Bias Curriculum: Tools for Empowering Young Children
Louise Derman-Sparks and Julie Olsen Edwards
Washington, DC, NAEYC, 2010
This essential book is full of suggestions for helping teachers and children respect each other as individuals and for confronting, transcending, and eliminating barriers based on race, culture, gender, and ability.

Teaching and Learning in a Diverse World: Multicultural Education for Young Children, Third Edition
Patricia Ramsey
New York, Teachers College Press, 2004
This essential resource examines children's understanding of race, socioeconomic class, culture, and gender. It provides practical suggestions on how to incorporate a multicultural perspective in our day-to-day interactions with children.

We Can't Teach What We Don't Know: White Teachers, Multiracial Schools, Second Edition
Gary R. Howard
New York, Teachers College Press, 2006
In this book, the author outlines what good teachers know, what they do, and how they embrace culturally responsive teaching. It addresses current issues such as closing the achievement gap and recent legislation such as No Child Left Behind.

What If All the Kids Are White? Anti-Bias Multicultural Education with Young Children and Families
Louise Derman-Sparks, Patricia G. Ramsey, and Julie Olsen Edwards
New York, Teachers College Press, 2006
In this book the authors tackle a frequently asked question: How do I teach about racial and cultural diversity if all my students are white? The text includes strategies, resources, and classroom examples for implementing learning themes in early childhood settings where most of the children are white.

Why Are All the Black Kids Sitting Together in the Cafeteria? And Other Conversations About Race
Beverly Daniel Tatum
New York, Basic Books, 2003
This book provides a new framework for thinking and talking about race and encourages us to get past our reluctance to talk about racial issues.

Peter Campbell recommends:

A Child's Work: The Importance of Fantasy Play
Vivian Paley
Chicago, University of Chicago Press, 2004
Vivian Paley taught preschool children for 37 years, much of that time at the University of Chicago's Laboratory Schools. She is the only kindergarten teacher to ever receive one of the MacArthur "genius" grants.

The Power of Play: Learning What Comes Naturally
David Elkind
New York, Da Capo Press, 2007
Elkind is one of the key authorities on developmentally inappropriate practices in early childhood education.

Mary Cowhey recommends:

All Families Are Different
Sol Gordon and Vivien Cohen
New York, Prometheus Books, 2004
Written by a clinical psychologist, this illustrated book for readers 7 and older defines families in multiple ways, considering economic and racial factors as well as including same-sex, divorced, and foster parents.

All Families Are Special
Norma Simon and Teresa Flavin
Boston, Albert Whitman and Company, 2003
A teacher tells her students she is going to be a grandmother, initiating a conversation about family diversity in which students share how their home lives are similar or different. Colorful illustrations complement an appropriately sensitive book for young readers.

I Will Be Your Friend: Songs and Activities for Young Peacemakers
Produced by Larry Long, J.D. Steele, and Ellen Weiss
Montgomery, Ala., Teaching Tolerance, 2003
This is a CD and songbook of great songs (lyrics and music) on themes like peace, inclusion, friendship, social justice, and more. It is available free (one copy per school) at tolerance.org/teach/resources/your_friend.jsp

Oliver Button Is a Star
GPN, 2002
This documentary weaves a reading and a musical production of *Oliver Button Is a Sissy* together with interviews with adults like arctic explorer Ann Bancroft, author/illustrator Tomie dePaola, and dancer Bill T. Jones, who recall their childhood experiences. It includes scenes where 1st and 2nd graders do activities about name-calling and challenging gender stereotypes.

That's a Family: A Film for Kids About Family Diversity
GroundSpark, 2000
Children's voices are central to this gentle approach to talking about and developing respect for family diversity.

Louise Derman-Sparks recommends:

Can We Talk About Race?: And Other Conversations In an Era of School Re-segregation
Beverly Daniel Tatum
Boston, Beacon Books, 2007
This is a must for understanding the dynamics of current systemic racism and its impact on schools.

Celebrate! An Anti-Bias Guide to Enjoying Holidays in Early Childhood Programs
Julie Bisson
St. Paul, Minn., Redleaf Press, 1997
This book offers strategies for creating a holiday framework and making choices about how to teach about holidays within an anti-bias education approach.

The First R: How Children Learn Race and Racism
D. Van Ausdale and J.R. Feagin
Lanham, Md., Rowman & Littlefield, 2001
This is a must-read for teachers who want to understand how young children construct their ideas about racism. It's based on a yearlong, observational study of preschool-aged children in a diverse childcare center.

Magic Capes, Amazing Powers: Transforming Superhero Play in the Classroom
Eric Hoffman
St. Paul, Minn., Redleaf Press, 2004
Hoffman examines superhero play in an anti-bias framework by exploring issues of power, social development, gender roles and fairness. He provides excellent teacher suggestions for early childhood classrooms.

The Skin That We Speak: Thoughts on Language and Culture in the Classroom
Lisa Delpit and J. Kilgour
New York, New Press, 2002
This is one of the best analyses of language oppression related to class and culture. It's helpful for understanding current political struggles about bilingualism.

That's Not Fair: A Teacher's Guide to Activism with Young Children
Ann Pelo and Fran Davidson
St. Paul, Minn., Redleaf Press, 2000
Pelo and Davidson suggest ways to engage young children in critical thinking and in taking action for fairness. Their book is grounded in a clear, developmental framework that respects children's co-construction of knowledge.

Jean H. Hannon recommends:

Constructive Guidance and Discipline: Preschool and Primary Education, Fourth Edition
Marjory V. Fields and Debby Fields
Upper Saddle River, N.J., Prentice Hall, 2005
This book challenged me to think hard about my interactions with young children and to teach with much more care.

Let's Begin Reading Right: Developmentally Appropriate Beginning Literacy
Marjory V. Fields and Katherine L Spangler
Upper Saddle River, N.J., Prentice Hall, 1995
Marjory Fields seeks to expand the reader's knowledge about appropriate literacy practices in early childhood education.

Laura Linda Negri-Pool recommends:

Soy Bilingüe
Sharon Cronin and Carmen Sosa-Masso
Calabasas, Calif., Center for Cultural and Linguistic Democracy, 2003
This book is full of information, stories, resources and research for teachers interested in creating bilingual and bicultural classrooms.

Theatre of the Oppressed
Augusto Boal
New York, Theater Communications Group, 1985
This book outlines Augusto Boal's "arsenal" for change. It is a resource for utilizing theatre as a means to engage people in social change.

Patty Hnatiuk recommends:

Building a Stronger Child Care Workforce: A Review of Studies of the Effectiveness of Compensation Initiatives
Jennifer Parke-Jadotte, Stacie Golin, and Barbara Gault
Washington, D.C., Institute for Women's Policy Research, 2002
The research and policy studies in this book address issues that face women in the workforce (including childcare workers) such as pay equity, benefits and working conditions. This book includes a comprehensive policy study about the effectiveness of a variety of childcare compensation initiatives in the United States.

A Center Piece of the Pre-K Puzzle: Providing State Prekindergarten in Child Care Centers
K. Shulman and H. Blank
Washington, D.C., National Women's Law Center, 2007
This is a key resource about the links being forged between childcare centers and pre-kindergarten programs in public schools.

Estimating the Size and Components of the U. S. Child Care Workforce and Caregiving Population: Key Findings from the Childcare Workforce Estimate.
A. Burton
Washington, D.C., Center for the Child Care Workforce, 2002
This is the first concrete assessment of the characteristics and numbers of people employed in the childcare industry.

Working for Worthy Wages: The Child Care Compensation Movement, 1970–2001
Marcy Whitebook
Washington, D.C., Center for the Child Care Workforce, 2002
This is a foundational resource about the childcare compensation movement.

Margot Pepper recommends:

September 11 and the U.S. War: Beyond the Curtain of Smoke
Edited by Roger Burbach and Ben Clarke
San Francisco, City Lights and Freedom Voices, 2002
This is an informative collection of essays by journalists, historians, activists, and political theorists providing the historical, political, and intellectual context for understanding the events and the consequences of September 11 and America's "War on Terrorism." The collection outlines the U.S. policies that contributed to the tragedy of 9/11, the consequences of the new war, and suggestions for options and alternatives, such as grassroots organizing linked to the antiglobalization movement and the strengthening of institutions like the International Criminal Court and the United Nations.

Taking Back Childhood: Helping Your Kids Thrive in a Fast-Paced, Media-Saturated, Violence-Filled World
Nancy Carlsson-Paige
New York, Penguin, 2008
This groundbreaking guide is based on early childhood development scholar Nancy Carlsson-Paige's 30 years of teaching, researching, and writing about young children. It helps parents to navigate the social currents such as media violence and rampant consumerism that shape—and harm—the lives of children today, and is a call to all of us to restore childhood to the best of what it should be.

Who's Calling the Shots?: How to Respond Effectively to Children's Fascination with War Play, War Toys and Violent TV
Nancy Carlsson-Paige and Diane E. Levin
Gabriola Island, B.C., Canada, New Society Publishers, 1989
After a historical analysis of the narrowly scripted play encouraged by today's merchandise-oriented children's TV, *Who's Calling the Shots* offers a wealth of suggestions and resources for helping children reclaim control over their play, avoid rigid gender and racial stereotypes, combat consumerism, and learn the skills for building a less violent future.

Melanie Quinn recommends:

In Defense of Children: When Politics, Profit, and Education Collide
Elaine Garan
Chicago, Heinemann, 2004
Elaine Garan lays out how millions of precious education dollars were inhaled by greedy textbook and test publishers instead of reaching the classroom in the form of quality literature and informed instruction. It is a must-read for teachers tired of being hoodwinked by No Child Left Behind and Reading First's false claims and who are ready to push back in defense of our children and our profession.

Raising Writers: Understanding and Nurturing Young Children's Writing Development
Ruth Shagoury
Danbury, Conn., Allyn & Bacon, 2008
This book uses early childhood literacy research to demonstrate that the current early literacy curriculum being pushed by federal education policies is a stark departure from established early childhood research in the field.

Silent No More: Voices of Courage in American Schools
Edited by ReLeah Cossett Lent and Gloria Pipkin
Chicago, Heinemann, 2003
This book tells the stories of brave educators who put their reputations and jobs on the line to do what was best for children and our profession. These activists have paved the way for a new breed of teacher who refuses to be intimidated and silenced. It is time for a revolution!

Cirila Ramírez recommends:

It's All in the Frijoles: One Hundred Famous Latinos Share Real Life Stories, Time Tested Dichos, Favorite Folktales and Inspiring Words of Wisdom
Yolanda Nava
New York, Fireside, 2000

This book is a rich collection of folktales, lullabies, poems, and dichos of Latino wisdom.

Parrot in the Oven: Mi Vida
Victor Martinez
New York, Harper Trophy, 1998
A vivid portrait of one Mexican American boy's life.

Rita Tenorio recommends:

All the Colors of the Earth
Sheila Hamanaka
New York, William Morrow and Co., 1994
A beautiful book that describes and celebrates the richness and variety of the many colors of skin. Hamanaka uses images of food, plants, and animals to connect the reader with the text. The message is clear: There is beauty and richness in every color. The children depicted in the book are very diverse and include children with special needs, mixed-race children, and children with albino characteristics.

All the Colors We Are: The Story of How We Get Our Skin Color
Katie Kissinger
St. Paul, Minn., Redleaf Press, 1997
This is a bilingual picture book—the text is presented in English and Spanish—about how people "get" their skin color. The text explores the basic facts about the roles that melanin, the sun, and ancestors play in making us different. The author uses photographs to explain the concepts in clear, child-friendly language that offers opportunities to explore this scientific concept with children.

Bein' with You This Way
W. Nikola-Lisa
New York, Lee & Low, 1995
One of the favorite read-alouds in my classroom, this picture book is a joyful, rhythmic chant that celebrates diversity. Familiar, straightforward observations about size, hair texture, eye and skin color help the reader to dispel the notion of "normal" and recognize that we are all unique. Also available in a well-translated Spanish version.

The Colors of Us
Karen Katz
New York, Henry Holt, 1999
When Lena decides to paint pictures of all of her friends, she is surprised to learn that brown is not just one color. In this picture book, Lena's mother takes her on a tour of the neighborhood to observe all the shades of "brown" skin. With new labels like "cinnamon," "chocolate," and "pizza crust," she begins to understand how four basic colors combine to make lots of variations. It serves as a great conversation starter on skin color.

Creative Resources for the Anti-Bias Classroom
Nadia Saderman Hall
Albany, N.Y., Delmar Thomson Learning, 1998
This excellent book connects developmental social studies skills for children ages 6–11 with the elements of an anti-bias curriculum. It's a must-have for every elementary classroom.

We Can Work It Out: Conflict Resolution for Children
Barbara Kay Polland
Berkeley, Calif., Tricycle Press, 2000
A good resource for the teaching of social skills. Through the use of photos and questions, Polland asks students and teachers to explore such issues as praise and criticism, jealousy, anger, and teasing. Lessons that start with the book can be extended in many ways with role plays, writing, and literature.

Whoever You Are
Mem Fox
San Diego, Calif., Voyager, 2001
A wonderful story that we use throughout the school year. With poetic language and mysterious, almost magical illustrations by Leslie Staub, this picture book tells the reader that "there are children all over the world just like you." Our students begin to see how all families experience the universality of love, joy, pain, and sadness.

Organizations and Websites

We asked the contributors to *Rethinking Early Childhood Education* to recommend some of the organizations and websites that they find useful in their work. Below are their recommendations.

Ellen Bravo recommends:

Center on Law and Social Policy, clasp.org
This DC-based organization researches policy to strengthen low-income families. They have done significant work on child care and early education, child welfare, and work-life issues.

Institute for Women's Policy Research, iwpr.org
This organization conducts rigorous research and disseminates its findings to address the needs of women, promote public dialogue, and strengthen families, communities, and societies. They have produced studies documenting the cost-benefit ratio of implementing paid sick days, as well as the costs of not having family leave.

Multi-State Working Families Consortium, valuefamiliesatwork.org
This is a network of 11 state coalitions working for policies that value families at work, including paid sick days, family leave insurance, and time for parental involvement in children's education. The consortium is a new model of collaborative fundraising, strategy and messaging.

National Partnership on Women and Families, nationalpartnership.org
This nonprofit, nonpartisan organization uses public education and advocacy to promote fairness in the workplace, quality health care, and policies that help women and men meet the dual demands of work and family. They coordinate a national coalition of groups working to pass the Healthy Families Act.

9to5, National Association of Working Women, 9to5.org
This is a national, grassroots organization of low-wage women working to win economic justice. They have been instrumental in involving low-wage women in efforts to win paid sick days and expanded access to family leave.

Mary Cowhey recommends:

Philosophy for Children, mtholyoke.edu/omc/kidsphil
This website offers information and resources about teaching philosophy to children, including question sets and video.

Syracuse Cultural Workers/Tools For Change, syracuseculturalworkers.com
This catalog includes posters, music, children's books, and calendars on issues like labor, the environment, diversity, peace, and children's and human rights.

Teaching Tolerance, teachingtolerance.org
This free magazine for teachers is published by Southern Poverty Law Center.

Louise Derman-Sparks recommends:

Applied Research Center, arc.org
This website has useful analyses of racism in education and suggests public policy and educational changes.

California Tomorrow, californiatomorrow.org
This organization offers resources for working with elementary, middle, and high school children on issues of culture and language.

Children's Book Press, childrensbookpress.org
This organization publishes preschool and primary bilingual children's books that feature children and families of color.

Gustavus Myers Center for the Study of Bigotry and Human Rights, myerscenter.org
This organization reviews new books and videos for adults about social justice issues.

Teaching for Change, teachingforchange.org
This website is one of the best places to begin looking for social justice teaching resources. It has great books, videos, and posters, as well as excellent links to other social justice websites.

Patty Hnatiuk recommends:

Childcare Resource and Research Unit, childcarecanada.org
Based at University of Toronto, this website offers information about the most recent policy studies and developments on issues in child care, including compensation, as they take shape in Canada, the U.S. and Europe.

Center for the Child Care Workforce, ccw.org
This is a project of the American Federation of Teachers Educational Foundation. It provides numerous print resources and a free monthly electronic newsletter: Rights, Raises, Respect.

Center for the Study of Child Care Employment, iir.berkeley.edu/cscce
The Center is housed at the Institute of Industrial Relations at the University of California at Berkeley. Longtime compensation activists Marcy Whitebook and Dan Bellm are the key researchers at the Center. The website makes available numerous research studies about the childcare workforce, including the 2006 study, *Roots of Decline: How Government Policy Has De-educated Teachers of Young Children.*

National Women's Law Center, nwlc.org
The Center focuses on major policy areas of importance to women and their families. It works to protect and to advance women's rights.

Sharna Olfman recommends:

Alliance for Childhood, allianceforchildhood.net
This international organization's mandate is to restore healthy play in children's lives and to reinstate play-based early childhood curricula.

Campaign for a Commercial Free Childhood, commercialfreechildhood.org
This coalition of organizations and groups across the United States is dedicated to reducing the impact of commercial culture in children's lives.

Margot Pepper recommends:

AdBusters, adbusters.org
AdBusters calls TV-Turnoff Week "Mental Detox Week" and encourages unplugging DVD players, iPods, laptops, PSPs and Xboxes for seven days.

Center for Screentime Awareness, screentime.org
This organization provides information to help people live healthier lives in functional families in vibrant communities by taking control of electronic media, rather than allowing it to control them. The website also has information on National TV-Turnoff Week, which takes place in late April each year. Included are shocking statistics on the detrimental effects of television and alternative activities and resources.

Valerie Polakow recommends:

Children's Defense Fund, childrensdefense.org
This national advocacy and policy organization acts as a watchdog for children's rights, with a specific focus on children in poverty. It publishes and posts excellent updated information and leads advocacy campaigns on behalf of children.

Columbia University Clearinghouse on International Developments in Child, Youth and Family Policies, childpolicyintl.org
This website provides cross-national and comparative information about family, child, and youth policies in wealthy industrialized countries.

Economic Policy Institute, epi.org
This nonprofit think tank focuses on economic inequality with a focus on improving conditions for working families in the United States. They provide useful data and living-wage budgets.

Human Rights Watch, hrw.org
This global organization is dedicated to protecting human rights and exposing abuses, violations, and injustice worldwide.

Innocenti Research Centre of UNICEF, unicef-irc.org
Innocenti publishes comparative cross-national research about children's rights and child well-being. It issues annual report cards on child poverty, child justice, sexual exploitation, and children's rights.

National Center for Children in Poverty, nccp.org
This is a national clearinghouse, based at Columbia University, that disseminates important information about children in poverty.

Index

ABC, 106
activism, x
  by children, 153–54
  children affected by, 184–85
  at El Centro de la Raza, 183–86
  by families, 185–86
  for family-friendly business policies, 199–200
  labor, 207–8
  against packaged curricula/assessments, xii–xiii
  teachers' attitudes toward, 49–50, 52, 53
  for UPK, xiii, 203
AdBusters, 224
adequate yearly progress (AYP), 58, 115
AFT (American Federation of Teachers), xiii, 204
AIDS awareness, 156
Alejandro-Wright, Marguerite N., 8
All Families Are Different (Gordon and Cohen), 219
All Families Are Special (Simon and Flavin), 219
Alliance for Childhood, 224
All of a Kind Family, 61
All Saints Day, 169
All the Colors of the Earth (Hamanaka), 20, 222
All the Colors We Are (Kissinger), 222
"All the Pretty Horses," 216
"All Work Together," 216
Amazing Grace, 178
American Federation of Teachers (AFT), xiii, 204
ancestors, remembering, 19
Annie E. Casey Foundation, 185
anti-apartheid movement, 151
Anti-Bias Curriculum (Derman-Sparks), 219
anti-bias curriculum/education. *See also* holidays
  biased remarks from children, 44–46
  biases in young children, 7–8, 17–18
  common questions/answers about, 9–12
  critiquing children's books, 46–47
  developmental appropriateness of, 11
  developmental themes, tasks, and goals, 13–16
  discrimination, challenging, 44, 47
  empathy development, 47
  factors in identity/attitude construction in children, 7–8
  gender stereotypes, exploring, 46
  integrated into existing curriculum, 11–12
  with *Kids Like Us* (persona) dolls, 23–28, 45, 47
  vs. multicultural curriculum, 10–11
  need for, 7–12
  potential for making things worse, 9–10
  prejudice, challenging, 44, 47
  prioritizing, ix–x, 1
  racial stereotypes, exploring, 46
  racism/sexism in children's books, 211–13
  research on play and gender, 67–73
  responsibilities of early childhood educators, 8–9
  stereotypes, challenging, 44
  stereotypes, recognizing, 46
  teachable moments, 4, 44–46, 47, 68
  teaching that color is beautiful, 3–6, 212
  for white children, 43–47
  and white privilege/superiority, 4–5, 43, 44, 72, 212
anti-racist curriculum, 18
  music in, 215–17
antiwar rallies, 185
Applied Research Center, 223
Armstrong, Louis, 217
At Long Last Records, 217
attachment theory, 135
attention skills, 77–78
auditory figure-ground perception, 78
authors of children's books, 212–13
AYP (adequate yearly progress), 58, 115

background noise, screening out, 78
Bain Capital, 206–7
Barbies (toy), 30, 32, 61
Bass, Rick, 124–25
Battle Arena (toy), 30
Beautiful Warrior, 178
Bein' with You This Way (Nikola-Lisa), 222
Bellavance-Grace, Beth, 179, 182
Bellavance-Grace, Karen, 179
Betty la fea, 104
bias. *See also* anti-bias curriculum/education; racism
  in children's books, 211–13

forms of, 25–26
as a universal experience, 26
Big Brother (toy), 30
The Big Pig's Bib, 100
Bisson, Julie, 165, 220
Black Sheep, 217
Blank, H., 221
block building, 65–66
Boal, Augusto, 220
book recommendations, 219–22
books, racism/sexism in, 211–13
Bowman, Barbara, 79
boys
block building for, 66
maternal role playing by, 67–69
playing dress up, 31
toys for, 30, 31, 32
brain development, 76–81, 83, 198
Bravo, Ellen, 197, 223
Bridges, Ruby, 153–54
Bright Horizons, 203, 206–7
"The Broken Pot," 116
Brown, Deborah, 207
Brown v. Board of Education, 177
Bruner, Charles, 201
Building a Stronger Child Care Workforce (Parke-Jadotte, Golin, and Gault), 221
Burbach, Roger, 221
Burton, A., 221
Bush, George W., 103, 107, 109, 110
business policies, family-friendly, 197–200
Butternut Hollow Pond (Heinz), 140

Cadwell, Louise Boyd, 85
California Tomorrow, 223
Campaign for a Commercial Free Childhood, 224
Campaña Quetzal (Seattle), 185
Campbell, Peter, 57, 219
Can Pat Nap? 100
Can We Talk About Race? (Tatum), 220
capitalism, 88, 92
Carlsson-Paige, Nancy, 221
The Carrot Seed, 181
Carson, Rachel, 121
Carter, Margie, 13, 119, 145
Case, Robbie, 80
causal (if-then) reasoning, 79–80
CBS, 106
CEDAW (Convention on the Elimination of All Forms of Discrimination Against Women), 191–92
Celebrate! An Anti-Bias Guide to Enjoying Holidays in Early Childhood Programs (Bisson), 220
Center for Screentime Awareness, 106, 224
Center for the Child Care Workforce, xiii, 203, 205, 206, 224
Center for the Study of Child Care Employment, 224
Center on Law and Social Policy, 223
A Center Piece of the Pre-K Puzzle (Shulman and Blank), 221
cerebral palsy, 147
change
resistance to, 50–51, 53
through guilt, 138
Charlotte's Web (White), 143
Chávez, César, 92, 186, 216
child care
administration of/infrastructure for, 205
commercialized/privatized, 202, 203, 205, 206–7
community-based, 205–6
cost of/subsidies for, 190–91, 194n.9, 202, 205
vs. day care, xv
deficit in, 190–91, 194n.5
vs. education, 205
funding for, 205–6
history of centers, 206
meanings of, xv
and poverty, 189, 193–94
public vs. private responsibility for, 190
right to, 189, 191–94
Child Care Employees Project, xiii
Childcare Resource and Research Unit, 224
childcare workers. *See also* teachers
career/professional development for, 202, 206
discrimination against, xiii
diversity among, 202
in Finland, 63
higher education for, 202, 204, 206, 207
people of color as, 206
perceived as unskilled (women's work), xi, xv, 205
rating systems for, 202
state requirements for, xi
turnover, xi, 205, 206
wages/working conditions for, xi, xiii, 68, 201–2, 203–8
"Children, Violence and the Media," 106
Children's Book Press, 223
children's books, racism/sexism in, 211–13
Children's Community School, Van Nuys, Calif., 65
Children's Defense Fund, 224
A Child's Work (Paley), 219
China's Bravest Girl, 178
Chinese New Year, 10, 167
Christmas, 10–11, 50–51, 53, 165, 168, 169
Cinco de Mayo, 10, 161, 166
Civil Rights Movement, 151, 216
Clarke, Ben, 221
classroom community, 152, 216
cognitive disequilibrium, 92
Cohen, Shirley, 9
Cohen, Vivian, 219

collaboration, ix, x, 159, 199, 204, 205–6. *See also* Legos
colorblindness, 9–10, 201
color of skin. *See* skin color
The Colors of Us (K. Katz), 20, 222
Columbia University Clearinghouse on International Developments in Child, Youth and Family Policies, 224
Commission on Gay and Lesbian Youth (Massachusetts), 179, 181
community in the classroom, 152, 216
competition, 31, 33, 59, 96
computers in preschool, 75–83
  age-appropriateness of, 75
  and brain development, 76–81, 83
  and children's power over play materials, 77
  effectiveness/cost, vs. other teaching materials, 81
  guidelines, 82
  and if-then (causal) reasoning, 79–80
  and intersensory integration, 77
  and learning in a social context, 76
  and memory, 78–79
  negative effects of, 76
  selective attention threatened by, 77–78
  software for phonics/math skills, 80–81
  software for toddlers, 75–76
  and symbol systems, learning, 80–81
  and visual imagery, 78–79
conflict-resolution strategies
  prejudice/discrimination addressed with, 47
conservation psychology, 133
Constructive Guidance and Discipline (Fields and Fields), 220
consumerism, 64
Convention on the Elimination of All Forms of Discrimination Against Women (CEDAW), 191–92
Convention on the Rights of the Child (CRC), 191–92, 193
Copland, Jim, 96–97
copyright date of children's books, 213
Council on Interracial Books for Children, 211
Cowhey, Mary, 177, 178, 180, 219, 223
CRC (Convention on the Rights of the Child), 191–92, 193
"Creating Balance in an Unjust World" (New York City), 97
Creative Resources for the Anti-Bias Classroom (Hall), 222
Cronin, Sharon, 220
cultural identity
  development of awareness of differences, 16
  explored through gender, 67–73
  welcoming children from nondominant cultures, 161–63
culture bias, 26
curricula. *See also* anti-bias curriculum/education
  and developmental/intellectual pursuits, x, 85
  in New Zealand, 119–20
  play vs. school-readiness approach, x–xi, xii, 57–59
  science in, disputes over, 134
  standardized, scripted packages, x–xi, xii, 59, 99–102
  teacher-proof, x, xi
Curtis, Deb, 13, 145

Dalai Lama, 185
Dalembert, Evelyne, 207
Davidson, Fran, 220
Davis, Martha, 191
death and loss, 155–57
"De Colores," 216
degree programs for childcare workers, 202
Delpit, Lisa, 220
Delta Education, 140
democracy cultivated as a way of life, xii
Denmark, poverty in, 192
Derman-Sparks, Louise, xvii, 1, 7, 13, 43–47, 219, 220, 223
desegregation, 153–54
DeWeese-Parkinson, Cathie, 175
developmental stages of children, 62–63, 83
differently abled children
  bias against, 26
  development of awareness of, 8, 14
  dolls with disabilities, 149
  fear of, 148–49, 150
  in inclusion classrooms, 147–50
  modifying the environment for, 9, 148
  parents of, 150
disabilities. *See* differently abled children
disassociation, 134
Discovery Channel, 116
Discovery Education, 116, 117, 118
diversity, 50–53, 182, 202. *See also* anti-bias curriculum/education
Dreamland, 217
Dumb and Dumber, 104
"Dying to Entertain," 106

early childcare educators. *See* childcare workers; teachers
early childhood education. *See also* Head Start; preschool
  challenges to, x–xi
  by country, 59, 63–64
  meanings of, xv
  necessity of rethinking, ix
  politics of, ix
  purpose of, xii
  social and ecological dispositions in children, fostering, ix–x (*see also* social justice and ecological teaching)
  words for describing programs, xv–xvi
Early Head Start, 205
early intervention (EI) specialists, 147, 148–49, 150
Easter, 168

ecology. *See also* social justice and ecological teaching
activism for, 129–30
attachment to land, 135–36
and consumption/stewardship/conservation, 131–32, 134
cultivating ecological identity, 125
despair about, 132
ecophobia/disassociation, 134–36
education as a barrier to nature, 133–36
endangered species, 143
food waste in art/play, 137–38
food webs, 140
and identity, 124
importance of teaching, xii
learning names in nature, 126–27
life cycles, 65–66, 134, 139, 143, 157
oath for, 185
pedagogy for, 128
professional development on, 131–32
respect for life, 141
sensuality of nature, embracing, 127
spider study, 139–43
urbanization and distance from nature, 133–34, 136
walking the land, 125–26
Economic Policy Institute, 224
ecopsychology, 133
Edwards, Julie Olsen, 43–44, 219
EI (early intervention) specialists, 147, 148–49, 150
El Centro de la Raza, 183–86
Elkind, David, 58, 83, 219
Ellipsis Arts, 217
ELLs (English Language Learners), 140
El Puente Academy for Peace and Justice (Brooklyn), 97
Emihovich, Catherine A., 9
empathy, 47
employee turnover, xi, 199, 205, 206
endangered species, 143
English Language Learners (ELLs), 140
environmentalism. *See* ecology
Erickson, Martha Farrell, 135
Erikson, Erik, 62
Estimating the Size and Components of the U.S. Child Care Workforce and Caregiving Population (Burton), 221
exclusion, social power via, 25

fairness
and gay marriage, 177, 179, 180, 181–82
and injustice, 151–54
with Legos, 89–90, 91, 94
meanings of, 152
families
activism by, 185–86
bias about structure of, 26
biracial, 177
business policies friendly to, 197–200
discussing diversity in, 182
family leave, 192, 193, 198, 200
family relationships in children's books, 212
low-income, xiii, xvi, 109, 147, 189, 190–91, 193, 201
migrant, 171–73, 175
parent-child attachment in, 135
with same-sex parents, 177–82
sharing their holidays in the classroom, 167, 168
teachers' learning from/standing with, x, 159
FAMILIES COUNT Family Strengthening Award, 185
Family and Medical Leave Act (FMLA; 1993), 193, 198
Feagin, J. R., 220
Fields, Marjory V., 220
Finch, Robert, 135–36
Finland, play vs. early academics in, 59, 63
First 5 Santa Cruz County, 172
The First R: How Children Learn Race and Racism (Van Ausdale and Feagin), 220
Fisher Price Playlab, 31
Flavin, Teresa, 219
FMLA (Family and Medical Leave Act; 1993), 193, 198
folk songs, 216
food for art/play, 137–38
food webs, 140
FOSS (Full Option Science System), 140–41, 143
Fox, Mem, 222
Fox News, 96–97
freedom, practice of, 1
Freire, Paulo, 1, 185
frontal lobe development, 77, 78–79
Full Option Science System (FOSS), 140–41, 143

Game Boys, 35–36, 39
Game Kids, 36–37, 39
Garan, Elaine, 221
Gault, Barbara, 221
Gaye, Marvin, 217
gay/lesbian people, 177–82
gay marriage, 177, 179, 180, 181–82
gender identity, 26
bias in toy stores, 29–33
development of, 8, 13
explored via play, 67–73
female teachers' attitudes toward, 70–73
stereotypes, 8–9, 46, 178
gender-neutral language, 213
GI Joes (toy), 32
girls
block building for, 66
fairness of educating, 151
self-esteem of, 31, 212
tomboys, 71–72
toys for, 30–31, 32
trying to be boys, 72–73
global warming, 185

Golin, Stacie, 221
Goodman, Mary E., 9
Goodridge v. Mass. Department of Public Health, 181–82
Gordon, Sol, 219
Gornick, Janet, 190, 191
Greenberg, Selma, 8–9
green urbanism, 136
Gustavus Myers Center for the Study of Bigotry and Human Rights, 224
Gutowski, Amy, 113, 115, 116
Gutstein, Eric, 97

Hall, Nadia Saderman, 222
Hamanaka, Sheila, 222
Hannon, Jean, 137, 220
Hanukkah, 50, 51
Head Start, xvi, 109–11, 147, 175–76, 190, 205
Healy, Jane, 64, 75
Heinz, Brian, 140
Henkes, Kevin, 157
heroes in children's books, 212
Hilltop Children's Center (Seattle), 67–73, 88, 95–96, 97, 128
Hnatiuk, Patty, 203, 221, 224
Hoffman, Eric, 44–45, 47, 220
Hofmann, Sudie, 29
holidays. *See also specific holidays*
  adding nondominant holidays to the curriculum, 166–67
  children's books about, 165
  decorations, 50–52
  holiday-themed curriculum, 10–11, 165–66
  principles for anti-bias practices surrounding, 167–70
  religious aspects of, 169
  stereotypes connected with, 169–70
  unfamiliar, 168–69
homes, straw/wood vs. brick, 41–42
homosexuals, 177–82
"Houghton Mifflin Reading," 100–102
House of Commons Education Select Committee (Great Britain), 63
Howard, Gary R., 219
Huerta, Dolores, 216
Human Rights Watch, 224
The Hundred Dresses, 178
Huxley, Thomas, 133

ICESCR (International Covenant on the Economic, Social, and Cultural Rights), 191–92
"If I Had a Hammer," 216
if-then (causal) reasoning, 79–80
illustrators of children's books, 212
The Importance of Being Earnest (Wilde), 116
inclusion classrooms, 147–50
In Defense of Children (Garan), 221
indigenous languages, families, and teachers, 175–76
individualism, 64, 72
infant mortality, 198
injustice. *See also* activism; anti-bias curriculum/education; bias; racism; sexism
  developing compassion about, 45
  developmental appropriateness of studying, 11
  and fairness, 151–54
  oppression of minorities/women, 211–12
  questioning, 96, 149–50
  and school desegregation, 153–54
  sexist toys as representing, 39
innocence, loss of, 61–62
Innocenti Research Centre of UNICEF, 224
Institute for Women's Policy Research, 223
insults, 103–4
International Covenant on the Economic, Social, and Cultural Rights (ICESCR), 191–92
Internet, 79, 105–6, 223–25
Iraq war, 97
Islam, Yusuf (*formerly* Cat Stevens), 217
It's All in the Frijoles (Nava), 221–22
It's Elementary, 178
"I've Been Working on the Railroad," 216
I Will Be Your Friend (Long, Steele, and Weiss), 216–17, 220

Jackie Chan, 104
Jackson St. School (Northampton, Massachusetts), 179
Jenkins, Ella, 216
Jones, Elizabeth, 159
Jones, Jacqueline, 110
José Martí Child Development Center (Seattle), 183–86
justice. *See* injustice

Kamerman, Sheila, 193
Katz, Jackson, 31
Katz, Karen, 222
Katz, Lillian, 82
Katz, Phyllis, 8
Kaybee Toys, 30
KB Toys, 207
Kids First, 207
Kids Like Us (persona) dolls, 23–28, 45, 47
Kilgour, J., 220
King, Martin Luther, Jr., 9, 107, 153, 186
Kissinger, Katie, 147, 222
Kohlberg, Lawrence, 8
Kozol, Jonathan, xvi, 55
Kwanzaa, 167

labor movement songs, 216
Labor of Love: Songs of Work and Play, 217
La Escuela Fratney (Milwaukee), 17, 18

Lakeshore Learning Materials Company, 149
Lalley, Jacqueline, 183
language bias, 25–26, 213
Lanham Act (1947), 206
Lawrence, D. H., 125
Leadership Empowerment Action Project, 205
Learning Stories (New Zealand assessment system), 119–20
Legos, 87–94
collectivity/consensus in use of, 93–94
fairness/equity issues surrounding, 89–90, 91, 94
investigation of, 88–89, 90, 93
outrage over ban on, 95–97
power/ownership issues surrounding, 88, 89, 90, 92–93, 94
removal of, 88, 89–90, 95–97
restoring use of, 93–94
and rule-making, 92, 94
trading game using, 90–92
Lent, ReLeah Cossett, 221
Leonard, Annie, 131, 132
lesbian/gay people, 177–82
Let's Begin Reading Right (Fields and Spangler), 220
Levin, Diane E., 221
liberation movements, 211
life cycles, 65–66, 134, 139, 143, 157
lifestyles in children's books, 212
Lil Bratz Fashion Mall (toy), 31, 61
Limbaugh, Rush, 96
LIS (Luxembourg Income Study), 192–93
literacy. *See also under* testing
among four-year-olds, 110
by country, 59, 63–64
early skills emphasized, xi, 58, 59, 63
natural activities involving vs. alphabet drills, 110
Spanish, 171, 172
Little Women, 61
loaded words in children's books, 213
logical thinking, learning, 79–80
Long, Larry, 216–17, 220
Lopez, Barry, 187
Louv, Richard, 129, 133
love, meaning of, 125, 129
Lowitz, Sadyebeth and Anson, 165
lunch program, zero-waste, 132
Luxembourg Income Study (LIS), 192–93
Lyman, Kate, 139, 155

Madison (Wisconsin), 140
Magaña, Hilda, 183–86
Magic Capes, Amazing Powers (Hoffman), 220
mainstreaming, 9
make-believe, loss of, 61–62, 64
Malaguzzi, Loris, ix
Mandl, Heinz, 80
"man," generic use of, 213
Manhattan Institute, 96–97
Maori culture, 119–20
marginalized children, welcoming, 161–63
Marshallese language/culture, 162–63
Marshall Islands (Micronesia), 162
Martinez, Victor, 222
Marvin's Magic Mind Blowing Card (toy), 32
maternity leave, 192, 193
math skills, 80–81, 110. *See also under* testing
Mattel, 30
McFarland, Gretchen, 78
M&C Toy Centre, 30
memory, 78–79
Me Pockets, 18–19
Mexican American identity, 161
Meyers, Marcia, 190, 191
migrant farmworkers' children, 171–73, 175
Miller, John J., 96
Milton Bradley, 31
minorities in children's books, 211–12, 213
Mixteco teachers, 175–76
Moore, Kathleen Dean, 125, 129
mothers, single, 32, 189, 190, 192, 193
Ms. Foundation for Women, 32
Muir, John, 133
multiculturalism, 10–11, 18
multimedia resources, 219–22
Multi-State Working Families Consortium, 199, 223
Murdoch, Rupert, 97
music for social justice, 215–17
Myers-Walls, Judy, 108
Mystery Date (game), 31

NAEYC (National Association for the Education of Young Children), 81
name-calling, 26, 178
names in nature, learning, 126–27
NAMES (AIDS Memorial) Quilt, 156
narrative's role in assessment, 120
National Association for the Education of Young Children (NAEYC), 81
National Association of Working Women, 223
National Center for Children in Poverty, 224
National Partnership on Women and Families, 223
National Velvet, 61
National Women's Law Center, 204, 224
nature-deficit disorder, 135–36
nature/natural history. *See* ecology
Nava, Yolanda, 221–22
NCLB. *See* No Child Left Behind
Negri-Pool, Laura Linda, 161, 220
New York City child care, 191
New York Collective of Radical Educators, 97
New York Post, 97

New Zealand assessment system, 119–20
Nikola-Lisa, W., 222
Nimmo, John, 159
Niña Bonita (Machado and Fara), 3, 4, 5–6
No, David (Solomon), 163
No Child Left Behind (NCLB), 58, 59, 62, 99, 111
Northampton (Massachusetts), 179
Nortonsmith, Heidi and Gina, 181–82
novelty, 125

OECD (Organization of Economic Cooperation and Development), 59, 63
Olfman, Sharna, 61, 224
Oliver, Mary, 130
Oliver Button Is a Sissy, 178
Oliver Button Is a Star, 178, 220
"Open Court Reading," 100
organization and website recommendations, 223–25
Organization of Economic Cooperation and Development (OECD), 59, 63
Orozco, José Luis, 215

Paley, Vivian, 219
parents. *See also* families
  burned-out, 64
  conversation time vs. television, 107
  of differently abled children, 150
  parent-child attachment, 135
  single mothers, 32, 189, 190, 192, 193
Parents Television Council (PTC), 105, 106
Parke-Jadotte, Jennifer, 221
Parks, Rosa, 92, 186
Parrot in the Oven (Martinez), 222
partner questions, 19
Passover, 168
PBS, 182
PDA (Pregnancy Discrimination Act; 1978), 198
peace, 108, 216–17
Peace Makes the World Go Round, 217
"Peace Train" (Islam), 217
Pelo, Ann, ix, xv, 35, 67, 87, 95, 96, 108, 123, 131, 180-81, 220
PeloJoaquin, Kendra, 87, 95, 96
Penn, Helen, 206
Peppard, Carissa, 199
Pepper, Margot, 103, 108, 221, 224
persona (*Kids Like Us*) dolls, 23–28, 45, 47
Personal Responsibility and Work Opportunity Reconciliation Act (PRWORA; 1996), 190, 194n.5
pets in the classroom, 143
Phil of the Future, 104
Philosophy for Children, 223
physical development of children, 63
Piaget, Jean, 62–63
The Pilgrim's Party (Lowitz and Lowitz), 165
Pipher, Mary, 31
Pipkin, Gloria, 221
place
  attachment to, 135–36
  exploring new perspectives in, 127–28
  finding the natural world in urban neighborhoods, 124–25
  as home, 124
  love of, 125, 127
  sense of, x, 121, 123–24, 125–26 (*see also* ecology)
  stories/histories linked to, 128–29
  telling stories that link us to, 129
play
  academic success predicated on, 62–63
  adult activities emulated in, 64
  block building, 65–66
  children's power over materials, 77
  developmental themes in, x, xi–xii
  vs. early academics/school readiness, x–xi, 57–59, 61–63
  with food, 137–38
  gender identity explored via, 67–73
  learning through, 63–64
  political/social aspects of, 69, 70, 72, 73
  purposeful, intellectual, 65–66
  vs. screen culture, 64
  time for/value of, x, 55, 59, 61–62
Polakow, Valerie, 189, 224
political/social identity, 69, 70, 72, 73. *See also* activism
Polland, Barbara Kay, 222
"Pop Goes the Weasel," 216
Postcards from Buster, 182
poverty levels, 189, 192–94
Powell, Roslyn, 191
power
  exploring, 90–92
  over play materials, 77
  and ownership, 88, 89, 90, 92–93
  via exclusion, 25
Power Brutes (toy), 30
The Power of Play (Elkind), 219
Power Team Elite (toy), 30
Pregnancy Discrimination Act (PDA; 1978), 198
prekindergarten, xv–xvi, 57–59. *See also* UPK programs
preschool. *See also* computers in preschool
  and extended care, xv
  in Finland, 63
  gender-specific play in, 37–38
  handicapped, 147, 150
  meanings of, xv
present, living in, 172–73
problem-solving strategies, 47, 66
PRWORA (Personal Responsibility and Work Opportunity Reconciliation Act; 1996), 190, 194n.5
psychosocial stages, theory of, 62–63

PTC (Parents Television Council), 105, 106
public vs. private schools, 96–97
put-downs, 26, 103–4, 178
Putumayo World Music, 217

Quinn, Melanie, 99, 221

racial differences. *See also* anti-racist curriculum
bias and exclusion, 25, 26
children's attitudes toward, 8–9
colorblind/color-denial approach to, 9–10, 201
developing awareness of, 8, 15, 18
discussing race with children, 17–21
racism. *See also* anti-bias curriculum/education; anti-racist curriculum
children's ability to discuss/understand, 21
in children's books, 211–13
effects on children, 17, 18, 21, 43
effects on teachers, 21
King's challenge to, 9
white privilege/superiority, 4–5, 43, 44, 72, 212
Raffi, 215
The Railway Children, 61
rain forests, 134
Raising Writers (Shagoury), 221
Rambo 81 mm Mortar Thunder-Tube Assault (toy), 30
Ramírez, Cirila, 171, 221
Rampage Transformer (toy), 30
Ramsey, Patricia, 11, 43–47, 219
reading. *See* literacy
recycling, 132, 134, 185
Reggio Emilia (Italy), ix, 90
relationships in children's books, 212
representational distance/competence, 80–81
Rethinking Schools, 97
Reviving Ophelia (Pipher), 31
Riding Freedom, 178
Ritalin, 63
role-playing activities, 19, See also *Kids Like Us* dolls
Romney, Mitt, 206
Rosa Parks Elementary School (Berkeley), 103
Rothstein, Richard, 109
rules, making/breaking of, 92, 94, 103–4

same-sex parents, 177–82
"San Sereni," 216
Sapon-Shevin, Mara, 9
science education, 30, 134, 140–41, 143
Scouting organizations, 136
screen culture, 64. *See also* television
The Secret Garden, 61
Seeger, Pete, 215
Segura-Mora, Alejandro, 3
SEIU (Service Employees International Union), 97, 207
self-image of children, 212
senses, integrating, 77
sensual awareness, 127
September 11 and the U.S. War (Burbach and Clarke, editors), 221
Service Employees International Union (SEIU), 97, 207
sexism, 29–33, 211–13
Shagoury, Ruth, 221
Shteir, Seth, 65
Shulman, K., 221
sick children/sick days, 197, 198–99, 200
Siegel, Irving, 80
Silent No More (Lent and Pipkin, editors), 221
Simon, Norma, 219
single incident bias, 26
skin color. *See also* racial differences
awareness of, and racial awareness, 8, 15
changing of, 3, 4–5
children's perception of dark skin as ugly, 4, 5
discussing, 19–20
and science, 20
teaching the beauty of color, 3–6, 212
writing about, 21
The Skin That We Speak (Delpit and Kilgour), 220
Sobel, David, 133, 134
social causal reasoning, 79
social context of learning, 76
social-emotional and dispositional learning, x, 145, 147–54
social identity. *See* political/social identity
social justice and ecological teaching. *See also* ecology
attack on, 95–97
characteristics of, ix–x
at El Centro de la Raza, 183–86
as intellectually/emotionally engaging, xii
with Legos, 87–94
music in, 215–17
need for, 97
as responsive to children, xi–xii
for social change, xii–xiii
songs for social justice, 215–17
Solomon, David, 163
"Somos el Barco," 216
songs for social justice, 215–17
Sosa-Masso, Carmen, 220
Soy Bilingüe (Cronin and Sosa-Masso), 220
Spangler, Katherine L., 220
Spanish immersion classes, 105
Spellings, Margaret, 182
SpongeBob SquarePants, 104
SRA/McGraw-Hill reading programs, 100–102
St. Cloud State University, 32
Steele, J. D., 216–17, 220
"Step by Step," 216
stereotypes

about holidays, 169–70
Asian American, 211
in book illustrations, 211
defined, 211
empathy about hurt caused by, 47
gender, 8, 9, 46, 178, 211
Native American, 170, 211, 212
of people of color, 211, 212
Stereotype or Fact game, 46
Stern, Sol, 97
Stevens, Cat (*later named* Yusuf Islam), 217
stimulus-bound children, 78
The Story of Ruby Bridges, 153–54
The Story of Stuff (Leonard), 131, 132
storytelling with *Kids Like Us* dolls, 23–28
stress, xi, 59, 62, 78
Sweden, poverty in, 192
Sweet Honey in the Rock, 215
symbol systems, learning, 80–81
Syracuse Cultural Workers/Tools for Change, 223

Target, 30
Tatum, Beverly Daniel, 219, 220
TDI (Temporary Disability Insurance), 193, 199
TEACH Early Childhood Program, 207
teachers
attitudes toward activism, 49–50, 52, 53
attitudes toward gender identity, 70–73
career/professional development for, 202, 206
diversity among, 202
higher education for, 202, 204, 206
learning from/standing with families, x, 159
political/social identity of, 73
racism's effects on, 21
rating systems for, 202
as role models, 148
self-censorship by, 179, 181
wages/working conditions for, xi, xiii, 68, 201–2, 203–8
teacher unions, 95, 97, 204, 206
Teaching and Learning in a Diverse World (Ramsey), 219, 220
Teaching for Change, 224
Teaching Tolerance, 223
Teaching Tolerance, 216–17
teasing, 25–26, 47, 178
television
aggression/violence on, 103–7
biases influenced by, 18
children's exposure to, 18, 106
vs. conversation time with parents, 107
and discriminating fact from fiction, 80
insults/put-downs on, 103–4
math used to analyze, 103–7
rule-breaking on, 103–4
selfishness on, 103–4, 106–7
TV violence and real violence/war, 105–8
Temporary Disability Insurance (TDI), 193, 199
Tenorio, Rita, 17, *20*, 215, 222
The Tenth Good Thing About Barney (Viorst), 156
testing
as accountability, 97, 109, 110
flawed, 114, 115–18
in Head Start, 109–11
literacy/math/science, xi, 57, 63, 109, 111
motor skills, 110–11
for prekindergarten, 57
reading, 106, 113–14, 117–18, 140
standardized, vs. play, x, 61, 62, 63, 65
teaching to tests, 110
ThinkLink, 115–18
validation/reviews of, 110–11
Te Whariki (New Zealand assessment system), 119–20
Thanksgiving, 169–70
That's a Family, 178, 182, 220
That's Not Fair (Pelo and Davidson), 220
That's So Raven, 104
Theatre of the Oppressed (Boal), 220
ThinkLink, 115–18
"The Three Little Pigs," 41–42
Through My Eyes, 153–54
"Time to Think," 217
Title IX (1972), 29
tokenism, 10, 211
tomboys, 71–72
tourist curriculum, 10–11
toys
gender-inclusive, 36–39
sexist/gendered, 29–33, 35–36
Toys 'R' Us, 29, 30, 33
Triqui teachers, 175–76
The Trumpet of the Swan (White), 180–81
Turtle Bay, 118
TV. *See* television
TV-Turnoff Network, 105, 106, 107, 224
TV-Turnoff Week, 106

Ucci, Mary, 83
The Ugly Duckling, 6
UMG Recordings, 217
United Farm Workers, 216
United Mine Workers, 216
United Nations, 192
United States
commercial childcare systems in, 206–7 (*see also under* childcare)
parental leave in, 193
poverty in, 192–93
rights of women and children in, 191–92
workplace standards in, 197–200
University of California–Berkeley, 140

UPK (universal prekindergarten) programs
activism for, xiii, 203
benefits for low-income families, xiii
vs. community-based childcare programs, xiii
funding for, 204
standardized curricula in, xiii
workforce development for, 207

Van Ausdale, D., 220
Viehauser, Emily, 35–36, 37–39
Viorst, Judith, 156
Virgie Goes to School with Us Boys, 151
visual imagery, 78–79
vouchers, 96–97

wage floor, meaningful, 200
WAGE$ Projects, 207
walking the land, 125–26
Wal-Mart, 30
Walters, Stephanie, 151
war, talking with children about, 108
War on Poverty, xvi
war on terror, 103, 106–7
war toys, 29, 30, 32, 96
Watsonville (California), 171–72
weapons, toy, 29, 30, 32
website and organization recommendations, 223–25
We Can't Teach What We Don't Know (Howard), 219
We Can Work It Out (Polland), 222
Weiss, Dale, 49
Weiss, Ellen, 216–17, 220
Weizenbaum, Joseph, 83
Weld, William, 179, 181
welfare reform, xv, 64, 190, 191, 193
"What a Wonderful World," 217
What If All the Kids Are White? (Derman-Sparks, Ramsey, and Edwards), 43–44, 219
"What's Going On" (Gaye), 217
wheelchairs, 148, 149–50
White, E. B., 143, 180–81
white behavior standards, 211
Whitebook, Marcy, 221
white children, anti-bias curriculum/education for, 43–47
White Knight, 101–2
white privilege/superiority, 4–5, 43, 44, 72, 212
Whitney, Trisha, 23
Who Cares for Our Children (Polakow), 189
Whoever You Are (Fox), 222
Who's Calling the Shots? (Carlsson-Paige and Levin), 221
Why Are All the Black Kids Sitting Together in the Cafeteria? (Tatum), 219
Wilde, Oscar, 116
Williams, Terry Tempest, xii
William's Doll, 178
Wisconsin Third Grade Reading Test, 140
Wolpert, Ellen, 41, 46
women. *See also* gender identity
roles in children's books, 212
sexualized in toy marketing, 33
single mothers, 32, 189, 190, 192, 193
wages/benefits for, 32, 189, 191, 192
Wonder, Stevie, 215
Words of Stone (Jenkes), 157
Working for Worthy Wages (Whitebook), 221
World Music for Little Ears, 217
"World Playground," 217
Worthy Wage Campaign, xiii, 203, 205
Worthy Wage Day, 204

The Young Martin Luther King Jr., 153

Zanes, Dan, 217

About the Editor

Ann Pelo is a teacher educator, program consultant, and author whose primary work focuses on reflective pedagogical practice, social justice and ecological teaching and learning, and the art of mentoring. After receiving a master's degree in child development and family studies from Purdue University, Ann worked as an early childhood teacher and teacher mentor for sixteen years at a full-day, not-for-profit childcare center in Seattle, Washington. During that time, Ann was active in the national Worthy Wage Campaign, an effort to improve the wages and working conditions of childcare teachers. Currently, Ann collaborates with early childhood educators, teachers, and program administrators in North America, Australia, and New Zealand, thinking with them about inquiry-based teaching and learning, pedagogical leadership, and the necessary place of ecological identity in children's – and adults' – lives.

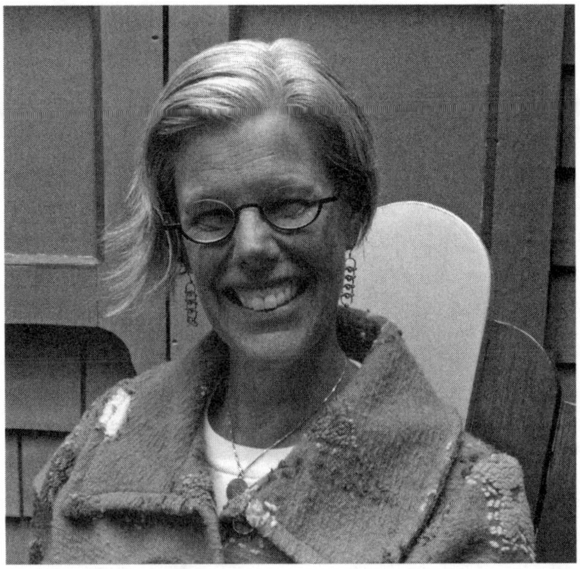

Ann is the author of a number of books, including: *From Teaching to Thinking: A Pedagogy for Reimagining Our Work*, with Margie Carter (2018); *The Language of Art: Inquiry-based Studio Practices in Early Childhood Settings* (2017); *The Goodness of Rain: Cultivating an Ecological Identity in Young Children* (2013); *Season by Season the Year Unfolds: A Guidebook for Developing an Intentional Culture in Early Childhood Programs* (2010); and, with Fran Davidson, *That's Not Fair: A Teacher's Guide to Activism with Young Children* (2000).

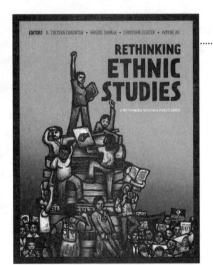

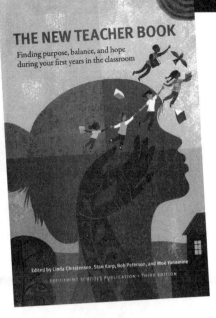

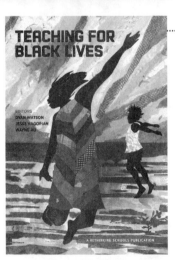

Resources from RETHINKING SCHOOLS

Rethinking Bilingual Education
Welcoming home languages in our classrooms
Edited by Elizabeth Barbian, Grace Cornell Gonzales, and Pilar Mejía

See how teachers bring students' home languages into their classrooms—from powerful bilingual social justice curriculum to strategies for honoring students' languages in schools without bilingual programs. Educators, students, and advocates speak to the tragedy of language loss and share inspiring work that centers on equity, builds solidarity among diverse communities, and defends and expands bilingual programs.

2017 • Paperback • 343 pages • ISBN: 978-1-937730-73-4
Print: $24.95*

Rethinking Popular Culture and Media SECOND EDITION
Edited by Elizabeth Marshall and Özlem Sensoy

Beginning with the idea that the "popular" in the everyday lives of teachers and students is fundamentally political, this provocative collection of articles examines how and what popular toys, books, films, music, and other media "teach." The second edition includes revised articles, nine new articles, and an updated list of resources.

Paperback • 340 pages • ISBN: 978-0-942961-63-8
Print: $24.95*

A People's Curriculum for the Earth
Teaching Climate Change and the Environmental Crisis
Edited by Bill Bigelow and Tim Swinehart

Engaging environmental teaching activities from Rethinking Schools magazine alongside classroom-friendly readings on climate change, energy, water, food, pollution—and the people who are working to make things better.

Paperback 433 pages ISBN: 978-0-942961-57-7
Print: $24.95*

Rethinking Multicultural Education
Teaching for Racial and Cultural Justice
Edited by Wayne Au

This new and expanded second edition demonstrates a powerful vision of anti-racist social justice education. Practical, rich in story, and analytically sharp, ***Rethinking Multicultural Education*** reclaims multicultural education as part of a larger struggle for justice and against racism, colonization, and cultural oppression—in schools and society.

Paperback • 418 pages • ISBN: 978-0-942961-53-9
Print: $24.95!*

*** Plus shipping and handling**
Use discount code RSBK19 for a 10% discount on your next order.

Rethinking Elementary Education

Edited by Linda Christensen, Mark Hansen, Bob Peterson, Elizabeth Barbian, and Dyan Watson

Offers practical insights about how to integrate the teaching of content with social justice, seek wisdom from students and their families, and navigate stifling tests and mandates. Some of the finest writing about elementary school life and learning.

Paperback • 320 pages • ISBN: 978-0-942961-52-2

Print: $24.95!*

Reading, Writing, and Rising Up SECOND EDITION

Teaching About Social Justice and the Power of the Written Word

By Linda Christensen

Essays, lesson plans, and a remarkable collection of student writing, with an unwavering focus on language arts teaching for justice.

SECOND EDITION • FULLY REVISED •

Paperback • 196 pages • ISBN: 978-0-942961-25-6

Print: $19.95* | PDF: $14.95

Rethinking Sexism, Gender, and Sexuality

Edited by Kim Cosier, Rachel L. S.Harper, Jeff Sapp, Jody Sokolower, and Melissa Bollow Tempel

There has never been a more important time for students to understand sexism, gender, and sexuality—or to make schools nurturing places for all of us. The thought-provoking articles and curriculum in this life-changing book will be invaluable to everyone who wants to address these issues in their classroom, school, home, and community.

Paperback • 400 pages • ISBN: 978-0-942961-59-1

Print: $24.95*

eBook and Kindle: $9.95: rethinkingschools.org/RSGS

Open Minds to Equality

A Sourcebook of Learning Activities to Affirm Diversity and Promote Equity / By Nancy Schniedewind and Ellen Davidson

Activities to help students understand and change inequalities based on race, gender, class, age, language, sexual orientation, physical/mental ability, and religion.

Paperback • 408 pages • ISBN: 978-0-942961-60-7

Print: $24.95*

ORDER ONLINE: www.rethinkingschools.org

CALL TOLL-FREE: 800-669-4192

Resources from **RETHINKING SCHOOLS**

"Whenever teachers ask me for resources, I refer them to the work of Rethinking Schools."

HOWARD ZINN (1922–2010)
Author of *A People's History of the United States*

Subscribe to the leading social justice education magazine.

Every issue of ***Rethinking Schools*** overflows with creative teaching ideas, compelling narratives, and hands-on examples of how you can promote values of community, racial justice, and equality in your classroom — while building academic skills. Plus: news and analysis by and for education activists.

"As a teacher and researcher, I rely on* Rethinking Schools *for information, insight, and inspiration. It has become an indispensable part of my reading regimen."

SONIA NIETO
Professor Emerita, University of Massachusetts Amherst

Use code RSBK19 to get 10% off your 1, 2, or 3 year subscription.

*** Plus shipping and handling**
Use discount code RSBK19 for a 10% discount on your next order.